THE CLASS PROJECT

THE CLASS PROJECT:
HOW TO KILL A MOTHER

THE TRUE STORY OF CANADA'S INFAMOUS BATHTUB GIRLS

BOB MITCHELL

KEY PORTER BOOKS

Mitchell, Bob
      The class project : how to kill a mother : the true story of Canada's infamous Bathtub Girls / Bob Mitchell.

ISBN 978-1-55263-929-0

      1. Parricide--Ontario--Mississauga. 2. Juvenile homicide--
Ontario--Mississauga. I. Title.
HV6542.M58 2008   364.152'3092271   C2007-902113-1

 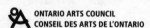

The publisher gratefully acknowledges the support of the Canada Council for the Arts and the Ontario Arts Council for its publishing program. We acknowledge the support of the Government of Ontario through the Ontario Media Development Corporation's Ontario Book Initiative.

We acknowledge the financial support of the Government of Canada through the Book Publishing Industry Development Program (BPIDP) for our publishing activities.

Key Porter Books Limited
Six Adelaide Street East, Tenth Floor
Toronto, Ontario
Canada M5C 1H6

www.keyporter.com

Electronic formatting: Alison Carr

Printed and bound in Canada

08 09 10 11 12 5 4 3 2 1

ACKNOWLEDGEMENTS

In alphabetical order, my heartfelt thanks to the people, and organizations, who made this book possible. Nick Bala, Eugene Bhattacharya, Alan Cairns, Mike Cantlon, Bruce Duncan, Jordan Fenn, Robert Jagielski, Dan Johnstone, Brent Magnus, Brian McGuire, Mike Metcalf, Jack McCulligh, Amy Moore-Benson, Anne Pecaric, Mike Pulley, Veronica Puls, Jonathan Schmidt, Steve Sherriff, Mark Totten, Tony Wong, as well as the Peel Crown Attorney's office, A Grenville & William Davis Courthouse reporters, monitors and staff, Peel Regional Police, the *Toronto Star* and all my friends and colleagues in the media.

DEDICATION

To my wife Kim and our children Jayson and Ashley.
Without your support and understanding this book
would never have been possible.
Maggie, clear the kitchen floor, and enjoy.
—Bob Mitchell

TABLE OF CONTENTS

FOREWORD

As a crime reporter and author for thirty years, I've sat through many fascinating murder trials. Canada's infamous "Bathtub Girls" ranks with the best, and in some ways, the most disturbing.

The 1995 trial of Paul Bernardo in Toronto, which became just as much the trial of his ex-wife and accomplice Karla Homolka, ultimately turned into a profoundly sinister and shocking psychological examination of how a twisted psychopathic sexual sadist could exert unfettered and cult-like control over another human being and have them engage in the most unspeakably wicked acts. Despite six months of exhaustive evidence, even a basic understanding of how Homolka participated in the fatal drugging and rape of her teenage sister Tammy, as well as her acquiescence in the confinement rape murders of teens Kristen French and Leslie Mahaffy, escapes most reasonable people.

The murder trial of Charles Ng in Santa Ana, California in early 1999 posed the same kind of questions. How could unabashed serial killer Leonard Lake exert full control of the enigmatic Ng, who saw himself only as Lake's Chinese houseboy and did not really know what Lake was doing with a string of female victims he confined in a dungeon-like shed on his Calaveras County ranch?

In 1998, I watched fugitive Canadian financier Albert Walker lie through his teeth in historic Exeter High Court in beautiful England. Walker tried in vain to weasel his way out of police allegations that he first stole the identity of an Englishman, Ronald Platt, and then took Platt's life when he took him sailing off the coast of Devon, hit him over the head with an anchor and then threw him overboard into the English Channel. The Walker case was also fascinating because of the control Walker exerted over his eldest daughter Sheena, whom Walker took to England when he escaped Canada in 1990 with untold millions in investor funds. When Walker was caught, he was with Sheena and her two children. Father and daughter were posing as man and wife; as mother and father.

The murder trial of two teenage females from Mississauga, Ontario—sisters who would become known as the "Bathtub Girls"—is in many ways as fascinating as the above cases, albeit for different reasons. The interest in the case is not so much about one person's control over another, but how two young girls set out to murder their mother amid complete indifference from their teenage classmates. It's as if conscience, compassion, and basic human morals were lacking in an entire group of people. Prior to killing their mom, the eldest girl told just about everyone in their social group that she and her younger sister were plotting the crime and intended to carry it out. That is why journalist Bob Mitchell, a veteran crime writer with the *Toronto Star*, decided the title *The Class Project* captured the essence of this incredible story. Everyone knew the girls were going to kill their mom. The big question remained: Why didn't anyone do anything to stop them?

Sitting in a courtroom along side Bob in late 2005 and early 2006, it was chilling to read a veritable book of emails, in which the girls discussed the details of the upcoming mother murder with their friends in such a cavalier way. When one teenage girl was asked on the witness stand why she did not tell police, her parents, or even her teachers about the unfolding plot, she responded she did not really take it seriously. "Everybody talks about killing their parents," she said, matter of fact.

It is disturbing to think such a broad section of youth in our society could become so detached from reality as to not take notice, or care, for whatever reason, when two highly intelligent sisters start talking about killing their mom. It was not until a year after the murder when the girls casually confessed their hideous crime to a family friend that the police would finally catch them.

At one point, Bob and I discussed working together as authors. We both realized the tale of the "Bathtub Girls" was a fascinating story that would make an interesting book. For various reasons I could not participate. But Bob stuck with it and has put together a compelling story that should give every parent-loathing teen pause for thought and one that will undoubtedly give every parent nightmares.

Alan Cairns

INTRODUCTION

In the fall and early winter of 2005, one of Canada's most sensational murder trials took place in Brampton, Ontario, a city northwest of Toronto. Two sisters, sixteen and fifteen, were accused of murdering their forty-three-year-old alcoholic mother on January 18, 2003 by drowning her in the bathtub of their rented townhouse in Mississauga, Ontario, a city of nearly a million people located immediately west of Toronto. Legal experts said it was the first time sisters had ever been accused in Canada of matricide.

The media initially dubbed them the "Pyjama Girls" because they made their first court appearance wearing flannel PJs under their winter coats—clothing they chose to wear the day the day of their arrest on January 21, 2004. They would become known as the "Bathtub Girls" during the mesmerizing trial that attracted intense media coverage, including some bizarre and unexpected American attention from the www.tuckermax.com Internet website.

For eight weeks, curious on-lookers packed the courtroom, including many high school students taking law courses, as well as interested attorneys. They sat spellbound as each day produced more and more chilling and disturbing evidence against the sisters born less than a year apart, who were described by a high school guidance counselor as the "smartest girls" he'd ever seen in his thirty years of teaching. The young brilliant girls got away with the crime for more than a year. They were eventually found guilty of first-degree murder on December 15, 2005. Six months later they were sentenced as youths to the maximum ten-year punishment allowed.

Before being sentenced noted Canadian forensic psychiatrist Dr. Phil Klassen remarked, "the most striking" aspect of the landmark Canadian murder case was the role a close group of academically gifted friends played, or for that matter, didn't play in the entire sinister enterprise. These friends didn't do anything to stop them and actually encouraged them.

"I've not seen one iota of resistance from anybody about the murder of their mother," Dr. Klassen said, testifying as a defence witness. He was equally stunned how their friends, none of whom had criminal records—and "weren't in any gang"—would be so "blasé" about the murder. He noted one friend who knew about the murder in advance likened it to "watching television or a movie."

For them it was all about "the drama, the excitement, the collaboration," Dr. Klassen said.

The younger sister told a probation officer preparing her pre-sentence report "none of her friends said it was a bad idea," and they supported the killing so much she felt she was "being swept along by the crowd."

As murders go, the killing of their mother wasn't gruesome, but the story behind this planned and deliberate killing, their reasons, their dysfunctional family and their callous and indifferent social network of friends, as well as how they were caught, is both a fascinating and alarming tale.

The Class Project: How to Kill a Mother is the story behind the headlines.

THE STORY

Canadian youth law protects the identities of anybody under the age of eighteen accused or convicted of a crime. As a result, the names of the two teenage girls have been changed along with the names of anybody whose identity would reveal their real names, including the name of their dead mother. Certain facts such as nationalities and professions have also been altered to prevent identification.

But all of the conversations and individual thoughts contained in this book were actually spoken and recorded in the hundreds of pages of transcripts and audio and video recordings examined for the writing of this book. Some situations under which they were said have been slightly recreated for literary purposes.

However, the names of expert witnesses, police officers and attorneys are real as is the story behind the infamous crime, a story told through interviews, court documents, transcripts, investigators, and personal observations.

THE KILLERS SPEAK FOR THEMSELVES

The following letters were written by Sandra Andersen, then age twenty, and Beth Andersen, then nineteen, to Judge Bruce Duncan the day before he passed sentence on June 30, 2006, as a result of finding them guilty of first-degree murder in the January 18, 2003 bathtub drowning of their mother.

Sandra Andersen

I am responsible for the deliberate murder of my Mother, Linda Andersen.

I'm no longer afraid of the truth. Taking my mother's life was the gravest and most defining mistake of my existence.

Her death has affected more people than I thought possible. My actions have changed countless lives forever. At the end of the day I will never escape from the truth. I have taken my Mother's life. What am I supposed to do? I do know that I realize I need help.

In the past I didn't see or feel that I belonged to a community. Years of abuse and neglect left me with a distorted perspective of the world and a strong case of independence. I naively believed that my Mother's life was linked with mine in a way that was no one else's concern.

Also, I came to believe my mother wouldn't stop drinking. That she was hopeless. I had no experience with solving life's harsh problems, let alone knowing how to help a very sick person. I didn't know how or where to seek the healing that my Mother, myself, and my siblings needed.

At sixteen, I was relatively mature for my age but my judgment was woefully underdeveloped and sometimes delusional. I was hurt and I was selfish. I made important decisions with serious and permanent consequences.

I came to be a walking textbook of mistakes. Thank God I learned from them, albeit painfully and slowly.

After my Mother's death I couldn't function naturally. The endless lies were killing me. I began to abuse drugs and alcohol. Those addictions ended on the morning of my arrest. The lies ended on the day of my conviction. As a result, I am thankful of my arrest and subsequent conviction.

If the intervention of the justice system was such a great event, why didn't I plead guilty? Simply, I was afraid. I didn't want to be labeled as a murderess for the rest of my life. I didn't want to go to jail. Also, I was too scared to tell my family that they were wrong when they automatically believed in my innocence.

I didn't recognize honesty as a safe direction in the right way. I want to stress that I am no longer afraid of the truth. I would give anything to retake my actions. My mother did not deserve to die. She was not as close to death as I imagined and she was far from hopeless.

Once again thank God for I have learned many priceless lessons. Now I see and feel that I have severely damaged my community, my family and myself. I am an emotional mess and in great need of catharsis. I am finally ready to accept the help that is being offered.

I will continue to share my story and I will repay my debt to society. I plan to enroll in university, to become a social worker. I want to live as a healer, as a teacher and help the members of my community cope with pain.

The purpose at the end of my path is for me to connect with the community in a meaningful way. I still have hope that I can lead a normal, successful life and find some peace before I die.

Beth Andersen

No matter what I do I can't change the past. The only thing I can do is to get up every morning and try to help as many people as possible, to spread as much love as possible, because in my mind that's the only true reason for living

I want to be able to help others not make the same mistakes I did. No one should suffer the way my mother, brother, my sister, and I have. The worst part is that children go through so much more pain than I and they still don't resort to murder. I need help. I'm not the same person that I was three-and-a-half years ago but I still need help. The person that I am now wouldn't give someone a dirty look let alone go out of my way to hurt them.

I feel sick at the thought of taking someone's life. I feel sick at the thought of what I've done. I'm not a bad person.

I want to see my little brother again. Three weeks ago I wrote a letter of apology to my mother's parents after not speaking to them for six months. I want to work things out with my family. I want to talk with them and then maybe over time feel like a family again.

We need counseling and family therapy. It's not healthy to not work through these problems. I'm sick of running. Right now I have trouble facing my past. I'm really scared to go back to it. The memories are so painful. I still choke up every time I talk about my mom or my brother Bobby but I want my family to know how badly I feel about everything that happened.

I want the opportunity to get better. Our mom's death was the product of greed, pain and ignorance.

At fifteen I couldn't see past my own nose. And took advantage of my mom's trust to end her life. There is no justifying what I've done. No matter how many times I say I'm sorry it won't bring my mother back. That to me is the worst punishment that I will never ever be able to escape.

At fifteen I had no foresight. I didn't think our 'solution' would affect so many people as it did. I didn't think I would miss her. I want my mommy back and that will never happen. For what it's worth, I'm sorry. I've been sorry for years but was too afraid to say anything.

I pled not guilty under the advice of my lawyers and family, not because I thought that I could get away with murder. Not being able to talk about how horribly I feel was killing me on the inside. I still feel awful but at least it's now out in the open.

I'm not a monster.

I can't sleep because of what I've done. I have nightmares. I feel as though my insides are being torn apart because of how my past hurts.

Please give me a chance to get better. Please don't send me to an adult facility where I can't get family therapy and where I would be turned into a cold, hyper vigilant ex-con.

Please consider letting me continue my treatment at Syl Apps. Through counselling at Syl Apps I've become more self-aware and have started figuring out where I've been making painful, hurtful mistakes and how I can change that.

Syl Apps provides family therapy which I really need if ever we're to be at least somewhat of a family again. Most important I'm able to help other residents here. Because of my age, I'm more like a big sister to many of the youths here, which enables me to help them in way that the staff can't. We connect on a different level and help each other.

If I stay at Syl Apps over the summer I and a few other long term youths would be trained for the mentorship program that starts in September. It is designed to help new intakes. Let me take advantage of this golden opportunity to turn their lives around. I would be helping in the tuck shop, a mini servery that provides home made lunches to staff and residents.

In September I would continue being a teaching assistant as well as begin university through correspondence. All of these inter-actions are teaching me how to be less selfish.

I have so much to offer this world but I need the right treatment to bring that out. I will never repeat our mistakes again, and maybe, someday, Your Honour, will believe me and accept me as part of society again.

GOOD LUCK.
WEAR GLOVES.

Sandra and Beth Andersen watched their mother Linda become inebriated throughout the day. By the late afternoon of January 18, 2003, she'd already been drinking heavily, consuming her favourite mixed drink of vodka and lemonade as well as a few glasses of red wine. She'd also popped several Tylenol-3 codeine-laced painkillers.

As their mother drank, Beth, fifteen, logged onto the MSN Instant Message chat room on their computer in their Mississauga townhouse using her familiar sign-on name of "Dearly Departed"—and the phrase "Screw the world." It was about 3 p.m. when Sandra, sixteen, noticed the computer was still logged on under her sister's user name.

She scanned the names of others chatting on line. The name "Southern Dream" stood out. Her best friend Ashley was signed on.

"Hey, it's Sandra," she typed. "So you coming to Jack Astor's?"

"Oh, are you going?" Ashley, also sixteen, typed back.

Sandra replied, "We're going at like sevenish, I guess."

Ashley suddenly realized the restaurant's significance.

"Oh my God!" Ashley typed. "Are you saying what I think you're saying?"

"No nothing yet—in like an hour," Sandra replied.

Ashley probed her friend further. "Is she trashed yet?" she asked.

"Getting there," Sandra answered.

Ashley had learned about Sandra's plan to murder her mother just two weeks earlier although the plot had been in the work for months. They'd just gotten off a bus at Mississauga's Square One Shopping Centre and were walking towards the mall with several other friends when she noticed Sandra and Jay were lagging behind. They were in deep conversation.

Were they sharing a "deep secret?" Ashley thought.

She detested "being kept in the dark" so she dropped back. She had to know what they were talking about. Why hadn't she been included?.

"So what's up?" Ashley asked.

"You really don't want to know," Sandra replied.

Ashley became more curious.

"Now, you really have to tell me," Ashley said.

"I'm gonna kill my mother," Sandra said. "On Saturday."

Ashley was stunned. She let out a "yelp" as if a dog was barking. But instead of stopping, Sandra and Jay kept walking towards the entrance of the mall and Ashley followed. Sandra never mentioned another word about what she'd just blurted out when they caught up with the rest of their friends. The rest of the day Ashley felt a bit numb. Sandra had been so calm, so nonchalant. She seemed deadly serious. But was it a real plan?

After all, Sandra once pretended to be pregnant just to gain attention from another boy whom she had a crush on at school. Sandra had also told her a few times how her mother "would be dead by the end of the year." But Ashley just thought she meant her mother would "drink herself to death."

Sandra, however, didn't murder her mother that Saturday. Over the next several days, Ashley would learn bits and pieces about her plan. The plot, unbeknownst to her, had been ever changing for months as Sandra and Beth accepted and rejected different ideas from Jay and Beth's new best friend Justin. They also searched various websites, seeking information from the Internet for different ways to kill their mother.

But by the afternoon of January 18, Ashley definitely knew some of the deadly details. They were going to get their mother drunk and give her painkillers. Once Linda was totally wasted, they'd get her into the bathtub and drown her, making it look like she'd been so drunk she accidentally drowned. They would use gloves. Sandra told her that her mother bruised easily. They needed to make sure they didn't leave any marks, particularly fingerprints, on their dead mother's body. Once she was dead, Sandra and Beth were going to meet her and Jay and Justin at Jack Astor's restaurant near Mississauga's Square One Shopping Centre, setting up an alibi.

Even though Ashley had talked several times with Sandra about how she and Beth were going to kill their mother, she never really expected her friends would go through with the plan. At least she didn't think they would. But now she knew it looked "pretty much" like their plans were in motion. So Ashley felt she needed to make sure Sandra and Beth had thought everything through to the bitter end.

After all, what are friends for?

"I have one thing to point out," Ashley typed. "That I don't think you've considered. I can't believe I'm saying this but have you thought about the time of death?"

"Yep," Sandra replied. "We have Justin's alibi plus we're leaving right after for the mall. And coming home late."

"Alright," Ashley typed. "Because you can't be home at the estimated time of death. So you should leave within an hour of doing it."

"Yeah, I'm pretty sure we thought of everything we could," Sandra typed.

"And when you get back, you're gonna call the police, right?" Ashley asked.

"No, we're gonna wait a while?" Sandra typed, being as sarcastic as one could online.

Ashley needed to be certain, especially for Sandra's sake, that she had planned everything down to the last second. She didn't particularly like Beth and didn't particularly care what happened to her. But Sandra was a different story. She was her best friend.

"Well, I can just see one of the two of you flipping out and not being able to get the police there," Ashley typed.

"We're probably going to be semi-drunk or stoned or something," Sandra replied. "And just be the silent type."

"Don't be semi-stoned," Ashley shot back. "Because if they think it, for some odd reason, couldn't they force a drug test and use it against you later, saying you were stoned so it would be easier for you to commit the act? Although I guess it doesn't matter since you would come up positive anyways."

Like her, Sandra and Beth regularly smoked dope. Ashley knew the drug would show up on a blood or urine test. But Sandra told her not to worry. "We always come home like that though—we're teens," Sandra typed.

"Teens in front of a jury who see two punks," Ashley replied.

At that moment, Ashley suddenly thought about her own

well-being. The police might think she was involved in their murder plot.

"Please don't get me in court though, alright?" Ashley asked. "Because I really don't wanna have to lie in court."

Again, Sandra told her not to worry. She had everything under control.

"That's only if they don't keep it an open and shut case of drunken drowning," Sandra said. "Don't worry."

Ashley still needed to be certain the sisters had worked out every little detail.

"She's gonna be in her bathroom right?" Ashley asked. "And where is Bobby?"

Sandra said her six-year-old half brother would be staying the weekend at his father's residence. "Otherwise, we wouldn't do anything," Sandra reassured her. Sandra then told her they got the Tylenol-3s from Justin.

"That's cool," Ashley typed and then asked Sandra to "run through" the plan for her one more time.

"Later," Sandra typed back. "Too lazy."

"I wanna hear your plan," Ashley insisted.

"Wouldn't it be better if you knew less?" Sandra typed.

"Not really, I'm involved no matter what 'cause I know about it," Ashley typed. "And technically, although I promise I won't, I should go to the police so I'm not an accessory to the crime. I won't go. Don't worry. So I may as well hear the plan."

But Sandra didn't want to talk about it online. "You can hear it at Jack Astor's," Sandra typed. Sandra previously told Ashley they were going to inherit some of their mother's life insurance money but she couldn't remember the exact details so she asked her how much money they stood to gain.

"When I'm eighteen, like seventy thousand dollars," Sandra

typed. "Unless it doubles or whatever 'cause it's an accidental death. It's seventy thousand each, too."

Ashley asked if she had checked out the insurance plan to make sure there weren't any catches. Sandra said they hadn't but "if we don't get money, shit happens." Ashley then suggested police might think their mother had committed suicide.

"Suicide is intentional," Sandra typed. "If she falls asleep she's not trying to kill herself."

"I know but if she falls asleep with three Tylenol-3s it might seem another way," Ashley said.

But Sandra had done her homework. Sandra knew exactly how many pills to give her mother, and how many pills not to give her, to avoid suspicion. And most important, to ensure their mother's death didn't look like she deliberately killed herself.

"People who want to OD take like fifteen," Sandra said. "Plus, if we have to argue for it, we will."

"But the insurance company would argue," Ashley said. "After an autopsy of the liver that she was drinking herself to her grave, a prolonged suicide."

Sandra then told her they would be taking her mother's bankcard. She thought there was $800 in the account. Ashley then reassured Sandra she was still behind her.

"I'm not trying to talk you out of it," Ashley typed. "I know it would be useless since I've tried before. But I'm just trying to look at every single aspect just in case somehow you missed one. I'm not saying you did. But you never know."

"Ah well, I'm not only doing it for the money," Sandra typed. "This probably seems weird but it's as if I'm gonna leave on a vacation soon. That's what I'm feeling."

"Well, the excitement part," Ashley typed. "I'd say that's called adrenalin."

"Does that make sense?" Sandra asked, wanting to know what Ashley thought about her feeling excited about murdering her mother.

"You're about to do something that will affect the rest of your life no matter how short you plan on living. And how much you hate the person," Ashley replied.

"Exactly," Sandra typed, and then told Ashley she should see the joint she was rolling. But Ashley warned her not to get too high because it would make her sloppy. Then Ashley asked if Justin was with them.

"Nope," Sandra replied, and then again told her not to worry about her getting high. "This weed is for Jack Astor's, I guess. I'm not dumb enough to do anything before."

Ashley then asked if she was going to smoke dope inside the restaurant.

"Yeah, do you want any?" Sandra asked.

"I dunno, it depends on whether you went through with it or not," Ashley typed. "Or how much I have to not care. I doubt it though so don't worry."

"Not inside," Sandra typed. "Okay, we'll do it before we meet you."

"When are you doing it?" Ashley asked. "You never answered, how long? 'Cause you're gonna have to wait for the pills to kick in."

"Yeah, we do it after she's completely unresponsive," Sandra typed. "Meaning they kick in—so that's gonna be in an hour?"

Ashley was surprised. "Oh, you've already given them to her?"

"Four of them," Sandra replied. "Plus a bottle of vodka. And wine."

"Oh my God," Ashley, now excited, typed. "How did you get her to take them?"

"She just takes them and forgets," Sandra typed. "She's stupid."

"Oh, you said they were like some sort of drug," Ashley said.

"They have codeine in them," Sandra typed. "And alcohol intensifies the effects."

"How is she right now?" Ashley then asked.

"Passing out," Sandra replied.

"Like barely moving?" Ashley asked.

And then Ashley gave her friend one more bit of advice.

"Well good luck—wear gloves," Ashley typed.

"Yeah, we got those too," Sandra replied. "Bye."

CHAPTER 1
FOUR MINUTES

Sandra had initially fantasized about burning her mother alive. The idea came to her when she was watching a television documentary on spontaneous combustion; how a person allegedly burst into flames in a chair. The idea of burning her mother to death was very intriguing. What if she waited for her mother to pass out on her bed from booze? Then she could douse her with wine, then light a cigarette and leave it on the bed, smouldering, until the covers caught fire. It would be so simple.

"But too gruesome and too horrible," Sandra told her friends.

As much as she hated her mother, Sandra didn't want her to suffer. She was already in enough pain from battling her alcohol demons. Besides, even if she was passed out when Sandra lit the cigarette, there was still a chance she might suddenly wake up once the flames started burning her flesh. Sandra couldn't take the chance because the thought of her mother's screams would surely haunt her forever.

What about smothering her? Sandra could suffocate her after she passed out from one of her drinking binges. But after giving it some careful consideration Sandra figured there was a good chance police and forensic experts might too easily detect a crime.

What about sleeping pills? Too many pills would look like the mother committed suicide. But her death had to look like an unfortunate accident—none of the insurance money would be paid out if she took her own life.

Then Sandra thought about drowning.

It would be a lot less messy.

Her little brother, Bobby, absolutely needed to be out of the home. She consulted the calendar. He would be away the weekend of January 17, when it was his turn to spend the weekend with Doug Landers, his biological father.

The drowning scenario began to take shape. She and Beth would draw their mother a bath and then let things play out. The girls hoped their mother would be so drunk and so sleepy from the Tylenol-3s that she would sink under the warm water in the tub. But Sandra realized she would have to play a more active role in her mother's death; she would have to physically drown her. She couldn't rely on her mother to pass out and fall into a coma.

What if her mother fought back? That's when Sandra decided to use pills laced with codeine. Her mother had used Tylenol-3s in the past, and the painkillers contained codeine, a narcotic she knew acted like sleeping pills if used in large quantities. The Internet provided her with a wealth of knowledge about how codeine reacted with booze and how many pills a person could consume before coming dangerously close to overdose levels. That was really important to the plan because she needed to be absolutely certain she gave her mother only enough pills to put her out, and not enough to kill her. This couldn't look like suicide.

Tylenol-3s could only be obtained with a prescription, and her mother didn't have any in the house. That posed a bit of a problem. Sandra needed to find a source for the pills. That's when Beth told her Justin had some extra Tylenol-3s. Sandra wasn't too keen on having another person know about their plan. She was certain she could trust Jay and Ashley. Both had been supportive. They wouldn't tell anybody or run to the cops afterwards. Her deadly secret would be safe with them. But she really didn't know Justin. In fact, she was a bit pissed at Beth when Beth said Justin had known about their plan for at least two weeks. But Beth vouched for him. Besides, it was the easiest way for them to obtain the Tylenol-3s.

"Justin has them readily available," Beth told Sandra as they went over various ways to get the pills. So Sandra agreed. Besides, it was Justin's idea to meet at Jack Astor's restaurant afterwards for a "nice celebration dinner." They would dine at the popular roadhouse-style restaurant near Mississauga's Square One Shopping Centre as part of their well-planned alibi for when their mother drowned, then return home several hours later. They'd call 911, crying and upset, telling the all-too-caring operator they had just discovered their poor drunk mother dead in the tub.

Sandra figured she could probably get away with giving her mother four to six pills. Any more, and her mother might OD on the pills alone. She could use her mother's alcohol cravings against her. She could exploit her weakness to end her miserable life.

Sandra was absolutely convinced she had created the perfect crime. She would get away with murder.

By the time Ashley chatted with her online that afternoon, Sandra had given her mother at least three and perhaps four Tylenol-3s. She'd been giving them two at a time every half hour, along with drinks of vodka and lemonade, which Beth mixed for her. When she was certain her mother was completely out of it, Sandra and her sister suggested their mother take a bath. After consuming six Tylenol-3s, several glasses of wine and nearly a full twenty-six-ounce bottle of Absolut vodka, Linda was nearly unconscious. She could barely stand as Sandra and Beth led her into the bathroom, helped her undress and got her into the tub. As Linda soaked, Sandra donned a pair of latex gloves, the kind her mother regularly used at the hospital where she had worked as a nurse. Sandra couldn't leave any finger-prints or marks on her mother's body. She knew she had to have to push her mother's head under the water.

"I have to use open hands," Sandra reminded herself. "She bruises so easily."

Even though she and Beth had figured out who would grab Linda's legs and who would take her arms after she passed out on the couch, which she always did when she got drunk, Sandra real-ized that carrying her mother might cause problems. They had to make sure Linda wasn't too out of it to walk into the bathroom.

At the last moment, Sandra wasn't sure she could go through with the plan. But her mother was nearly unconscious from the alcohol and the codeine. It was now or never. Or at least now or wait until the next time she had the nerve.

In the days leading up to the murder, Sandra felt waves of emotion running through her. She was anxious. She was agitated. But she was also excited. She had convinced herself that her mother's spiraling descent into alcoholism had forced her hand. She and Beth were mercy killers. The murder was something they had to do.

Sandra was surprised how easy it was to get her mother undressed and into the tub.

It was just after six in the evening.

Linda was so out of it she climbed into the tub and lay down with her head against the taps. There was no point trying to coax her to lie the other way around. The most important thing was to get her head under the water and keep it there for several minutes. It didn't matter which way her body was facing in the tub.

"Turn over, Mom," Sandra said.

Beth watched from the doorway of the small bathroom. Sandra didn't want to be looking into her mother's eyes when she pushed her head under the water. Linda slowly turned onto to her stomach. Her head was under the faucet.

Sandra took a deep breath, gently pressed on the back of her mother's head, and pushed her face under the water. She had to keep her mother's head submerged for two to six minutes to make sure she drowned. She split the difference.

"Four minutes should be enough."

She began to time her mother's drowning.

It would be horrible if she survives, Sandra thought as she held her mother's head under the water. *I can't take any chances.*

Thoughts roared through her mind.

I'm killing my mother.

She's dead already.

She's drinking herself to death.

She's hopeless.

She's going to die from drinking very, very soon anyways.

Sandra kept reminding herself that her mother had lost her job because of her drinking. Linda really was drinking more every day.

She's out of control.

She's not my mother.

She's just a drunk.

Beth stayed in the doorway as Sandra watched each minute pass. All she needed to do was hold her mother's head under water for at least four minutes. Then it would be all over, and they could set up their alibi.

The phone rang.

Beth ran from the bathroom, leaving Sandra alone, holding her mother's head under the water.

"What are you doing?" Sandra screamed. "Where are you going? Come back here!"

Beth ran to the phone.

It was Ashley.

"This isn't a good time," Beth said, and hung up the phone.

Linda's body twitched and went into convulsions under the water. Sandra knew to expect this. But seeing it live, in person, was a whole lot different than reading about it.

This isn't what I expected.

Except for the twitching, Linda never put up a fight. She didn't struggle. It was far easier than Sandra expected.

By the time Beth returned from answering the phone, Linda Andersen was dead.

CHAPTER 2
THE ALIBI

Beth and Sandra fled their home as quickly as possible. They locked the front door of the townhouse, then headed down the street to a nearby bus stop. They had their mother's bank card. They would later tell police their mother had given them her card to use for dinner.

Sandra and Beth were at the bus stop when Ashley got out of her mother's car.

"It's done. We did it," Sandra told Ashley as they boarded a Mississauga Transit bus at about 7:00 p.m. to go to Square One Shopping Centre. Sandra never said she murdered her mother, but Ashley knew Linda was lying dead in her tub.

This is so surreal, Ashley thought as she stared at her friends. *Oh, my God.*

After their online chat, Ashley thought the sisters would go ahead with the murder. But it wasn't until the moment at the bus stop that she knew for sure they had killed their mother.

Sandra and Beth looked at the other passengers on the bus and then stared at each other.

"They have no idea what we did," Beth whispered to her sister.

It was Justin's idea to meet afterwards at Jack Astor's restaurant. They figured people would remember them if police asked questions. The dinner would work perfectly as their alibi. They would be out of the house with their friends when their mother got drunk and accidentally drowned.

They got off the bus. Just before they got to the restaurant, Sandra reached into the pocket of her winter coat and pulled out the latex gloves. She threw them into a nearby garbage can. She also tossed away a small plastic sandwich bag containing two Tylenol-3 pills.

Justin was waiting in the restaurant's lobby. He'd gotten there about ten minutes earlier. He had called Beth on her cellphone while they were on the bus to see whether everything had gone off as planned. In the lobby, Sandra seemed upset. She was shaking and told Ashley that Justin had provided the pills.

"She was really out of it," Ashley said, recalling what Beth had told her as they waited for the red light to blink on the paging device to let them know their table was ready.

Suddenly a song by Canadian folk-rock band Great Big Sea started playing. They stared at each other when the words "It's the end of the world as we know it (and I feel fine)," came through the speakers.

In the lobby, Ashley learned that Justin's mother used Tylenol-3s to treat some kind of chronic back pain. It had been easy for him to get the pills.

Sandra told Ashley she was really angry with Beth because she wouldn't help and ran out of the bathroom to answer the phone. Sandra said she screamed at Beth not to leave her alone.

Throughout the dinner, Sandra was mostly quiet and withdrawn. She appeared far more upset and anxious than Beth, who spent most of the dinner talking and flirting with Justin.

Sandra barely touched her salad and stared aimlessly at her plate.

I'm in constant pain, Sandra thought. *I'm really, really deep in my hopelessness.*

Ashley noticed how unaffected Beth seemed.

Sandra looks shocked and really bothered, she thought, *but it's as if Beth is out on the town, like it's just a normal night out for dinner. Beth's just eating away, having a good old time with Justin. She's not bothered one bit. She's such an evil one.*

Ashley needed to know all the juicy details. Sandra finally explained how they convinced their mother to take a bath. How she held Linda's head under the water in the tub. How Beth stood watching from the doorway.

"Her body twitched for a long time," Sandra said, and then explained how weird it was to kill a person. "It wasn't the way I expected it."

As Sandra talked, Ashley felt mesmerized, almost as if she were a zombie. She was eating and listening but also just going through the motions. She was there but not there. In her mind she knew Linda was dead, but she couldn't make her mind believe that Sandra and Beth had murdered her.

"It's like watching a movie I'm starring in," is how Ashley described it.

Ashley never liked Beth, and wasn't really surprised "the Goth girl" (her phrase for Beth) didn't seem upset, because Ashley never saw Beth show much emotion about anything.

As she sat at the table, Ashley thought, *Beth's so evil. It wouldn't surprise me one bit if she pulled the strings, not Sandra.*

Ashley had met Justin a couple of times. He was dating another girl, but Ashley suspected his relationship with Kelly was history by the way he was carrying on with Beth. Ashley knew Beth had recently gone shopping in downtown Toronto for clothing she hoped Justin would find sexually appealing. Beth and Justin saw each other every day at school. They might not be officially dating—exclusive to each other—but Beth was obsessed with Justin, and doing whatever she could to impress him.

The conversation eventually turned to which of the sisters was more upset. At one point, Sandra accused Beth of not feeling anything and criticized her for the role she played, or didn't play, in their mother's murder. Beth accused her big sister of pretending to be upset when she was glad it was over.

"Mother's dead," Sandra scolded Beth.

"You're not upset," Beth countered.

"You weren't the one who did it," Sandra said. "I was."

"I was involved with you," Beth replied.

"But I was the one who held her head under the water," snapped Sandra.

"She was relaxed," Beth said. "She didn't even struggle much."

Sandra and Beth cooled down, and their conversation turned to their alibi. They would be crying when they called 911. They would be in tears when the police arrived. They told Justin and Ashley how they had plied their mother with alcohol and fed her Tylenol-3 pills before drowning her.

A few hours later, Sandra figured there was no point staying any longer so they paid their bill and left to catch the bus home.

Justin went home. But Ashley met another friend and went to the movies.

CHAPTER 3
AND THE OSCAR
GOES TO . . .

It was about 10:30 p.m. when Sandra and Beth returned to their townhouse. After removing her winter coat, Sandra climbed the stairs and knocked on the bathroom door.

She pushed open the door. Her eyes immediately zeroed in on the tub and her dead naked mother, still on her stomach under the water. The reality of what she'd done finally hit her.

Mother is really dead.

Beth was supposed to make the emergency phone call. She had boasted about how she would do it during an online chat with Justin five days earlier. When it came time to make the call, Sandra had to do it. In the days leading up to the murder, the sisters had rehearsed over and over what they were going to say and how they were going to say it. They had also practised telling Ashley, Jay, and Justin. They had to be convincing. They couldn't slip up. They had to make sure nobody suspected what really happened in their bathroom. They even practised crying. They were good actors, good at lying, and very good at manipulating people. Sandra and Beth told their friends they had to act all freaked out and play the role of poor grieving motherless kids to get away with their perfect crime.

Sandra dialed 911 at 10:33 p.m.

"Emergency, police, fire, or ambulance?" the 911 operator asked.

"I don't know," Sandra replied, sobbing into the telephone.

"What's the problem?" the operator asked.

"I think my mom is dead in the tub," Sandra said.

"You think your mother is dead?" the operator asked.

"Yeah, she's—" Sandra began, then told the operator she and her sister just got home.

"How old is your mother?" the operator asked.

"I don't know," Sandra said then looked at Beth for the answer. "How old is Mom?"

"She was born in 1959," Beth said.

"She was born in 1959," Sandra told the operator.

Beth started adding up the numbers in her head. "So she's forty-three," Beth told Sandra, who relayed the information to the operator.

"How old are you?" the operator asked.

"I'm sixteen," Sandra said.

"And did she have a medical problem?" the operator asked.

"No. I don't know," Sandra answered. "I don't think so."

"Okay, well, how, uh, what has she done?" asked the operator. "Has she done something to herself?"

"Well I got, uh, well, I, because we left earlier to go, like go out with other friends, and she was drunk and now she's in the tub, like not moving," Sandra said, sobbing and sounding panicky.

"Okay, I need you to calm down, just a little bit, okay?" the operator told her.

"'Kay," Sandra replied.

"Because I don't know what you're saying," the operator said. "You left and she was drunk, and then what?"

"And now she's just, like—she wanted me to draw her a bath, and now she's like—dead in there," Sandra said.

"Where is she?" asked the operator. "She on the bed?"

"She's in the washroom in the tub," Sandra said. "In the bathtub."

"She's in the tub?" the operator asked.

"Yeah," Sandra replied.

"Does she have a pulse?" asked the operator.

"I don't know," Sandra answered, sounding scared and nervous. "I don't wanna touch her, 'cause she's under water."

"She's under water?" asked the operator.

"Yeah," Sandra replied.

"Okay, do you know anything about CPR?" the operator asked.

"No," Sandra answered.

"Do you wanna grab her and pull her out of the water?" asked the operator.

Sandra never expected that question.

"I haven't like, like—" Sandra began to cry again.

"Her head is under the water?" the operator asked. "Is that what you're telling me?"

"Yeah," Sandra answered.

"Can you get it out?" asked the operator. "We have everybody on the way but it would help if you got her out of the water. Can you do that?"

"Well, how am I supposed to get her out of the water?" Sandra asked. "Just like, lift her up or—"

"Just can you slide her head up so she can maybe get some oxygen?" asked the operator.

"But she's not moving at all," Sandra said.

"Pardon?" asked the operator.

"She's not moving at all," Sandra repeated, almost hysterical.

"Okay, just calm down," the operator said. "I have lots of help on the way. Okay. Is your front door unlocked?"

Sandra turned to her sister. "Is the door unlocked?" she asked.

"Um, should I unlock it?" Beth asked.

"My sister's gonna unlock it," Sandra told the operator, who reminded her that help was on the way. Again the operator asked Sandra if she knew CPR.

"No," Sandra told her.

"You don't?" the operator asked.

"We had it in gym class in grade nine but I didn't even pay attention," Sandra said.

"And you don't wanna try it?" the operator asked.

"No," Sandra said.

"You sure?" the operator asked.

"Yeah, yeah, I don't wanna touch her, she's not—" Sandra was becoming hysterical.

"All right, all right, all right, calm down," the operator said.

Moments later Peel Regional Police Constable Blair Horner knocked on their front door, and Beth opened it.

"My mom's, like, in the tub upstairs," Beth told Horner, pointing up the stairs to the bathroom on the landing.

"Is that the police?" asked the operator.

Sandra didn't answer.

Horner asked if anybody else was in the house.

"Just us," Sandra told him.

"Just us," Beth said.

Horner asked what happened.

"We got home, not even five minutes ago, maybe," Beth said.

"Anyone else in the house then?" Horner asked.

"No," Sandra answered, then hung up the phone.

The officer then climbed the stairs.

CHAPTER 4
A BOOZE BATH

Constable Blair Horner was the first officer on the scene, at 10:36 p.m. His initial task was to determine what happened and whether the young girls were okay. Both girls seemed extremely upset. Horner thought this surely had to be the worst moment of their lives. They told him they had found their mother face down in the bathtub when they returned home after dinner with friends. Their mother was an alcoholic, and she suffered from depression.

"She seemed all right when we left the house," an emotional Sandra told Horner.

Their mother had been watching television and had given them her bank card so they could pay for dinner.

Beth was crying and very distraught when she opened the door for Horner. After getting a few brief details Horner told them to remain in the foyer while he went to check on their mother in the bathroom. He found Linda naked in the tub, face down in the water, her left side slightly lower than the right. Her legs were bent, and her right arm was hanging over the edge of the tub.

To Horner, the woman was obviously dead, although he never checked for signs of life. He thought it was strange for somebody to drown face down in her own bathtub. It was also a bit odd that her head was facing the faucet. The tub held about six inches of water, and the dead woman's skin appeared very pale, almost grey. As he scanned the bathroom he noted its condition, the half-filled orange glass of clear liquid, and various bathroom and toiletry items on the edge of the sink. There was also a single unlit cigarette on top of the medicine cabinet, but there was no ashtray in the bathroom. Horner also noticed that the faucet was dripping. He saw what appeared to be a small bit of vomit or fecal matter at the bottom of the tub. Underwear and a T-shirt were on the floor beside the tub.

It wasn't unusual for police to arrive at an emergency call before paramedics. When Horner received the call to attend the townhouse he was patrolling the neighbourhood in his cruiser.

Constable Mike Farley was the second police officer to arrive. As he entered the home, paramedics were making their way up the staircase towards the bathroom. Farley noticed two young girls standing in the foyer, crying and consoling each other.

As Mississauga firefighter captain Al Moore entered the bathroom with paramedics Peter Hayes and Bill Hueston, he thought it was odd the dead woman was face down in the tub. Usually if friends or relatives are in a home where somebody drowns in a bathtub, the first thing they do is take the person out of the water and try resuscitation. But there were no indications that anyone had tried to take the woman out of the tub.

Linda was still warm to touch but had no pulse when Hayes and Hueston lifted her from the bathtub and laid her in the doorway on a yellow blanket. Hayes noticed the water appeared clean and felt warm but not hot. Linda was a rather large woman, and it wasn't easy for them to lift her out of the tub.

When Hayes later made his notes he claimed the deceased woman was sitting up in the tub with her head slumped over. Hayes thought she had been lying down in a reclining position with the water at chest height and her face out of the water, her left hand dangling over the edge.

"She looked as if she had passed out," Hayes wrote in his notes.

Hayes tried to pry open her jaw to clear her airways in case there was a chance to save her life. But he couldn't move her jaw. Rigor mortis had already set in. Rigor almost always starts in the jaw and usually begins between four to six hours after death.

As was standard practice, Constable Farley separated the two girls so they could provide independent statements without relying on each other for information. He wanted to get a complete and accurate picture of what happened, and of the events leading to the tragedy.

Constable Mike Pulley arrived and began searching for any medication Linda might have taken to explain how the accident happened. He knew Horner had checked the kitchen and hadn't found any medication with Linda's name on it, but had not looked into the medicine cabinet in the bathroom. Pulley found a bottle of pills in the bathroom cabinet. It contained cyclonamine, a drug nobody at the scene had heard of. Detective Richard Schock, in charge of the sudden death investigation, checked with a local European pharmacy the next day and learned the drug wasn't usually prescribed in North America. It was widely prescribed in Europe to treat low blood pressure and to control hemorrhage bleeding. Its side effects included nausea and skin irritation, but there were no cautions about using it with alcohol.

As far as Pulley was concerned, the tragedy appeared pretty much as advertised.

"It seemed like a straightforward sudden death," he said.

Of course, like all officers, Pulley kept an open mind. The death could have been an accident or a suicide, which is why he went looking for prescription drugs such as sleeping pills. But he never thought a murder had taken place. As he searched the home, nothing jumped out. He noticed an empty twenty-six-ounce bottle of vodka on the dining room table. When he went down to the basement where Sandra and Beth were being interviewed, he noticed one dark and dreary basement bedroom with death-theme drawings on the walls. Pulley also looked into the kitchen cupboards and refrigerator but found no drugs. There was nothing unusual about the home, although it was a bit messy. Later, when he looked at photos of the bathroom, he noticed that the shower curtain was inside the tub. Normally, people put it on the outside when taking a bath.

In their interviews with Farley and Horner, both girls told the same story. Their mother often passed out from drinking. She had suffered from depression for several years. Sandra told Horner that she and her sister had gone to dinner at Jack Astor's around 6:00 p.m.

"She was drunk but still let us use her bank card," Sandra said. She said they met a friend at the bus stop and took a bus to Square One, where they met another friend for dinner. They went straight home afterwards and arrived about 10:30 p.m. She discovered her mother dead in the tub and called 911 a few minutes later.

To Horner, Sandra seemed composed, and her voice was clear and understandable during their fifteen-minute interview. She didn't appear drunk. She was less emotional than when he first entered their home. During the interview, Sandra never cried once. That was a bit strange, he thought, considering she was the one who found her mother. Still, he knew from experience that people handle tragedy differently. He had no reason to believe Sandra was lying to him. There was nothing to suggest anything but an accidental drowning.

Beth, meanwhile, told Farley that she got up about 2:00 p.m. and spent much of the afternoon chatting online with friends. Their mother had spent most of the afternoon drinking and watching movies on television. Beth couldn't remember exactly when they returned home after dinner but said Sandra called 911 about five minutes after she found Linda. They had to unlock the front door when they returned home. Beth never touched her mother's body. Their younger brother, Bobby, was staying with his father.

"My mom didn't seem upset about anything when we left earlier," Beth told Farley.

Beth had helped her mother fill out a new job application form for another hospital position. Even though her mom had been depressed, Beth told Farley she believed things were getting better over the past couple of weeks because her mother was looking forward to getting a new job. Farley noticed that Beth also didn't seem as distraught as she had initially.

"She was much calmer and quiet," Farley said. "Not hysterical or crying."

Farley didn't think there was anything suspicious about her demeanor. There was nothing to suggest her grief wasn't genuine.

Sergeant Bernie Webber, one of Canada's top blood-splatter experts, arrived about 11:30 p.m. He'd been told a woman was found face down in a tub that had a water temperature of about seventy-two degrees Fahrenheit. There had been a half-empty glass of vodka on a sink near the tub.

Because drowning in a bathtub is so very rare, police automatically considered Linda's death suspicious. It was Webber's job to see if he could find anything that might send the case into an entirely different direction. As a forensic investigator, it was his job to "always think dirty." But he couldn't find anything. Still, as he drove to the home his initial mindset was "Nobody drowns in their own bathtub."

There were no signs of a struggle in the small bathroom. There were so many toiletry items on the counter that something would have been knocked over had there been a fight. The shower curtain was inside the tub, but maybe it had been moved when Linda was lifted from the water. The relatively small amount of water in the tub didn't concern him either. There would have been water displacement when Linda was removed; her body would have raised the water level several inches. Face up in the tub or face down, there would have been at least eight inches of water, the average distance from the back of the head to a person's nose.

To Webber, there was nothing to suggest the bathroom was a crime scene.

"An accidental death or death by misadventure," Webber wrote in his notes.

Webber had attended the scene under the coroner's authority, not under the direction of a homicide investigation, which meant his work was confined to a narrow and specific area. His job was to assist Coroner Dr. Robert Boyko, not to pick apart a crime scene. He took photos and gave the bathroom a cursory look. Had he found any reason to believe the drowning was anything but an accident, all officers would have immediately stopped what they were doing and the entire home would have been cordoned off as a crime scene until a formal search warrant had been secured, as required by law, from a Justice of the Peace.

But that didn't happen. When Webber arrived, Linda was lying under a blanket in the hallway. An officer said she had been face down in the water. A paramedic said she had been sitting up. Sandra said she found her mother face down. Webber understood why Linda had been removed from the water. The preservation of life took precedence over the gathering of evidence.

But Webber knew it was rare for a person to drown in her own bathtub; he expected to get a call the next day telling him to go back to the home and investigate a crime scene. He thought the autopsy might uncover a bruise on the back of her head or other suspicious marks that hadn't been visible when Linda was found. Webber left word with the officer who attended the autopsy to call him the minute anything untoward turned up.

With no crime scene, police never seized any items from the bathroom. They never checked any glasses for DNA or lifted any fingerprints. They didn't examine every nook and cranny, shift through the garbage, or rip apart the bathroom looking for evidence that would prove murder.

Webber never thought Linda had drowned accidentally; he thought it more likely she had committed suicide. He knew people often found ingenious ways of killing themselves— including drowning in their own toilet. But there was nothing to suggest Linda took her own life.

Two days later, on January 20, at about 10:00 a.m., Dr. Tim Feltis, a forensic pathologist at Credit Valley Hospital in Mississauga, conducted the autopsy on Linda Andersen. Dr. Feltis knew Linda had been officially pronounced dead at the scene at 11:55 p.m. by Dr. Boyko. He knew alcohol might have been involved and that Linda suffered from depression. Dr. Feltis had performed more than three thousand autopsies, more than a hundred of them homicides. Andersen's death seemed a bit unusual because she had been found face down in the tub. But he ruled that cause of death was fresh-water drowning due to excessive alcohol in her system.

At the time of her death, Linda's blood alcohol level was 415 milligrams of alcohol in 100 milliliters of blood—a potentially fatal level and more than five times the legal limit for Ontario. He also found what he called a "hallmark sign" of fresh-water drowning: pinkish-white, frothy fluid in her throat, lungs, and sinuses. And there were bursting blood vessels in her lungs, also a sign of drowning.

Even though everything pointed to an accidental drowning after a large consumption of alcohol, the police and Dr. Feltis were suspicious. People generally didn't drown in their own bathtubs, and when they did, they usually were not face down.

Dr. Feltis checked Andersen's neck muscles for signs of hemorrhaging, which might indicate she'd been held underwater against her will. He expected to find "minor twitching," a sign that the brain lacked oxygen during a drowning or hanging. He didn't find any trauma.

The autopsy didn't tell him whether her death was an accident, a homicide, or a suicide. But the alcohol found in her blood would have lowered her blood oxygen level so her body could no longer sustain life.

He concluded Andersen was alive and still breathing, although likely unconscious, when she began to drown. There was no evidence she'd been held against her will. He noted that there likely wouldn't be any signs of bruising or trauma if her head had been gently pushed under the water.

Dr. Feltis estimated the time of death as four to six hours before her daughters discovered her at about 10:45 p.m.

Horner reported he had found Linda face down in the tub. Paramedic Hayes reported finding her sitting up with her head above the water. For investigators, that posed a bit of a problem. They had to conclude that somebody simply forgot they had moved her when they started to work on her while she was still in the tub.

No drug tests were ordered. Linda's blood alcohol was enough to induce unconsciousness and drowning. Dr. Feltis examined Linda Andersen's liver and found that she suffered from alcoholic hepatitis—the early stages of sclerosis of the liver. She did not have cirrhosis of the liver, a fatal disease.

Police maintained the scene until they received the results of the autopsy. Investigators had no reason to suspect foul play, so they did not order a toxicology test. Still, blood samples were taken from Linda's heart and veins and stored as a matter of procedure. Investigators took a second look at the townhouse a few days later, but her death remained classified as an accidental drowning.

CHAPTER 5
NOT EXACTLY
THE BRADY BUNCH

If Sandra and Beth had a vote, Linda would never have won a Mother of the Year contest. Then again, they wouldn't have taken home any trophies as Daughters of the Year.

Linda certainly had big problems, and her co-workers at the hospital where she had worked had known she was having trouble with her daughters. Many of those co-workers left the funeral feeling they would have hit the bottle, too, if they had to deal with Sandra and Beth every day.

Linda was well-liked by many of her co-workers, who considered her a hard-working nurse. She always smiled, got along with everybody, and went out of her way to help others. One co-worker said Linda would "light up" whenever she talked about her daughters, and called them "academically gifted students."

Could Linda have been talking about the girls who showed up at her funeral with green and pink hair, dressed in dark, ragged-looking clothes? The two teenagers giggled and laughed with their friends just a few feet away from Linda's open casket.

Linda's co-workers left the funeral feeling appalled by the way Sandra and Beth acted. Linda had told some of them how little respect her daughters gave her, but they were shocked by what they saw. But none of the hospital workers imagined the girls had murdered their mother.

"They were very disrespectful," said Charles Boswell, one of Linda's closest friends at the hospital. "They looked as if they would rather be somewhere else with their friends. They seemed casual, almost upbeat. They had smiles on their faces when this young guy walked in. They didn't look sorry. It seemed as if they couldn't wait to get out of there. Everybody else, [Linda's] co-workers, family, and other close friends, were crying. But they weren't. Linda seemed like a nice person who was working her fingers to the bone for her kids. She tried hard to provide for them. She seemed like a good mother to me."

Kim Wiley, another close friend from the hospital, said the girls "didn't look very grief stricken [or] very saddened by their mother's death. They sat in the church pews with their backs to their mom and laughed with their friends the whole time. The girl with the green hair laughed especially loud. Nobody believed they could laugh while their mother was lying dead in the open casket. It was strange that the people she worked with were grieving more than her own daughters."

Several co-workers were stunned by the girls' dark shabby clothes. They also didn't think it was appropriate show up with spiked hair.

Co-worker Jill Ponti described Linda as an "energetic, kind-hearted person who was always very pleasant to be around." Jill didn't remember seeing Linda in a bad mood during the two years they worked together. She found it odd that Linda's daughters didn't seem distraught.

Another hospital worker, Kim Lancaster, was disgusted. "They looked hard and unemotional and they weren't crying."

Mike Morden, another hospital friend, thought Linda's

daughters were "very unemotional," particularly the older daughter. "They and their friends were giggling and laughing with each other."

Hospital worker Joey Randford also noticed Sandra and Beth laughing and giggling with their friends. "They didn't seem distraught when I offered them my condolences. Their behaviour angered me."

Another hospital co-worker, Mandy McPherson, thought the daughters were trying to be cool. "But it didn't seem ... as if they were at a funeral. Their hair was radically coloured. They kept whispering to each other. They seemed excited and were giggling and smiling. It was just weird."

Edward Brockman, a lawyer Linda had been dating, thought her daughters acted strange and that their attire was peculiar. "It looked as if they were ready to go out on a night on the town."

Even though she had just turned sixteen the summer of 2002, in many ways Sandra was the sole parent in the very dysfunctional household she shared with Linda and with Beth and Bobby, when he wasn't living with his father.

In fact, she later told a probation officer it was the worst summer of her life.

Like Cinderella, Sandra cooked and cleaned her home and took care of Bobby, but there was no glass slipper and no Prince Charming to take her away from her unbearable life.

Linda's drinking was worsening. Sandra couldn't have a normal conversation with her; every attempt ended in a shouting match. Sandra talked to Linda only to ask her for money or to comment on her drinking. Linda denied that she had a problem. But she drank daily, enough to be fired from her nursing job at a local hospital. She had been booking off, sometimes not showing up. Some co-workers complained she came to work with alcohol on her breath.

Most days Linda started drinking in the morning, then drank until she passed out on the living room couch watching television, where she sometimes sprawled half-naked in front of Sandra, Beth, and their friends. Drinking dulled the pain of a failed relationship: Linda realized her dates with lawyer Edward Brockman were really a series of one-night sexual romps.

Sandra hated her life, and she blamed her mother. She and her siblings lived in a rented townhouse in what Linda's daughters called the "Mississauga ghetto." Her mother spent all her money on alcohol, not on Sandra, Beth, and Bobby. Most summers, Linda had sent Sandra and Beth to visit their maternal grandparents in Holland. But this summer, Sandra had a crush on a certain boy. She needed to work on him the entire summer. So there was no way in hell she was going to be shipped off to Holland. Sandra and Linda battled daily about where Sandra would spend the summer.

As a child, Sandra had been a bit of a loner. She was intellectually gifted but introverted, and had so few friends she often made up imaginary ones. But Sandra had become popular during the recently completed Grade 10 school year and had many amazing friends. There was no way she was spending the entire summer away from people who accepted her even though she lived on the other side of the proverbial tracks. Her friends came from families where money never seemed to be an issue. They lived in big houses, had nice clothes, nice furniture, and all the food they'd ever want to eat, and they never had to do a damn thing for their parents. Some had swimming pools. They didn't live in millionaire homes, but they had access to money and enjoyed a far better lifestyle than Sandra. They wore designer jeans, bought their clothes at trendy upscale stores, and sported Nike running shoes, while Sandra and Beth made do with hand-me-downs or if lucky, got to pick their clothing off of the rack at their local Value Village.

Sandra believed she deserved the lifestyle her friends had.

"I feel like a monster," she later told a psychiatrist when she compared the difference between her lifestyle and her friends.

But Sandra and her friends did have one thing in common; they liked to party hard. They frequently skipped school. They smoked pot and drank. Sometimes, they even went to school drunk or got high during lunch.

Sandra belittled her mother for thinking Edward Brockman, nearly twenty years her senior, would marry a fat woman like her. But if by some miracle they got married, maybe Sandra's life would get better. The family would have nicer things, better clothes, and certainly Sandra would have a lot more spending money to waste on booze and pot. Perhaps they'd even get a new home with a swimming pool. Still, Sandra hated how her mother drooled over Brockman. Linda once told her daughter that Brockman was the best lover she ever had, and that they had had anal sex. Sandra yearned for heart-to-heart mother-daughter talks, but hearing Linda discuss her fucking techniques wasn't what Sandra had in mind. Sometimes when she was drunk, Linda asked Sandra to send emails to Brockman, which of course Sandra never did. Linda also confided that she'd stopped taking her birth control pills because she hoped Brockman would marry her if she got pregnant. Sandra needed another little kid to look after as much as a she needed a bullet in her head, although she thought that would be a dramatic way to end her own life when she decided her time was up.

Although Sandra drank with her friends, she regarded her alcohol consumption as merely social drinking, not something she absolutely needed to do to get through each day. Anyways, Sandra preferred pot to booze. Smoking dope "was cool" and allowed her to fit in with her "amazing stoner friends." She and Beth both knew their mother was in denial. Linda hid bottles of booze in their home and denied she was an alcoholic. When Sandra and Beth mentioned their concerns to their father, Walter, who divorced Linda in the mid-1990s, he told them to call the police if things were that bad, which of course they never did.

Linda had no job and was in a dead-end relationship, and alcohol seemed to be her only salvation. She let her motherly duties slide, and those duties fell on Sandra's shoulders. Before she lost her job, Linda would phone several times each day to check up on Sandra. Sandra hated that. But now Linda was at home and always in Sandra's face. And that was far worse.

Sandra resented having to clean the house and cook. She was also expected to take care of Bobby. (Linda's abusive relationship with Doug Landers had ended two years earlier, when Doug put a knife to Linda's throat during one of their regular shouting matches.) Sandra told everybody how much she loved Bobby, but she later told a probation officer that taking care of him cut into her drug time.

In the summer of 2002, Linda sent Bobby to Holland with Beth, but Bobby stayed for only a few weeks. When he came home he once again became Sandra's full-time responsibility when he wasn't with his dad.

Beth returned home from Holland at the end of the summer, and Sandra's hatred for her life and her mother was deeper than ever. She was also becoming concerned about her future. Sandra dreamed of being rich and famous, of being a millionaire, a movie producer, a rock star, a flight attendant, a paramedic, an ambulance driver, a novelist—but she believed her dreams would never be possible because of the life she lived. She felt hopeless. She pitied her mother and hated her at the same time. She knew things would never change, and she was convinced no one would help her and Beth—not their relatives or Linda's friends or society. Sandra cried herself to sleep many nights, believing she was all alone and that nobody cared about her or Beth.

Sandra often fantasized about killing herself and romanticized her death—jumping out of a building or slicing her wrists. But she told a probation officer she had more potential than Linda had, so taking her own life didn't make a whole lot of sense. Besides, she believed it would only be a matter of time before her mother's drinking led to cirrhosis of the liver. If booze didn't soon put Linda in a cold grave, the woman would kill herself while driving; she often drove drunk.

"It was inevitable," Sandra told a psychiatrist and a probation officer. She also told a probation officer she had prepared herself for "life without mom." But watching Linda die was like living in hell.

At the end of the summer, Sandra was going for walks in the middle of the night in her pyjamas. She smoked more and more pot and thought about what she could do to make her life better. Mostly she thought about Linda, who had stopped being a mother. She wasn't there for her children anymore. Her alcoholism was out of control. She was gaining weight. She was having trouble functioning. She was often out of a job. She wasn't earning money. She was embarrassing. She masturbated in front of Sandra's friends.

Sandra told a probation officer that her mother was sinking and had no escape, so she (Sandra) decided to speed up the process. She fantasized that her friends would come live with her in the townhouse, where they'd be one big happy family after Linda died. If that didn't work, Sandra and Beth could live with their aunt Martha, who was an architect. Martha would give them the lifestyle they deserved. They'd have nice clothes and a nice home they could bring their friends to without embarrassment. Aunt Martha didn't sprawl half-naked on the living room couch and she didn't swear or yell at her in front of her friends. She would also have more access to pot. Her cousin Derek always seemed to have a ready supply. One day she would also try more harder drugs.

Sandra and Beth would eventually get their share of Linda's $200,000 life insurance, although the money would be held in trust until they were eighteen. But Sandra was sure Aunt Martha would give them an allowance.

"It's a nice plus, a bonus," she told Beth and their friends.

Sandra wanted to have Beth on her side, but with or without Beth's help, she had made up her mind. After years of feeling depressed and unloved she had finally suffered enough.

Sandra knew what had to be done. She knew somebody needed to die.

"Mother is a hopeless alcoholic," she told a probation officer. "It's either her or me."

CHAPTER 6
AN APPEALING IDEA

Sandra knew she had to convince Beth that killing their mother would be the best thing for them and Bobby. It would also be the best outcome for Linda.

They would have so much freedom once Linda was gone. They might get to live in their townhouse with their friends. They wouldn't have to answer to anyone. They could stay out as long as they wanted, and come and go as they pleased. They didn't need anybody but themselves and Bobby. They could take care of each other. If they wound up living with Aunt Martha, they would have easy access to their cousins' stash of drugs.

Beth was totally cool with the idea of taking care of Bobby. Neither thought their mother was taking care of him. Bobby would be so much better off without his mother in his life.

Beth initially didn't like the rest of her big sister's plan, but she soon came on board.

"You can't stop me, and I'm going to do it with or without you," Sandra told Beth in late fall 2002. They were sharing a joint in the bathroom in which they would murder their mother four months later. Sandra made sure Beth knew she had no choice in the matter.

"I have authority over her," Sandra told a probation officer. "I was going to kill her [Linda] anyways."

Sandra saw Beth as "a delicate flower—straitlaced but sharp as a whip." She knew how easily Beth could be hurt, and that she was more a follower than a leader. Sandra was the leader, not Beth, especially when it came to this plan.

"I can make her do almost anything," Sandra told a psychiatrist.

That day in the bathroom Sandra reminded Beth how many times their hopes had been dashed when their mother lost a job. "Even if she gets another job, she's going to lose it too," Sandra told Beth. "There's going to be no ifs and buts. You might as well help me because you're not going to stop me."

"Are you sure?" Beth asked. "Is this truly necessary? Is there no other way?"

"Trust me," Sandra replied. "This is happening. There's nothing you can do about it. We're looking out for Bobby's welfare. He'll be better off without her. Her death will have true meaning. Don't worry, Beth. I'll take care of you. I'll take care of everything."

Sandra told Beth that during the summer Linda was always drunk, slept in most days, and sometimes was drunk in the morning. She reminded Beth that their mother drove while drunk. If she got into an accident, there was a very good chance she might kill them or someone else. Beth remembered the day Linda drove drunk and talked about killing herself—and Sandra and Beth—by driving off a bridge.

Beth thought about Sandra's plan. The more she thought about it, the more merciful it seemed. It started to make a whole lot of sense for them to control how their mother died.

Even if Beth didn't want to kill her mother, she knew Sandra was right: Beth would not be able to stop her. In many ways,

Sandra was Beth's only role model. But even as she looked up to Sandra, Beth often felt frustrated by her older sister, who pushed Beth's buttons and set her off.

"It's hopeless to try and stop her," Beth told a probation officer. "Trying to stop Sandra is like trying to stop a tidal wave. So why try?" Beth also told a probation officer she found the idea of killing an alcoholic mother appealing. There was no malice involved. They were killing their mother to end her pain of alcoholism.

Mother is drinking herself to death.

She will soon be dead from cirrhosis of the liver.

"There was no hope for her anyways," Beth told the probation officer. "Drastic actions are called for in drastic situations. We're not doing this out of anger. It's a mercy killing." She said all her mother ever did was "sit around the house naked, drinking and smoking, soiling herself and hurting everyone."

Linda used to tell Beth and Sandra to go to bed at 3:00 p.m. She also told them "I drink because of you."

Beth remembered how that felt. "This sucks," she told a probation officer. "Why won't she stop?"

Beth wished she could run away from her life, but she would have to leave Bobby behind. And she could never do that. Beth was just ten when Bobby was born, but she often felt Bobby was her son, not her brother. She swore the first word that he ever spoke was her name. She knew Bobby trusted her with his life.

Beth and Sandra sought help for their mother's alcoholism, but it was pointless: family members would tell them "Have faith, things will get better." But things never did, Beth told a probation officer.

Beth didn't have many close friends growing up. By the time she was ten she'd changed schools at least four times, and her geographically unstable life made it difficult for her to develop any lasting friendships. Mostly the family was forced to move because Linda couldn't afford the rent. Moving to a new location and a new school, where she had to try to fit in, upset Beth.

She envied her rich friends and their lifestyle—"They have spending money and I have none," she told a probation officer—and was embarrassed about wearing hand-me-down clothing, or wearing the same clothes to school over and over again.

By the fall of 2002, Beth had friends, one of them Justin, a Goth rocker. He wasn't her boyfriend yet, but Beth had big plans for him in her future.

She had once looked forward to spending summers in Holland with her grandparents. But as she grew older she realized they were aging and dying, and that made her feel quite depressed.

She was thirteen or fourteen when she realized her mother was always tired because she was a drunk, and not because she was overworked. Still, Beth blamed herself for her mother's problems. She was a failure because she couldn't get her mother to stop drinking. "If I'd been a better daughter then maybe she wouldn't have become an alcoholic," Beth told a psychiatrist.

Beth believed Linda wanted to be a good mother. But the booze wouldn't allow Linda to be the kind of mother Beth and Sandra wanted her to be. She missed weeks of work because she was drinking. She never seemed to be emotionally there for either of them, especially when she was drinking, which was almost always. It hurt Beth that her mother neglected her and Sandra; worse, even when she was sober, she neglected Bobby. Like her sister, Beth had many happy memories of her early years, but those memories faded as she got older.

Beth didn't like Edward Brockman, although her thoughts

about him were based on things Sandra said. It was Sandra who told her about their mother's frequent sexual romps with the lawyer and that Linda became infatuated with him after giving him a blow job in his office.

Beth became bored easily, but planning her mother's death certainly wasn't boring. Even though she and Sandra seemed at times to have a psychic connection, the way twins sometimes have, for most of the time, they lived separate lives. They had their own friends and liked different activities. They went to different schools. Beth thought Sandra was often self-serving and went out of her way to hurt people. She hated how Sandra took credit for things Beth had achieved. Beth felt overwhelmed by despair and futility when she thought about her mother's alcoholism, and also when she had to deal with Sandra. But in planning their mother's murder, at least they shared a special bond, one few sisters have shared.

Beth told a probation officer that she thought her mother's life was full of broken hopes, and that Linda was miserable. "She can't hold a job. She's going downhill. She's suicidal," Beth said. "I've got a right to hate her. She's not a mother. She's an alcoholic."

Beth described her own life as "shitty and hopeless," and said her mother's alcoholism was messing up her children's lives.

"You finally break down after a lifestyle such as this," Beth told a psychiatrist. "You can only bear the stress for so long."

In the end, Beth realized Sandra was right. "Mother wasn't even a human being any more," she told a psychiatrist. "She was just a drunk."

Sandra and Beth had always been good students. They took pride in being better than all their friends, even better than each other. But life for the two young teenagers was changing fast in the months leading up to their mother's murder.

Their world deteriorated as their mother sank deeper and deeper into alcoholic despair. Sandra remembered something her maternal grandparents told her a few years earlier, when she and Beth were in Holland and their parents were waging a bitter marital war.

"As long as you get good grades, then everything else will follow," her grandmother said.

So Sandra obtained good grades. She taught herself how to play guitar and was taking violin lessons, becoming a well-rounded young teenager. She cleaned the house and took care of Beth and Bobby like a good sister should. She was an obedient and well-behaved child. As her mother's alcoholism worsened, Sandra made excuses for her. But as she grew older, her life became worse, not better. Her mother's drinking increased, and other family members turned a blind eye to Sandra's pleas for help. She sometimes pretended she wasn't related to her mother, and spent most of her time in her own room, crying and wondering if any of her classmates lived like she and her sister did.

Sandra thought she'd done everything her grandmother told her to do but her grandparents' promise wasn't coming true. Sandra stopped being the good girl and dramatically changed her appearance and attitude. By the end of Grade 10 she was on a rebellious path. She stopped studying, skipped classes, and deliberately failed courses. She craved attention from her mother and hoped Linda would notice that she skipped school and got poor grades.

"Any reaction, even anger, would be better than nothing," Sandra told a probation officer. But Linda seemed not to notice or care that Sandra's grades were slipping and her life was going down the proverbial toilet. Sandra began to despise Linda.

Sandra also began to abuse drugs and alcohol with her like-minded friends. She stopped caring how she looked and started dressing like a bum. Walter, Sandra's father, had promised to give her money if her grades and attendance were good. If her grades fell or she skipped classes, she would owe him. The more she rebelled, the more money she owed her father and the less she saw of him. Sandra also stopped doing her household chores and rarely told her mother where she was going or when she would return home. Sometimes she stayed out all night, often at her aunt Martha's home.

When her mother passed out from excessive drinking, Sandra would steal money from her purse, then convince Linda she had told Sandra to take the cash. Sandra also cashed a Canada Savings Bond her mother had bought in her daughter's name. Linda discovered the bond had been cashed when she needed the funds for a nursing upgrade course.

Sandra hated who her mother had become; she told a probation officer how bitterly betrayed she felt. She wanted to hurt Linda and make her understand how it felt to be abandoned and betrayed.

Beth also believed her grandparents when they told her that if she got good grades her life would get better. Getting good grades meant she was a good person, and Beth needed to be a good person. So she worked very hard to get good grades. Instead of partying with her friends she stayed home and hit the books. As she grew into her teenage years she realized that good grades didn't change the way she and her sister were living. She also realized there was another life out there. She knew she would be a good person even if her grades slipped or if she skipped school. Her mom never went to any parent-teacher interviews and didn't seem to care if Beth failed or passed.

When she was fifteen, in the months before her mother's murder, Beth deliberately underwent a dramatic change in personality and appearance. Like Sandra, she realized there was a huge social price to pay for being a studious goody two-shoes— she had to hang out with nerds, and she didn't like them.

"Studying is for nerds," she told a psychiatrist.

She decided it was far cooler to skip classes and stay out late. She started spiking her hair and dying it different colours, red one day and blue the next. She moved from the skater phase to the black-dressing Goth style and hung out with rockers and stoners, people she could rant to who never asked her tough questions.

By the fall of 2002, like Sandra, she had stopped caring about school, and her grades had dropped dramatically. She'd been in enrichment classes since Grade 4; now she was getting detentions for skipping classes. The once hard-working, intelligent, logical student, with an IQ in the ninety-ninth percentile, deliberately became a defiant dumb-ass almost overnight. Her musical interests turned to Nine Inch Nails and Marilyn Manson. She wanted to impress Justin, her new Goth rocker friend. (She lost her virginity to him in May 2003.) She figured nobody cared about her, so why should she worry about her future.

"Life is hopeless," she told a psychiatrist. "I'm not going to amount to anything anyways."

Like many young teenagers at odds with their parents, Sandra and Beth couldn't see anything positive about their mother. It never entered their mind that Linda was away from home, and always so tired, because she was working two jobs and going to school at night so she could provide for them. All they saw was a drunk passed out on the couch. They never forgave her for bringing Doug Landers into their home. They had to to endure his abuse for several years.

Sandra and Beth sought help from their aunt Martha, but they came to believe she didn't take their concerns seriously. Sandra once complained so much to her mother about her drinking that Linda attended an Alcoholics Anonymous meeting, and she took her sister, Martha, with her. Linda told Martha she felt guilty about drinking beer after work because her daughters were very concerned. But after the AA meeting, Linda decided she had nothing in common with the other people at the meeting, and she never went back. She continued to drink, and she was adept at hiding her alcoholism from her sister. Martha never witnessed any of the behaviour her nieces bitterly complained about. Linda and Martha talked on the phone almost every day, and Martha thought her sister was a good mother, one who provided for her children, cared deeply for them, and never complained about them. Martha believed her nieces enjoyed a good life. She knew they were involved in dance and swimming classes, martial arts lessons, and horseback riding—Linda often went riding with them on Sunday afternoons. Martha knew Linda was struggling financially and lived from paycheque to paycheque; she often lent Linda money, and Linda always paid her back. Martha thought her nieces were materialistic and demanding; they rarely appreciated all their mother did for them.

In the spring of 2001, Sandra called the Children's Aid Society (CAS). Things were getting way out of hand between Linda and Doug Landers, Bobby's father; the couple often argued after drinking heavily. One day Doug slapped Linda across the face. Beth and Sandra wanted to run away, and Sandra called the

CAS. A social worker showed up at their home. But according to court documents, Sandra and Beth said nothing bad about their mother. They never mentioned her drinking problem. Linda praised her daughters and told the social-service worker how delicate and responsible they were—they always looked after their little brother while she was at work. Linda lied about her drinking problems and about her life in general. It was a big charade.

In June 2001, Sandra called the CAS a second time. She told authorities that her mother was an alcoholic, and that Linda had made Sandra and Beth lie to the first social-service worker. Court documents show that Sandra insisted their mother often drove drunk, and that she threw things at her daughters.

According to the documents, Sandra said, "She's mean. She ignores me and treats me as if I don't even exist." Sandra also said she was fed up with having to always look after her sister and younger brother.

"There's no discipline in our home," she said, and claimed her mother embarrassed her when her friends were over, and sometimes threatened them. But CAS officials never believed Linda's children were neglected or in danger.

CHAPTER 7
BEST FRIENDS

At the time of Linda's murder, Donny was Sandra's boyfriend, but her best male friend and confidant was Jay. They were so close she told him her darkest secret—that she had decided to murder her mother—even before she told Beth.

Jay, like Sandra, was sixteen. They were sitting in their high school cafeteria when Sandra told him killing her mother was a good idea because it would put Linda out of her misery. Sandra added that Linda's life insurance policy would be a plus—in her words, a "kind of bonus."

Jay was shocked.

He knew how much Sandra hated that alcohol had taken control of her mother. But he'd never thought Sandra would take such drastic action, or believe the only solution to her problem was to kill her mother. He realized later that Sandra seemed casual about ending her mother's life.

Jay often hung out at Sandra's townhouse with their friends, smoking dope and drinking, usually when Linda wasn't home. Sandra complained that her mother was always drunk and couldn't take care of Bobby, but she thought there was nothing

she could do to stop Linda's drinking. Still, Jay never really
noticed any problems. To him, Linda seemed pretty sober. But
he didn't live with her.

Jay had known Sandra since Grade 7, when they were in
French immersion classes. They became close in Grade 10. Jay
met Beth through Sandra, and in December 2002, a few months
after Sandra revealed her murderous plans, he was dating Beth,
although their budding romance lasted only three weeks.

Even though they weren't romantically involved, Jay and
Sandra were so close that he helped her pull off a big practical
joke on their classmates. Sandra spread a rumour that she was
pregnant with Jay's child. She told a psychiatrist about watching the pregnancy rumour spread throughout the school. She
got a kick out of how much attention she received, not only
from her classmates but also from some of her teachers. Sandra
concocted the story to see whether she could get any reaction
from a particular boy. Jay didn't mind playing along with her.
He told people he was so drunk he didn't remember having sex.
Jay knew the pregnancy story was just a big joke, but he didn't
think Sandra was kidding when she told him she wanted to kill
her mother.

When she told Jay her plans, Sandra wasn't sure exactly
how she would commit the murder. But she had big ideas for
afterwards. She would quit school and travel around the world
using Linda's life insurance money. She also planned to take Jay
and some other close friends on a big "European vacation" to
Amsterdam once she turned eighteen.

Sandra insisted that the insurance money wasn't her reason
for killing Linda. But Jay thought it was weird that she seemed
so happy to tell him she was going to take him and her friends
to Europe with the blood money. Sure, it would be great to go

on the European junket, but Sandra would be using money she got from murdering Linda.

It seemed so callous and surreal.

Sandra's friend Ashley also dreamed of being lots of things, and she knew Sandra loved to tell wild stories to gain attention. Ashley thought it would be awesome to become an actress and play Buffy the Vampire Slayer. Sandra dreamed of being a writer and winning the Nobel Prize one day.

"Sandra was absolutely convinced she was going to discover something one day or do something absolutely fabulous, become famous and win the Nobel Prize," Ashley said. "She also wanted to be a millionaire, but who doesn't?"

So when Sandra told Ashley she wished her mother was dead, or that she wanted to kill her mother—something Sandra said frequently—Ashley passed it off as teenager talk. Sandra seemed pretty serious but Ashley assumed it was another prank, a way to get attention.

But Ashley understood why her friend might have such deadly thoughts. She knew Linda had emotionally abused both her daughters for many years.

Ashley didn't get along with her own mother, even hated her on some level. Ashley thought her mother was hypocritical and far too judgmental about everything. She described their relationship as "complicated." Like Sandra, Ashley wished her mother were dead on more than one occasion. But to Ashley it was just a phrase, something all rebellious teenagers said now and again.

"Who hasn't?" Ashley said. "People say all kinds of things when they're angry, when they're hot, things they really don't mean."

But as bad as her relationship was with her mother, Ashley never had to deal with a mother who was drunk all the time. She couldn't put herself in Sandra's or Beth's place.

Sandra never hid her feelings. She told Ashley many times that Linda would suddenly start talking about her sexual adventures, especially with her lawyer friend. Linda often left sex toys around the house, and laughed hysterically when Bobby ran around playing with one of the gadgets. Once Ashley and Sandra and their friends watched some of Linda's 1970s porn tapes.

"They were pretty funny," Ashley said.

Ashley felt sorry for Bobby. He seemed thin, maybe malnourished. He looked like the poster boy for neglect. Sandra once told Ashley her mother was so drunk she passed out when she was alone with Bobby, and stayed passed out for several hours. Once Linda called Ashley a whore in Danish; once she threw a beer bottle at the teenager. Linda was always throwing things at Sandra and Beth. Sandra told Ashley that Linda once threw the TV remote control at Sandra and nearly struck her on the head. Ashley didn't like Linda. She described Linda as "a horrible and unfit mother" who neglected her daughters and didn't seem willing to take care of Bobby. Ashley never saw Linda being generous or loving towards her children. Sandra told Ashley many times she never thought Linda really loved her.

"Just because you gave birth doesn't mean you're meant to be a parent," Ashley said.

Sandra and Ashley met in Grade 5 when they were in French immersion classes. Ashley was the loud girl; Sandra was quiet and reserved, the kind of kid nobody really noticed. They were eleven. By the end of the year they were friends. Sandra invited Ashley to go gliding with her father north of Toronto. They didn't develop a close bond until they went to the same high school and started hanging out in Grade 9. There were about thirty-five students in French immersion classes. Gradually, different cliques developed, and Sandra wound up in one of Ashley's many groups. Jay was also part of their clique.

By Grade 10 they were confiding in each other. They frequently talked on the phone and used the Internet to communicate with each other and their friends. In Grade 10, Sandra decided she wanted to start dressing as a rocker, just like Ashley. She usually went to school dressed in blue jeans, tapered at the ankles instead of flared. She had long brown hair, usually tied back in a ponytail. Ashley took her shopping, and Sandra started emulating her rocker style with baggy pants, skater shoes, and lots of jewellery. Ashley hadn't thought Sandra would dress cool—she certainly wasn't the most popular girl or "Queen Bee" at school. She liked to dress like pop star Gwen Stefani had in the early days of her career. Sandra fit in better when she dressed the way Ashley did. Before that, she wore the clothes her parents bought.

"I'm not sure I had a positive influence on her but I definitely had an influence," Ashley said. She didn't want to take credit for the way Sandra started dressing. But she suggested that Sandra cut her hair, dye it red, and spike it at the back with longer bangs in the front. In no time Sandra was picking out her own rocker and skater clothes without Ashley's help, and dyeing her hair blue one day, green the next, then purple. Beth also asked Ashley for fashion advice. She had moved on from the skater phase and wanted to dress Goth to impress Justin. Ashley took her shopping. Beth bought some black tight-fitting and slutty clothing, the kind of outfits she hoped Justin would find sexually pleasing.

Ashley had some fun times with Sandra, and once even with Linda, who took them to work one night during an overnight shift at the hospital. Linda allowed them to dress in scrubs and pretend to be nurses.

"We even gave x-rays to about ten people," Ashley recalled. "We gave ourselves ultrasounds and we weren't pregnant."

Ashley and Sandra shared a disturbing moment in a dark Mississauga movie theatre when they took turns giving oral sex to their friend Larry. He later briefly dated Beth, then eventually had intercourse with Sandra.

In Grade 10, drugs and booze became part of their lives. The close group of friends regularly partied most weekends and after school at Sandra and Beth's townhouse. When Linda was out they smoked pot and drank alcohol. Ashley was at Sandra's place almost every day after school. She and Sandra shared their first joint. One time Sandra invited her friends to party at Aunt Martha's house, where, as Ashley recalled they "got stoned and ordered lots and lots of KFC." It only cost about ten dollars to get high. The group pooled their money and bought weed from other students. Sometimes Sandra purchased pot from a neighbour in their townhouse complex.

Ashley, Sandra, and Beth once earned some pot money by selling chocolate bars in front of Canadian Tire for an organization called Students Against Drugs. They could hardly keep a straight face as they gave their pitch to unsuspecting buyers:

"Hello. We're from Students Against Drugs. And by selling these chocolates it's giving us a chance to be responsible and productive young teenagers instead of hanging out on the street and smoking pot."

They sold the chocolate bars for $3 and got to keep $1. They'd make about $60 a night, and usually spent it on pot.

"I kind of felt guilty, like it was blood money, but we usually got stoned," Ashley recalled.

In Grade 10, the sisters were still hiding their pot from their mom, usually in Beth's bedroom closet in the basement. Linda got very upset if she caught them with drugs. Ashley said once they were smoking pot with the window open when their mother suddenly came home. A neighbour, Ricky Rodriguez, spotted her and smoked a joint outside the same window to make it look like the pot was his.

At Sandra's house, Ashley saw Linda's alcoholism up close. Ashley rarely saw her when she wasn't drunk. Ashley knew Sandra hated that there never seemed to be any food in the house. Almost every time they partied, they'd end up buying their own food, ordering pizza and chicken fingers. Sometimes they'd go to the grocery store and buy food and cook meals such as ribs; otherwise they'd have starved.

By early January 2003, Sandra and Beth had pretty much decided how they were going to kill their mother. She needed to die on a weekend, when Bobby wasn't home. Alcohol was going to play a crucial role. So were sleeping pills. Linda usually drank throughout the weekend, so getting her drunk wouldn't pose any problem. It was essential that her death look like an accident. It couldn't look like she deliberately overdosed on pills and booze. There would be no bonus money from life insurance if it looked like suicide.

Jay, Ashley, and Justin knew about their plan, although they didn't all know every detail. They all knew Linda was going to be drowned in the bathtub after she got drunk.

"So how's life?" Jay asked Beth just after 9:00 p.m. on January 2, 2003 during an online chat using the popular MSN Instant Messaging communication system. "Getting any better?"

"How would it?" she answered. "No. I'm still just peachy." Then Beth asked Jay if he was still going to help with the alibi.

"Yeah sure," he replied. "Still planning that one out?"

"Yep," Beth answered. "Drowning. Tub."

"Uhhhh, that's like one of the worst ways though," Jay wrote.

"Fell. Hit head. Drown. Sleeping pills. She won't be able to move," Beth typed.

"'Kay cause you can't leave any marks," Jay answered. "Like pressure of your hands on her."

"I know," she replied. "No shit dip shit."

"Shut the fuck up," Jay typed back. "I'm trying to help. Cuz like even the slightest pushing on her. People could probably tell."

"Well thanks for crediting me with so much intelligence," Beth shot back. "It's obvious dammit!"

"You can't just leave her in the tub passed out," Jay told her.

"Why not?" Beth asked. "Not for long. Few hours maybe."

"I don't think that would work," Jay said. "But if you want to try. Go ahead. Cuz it's not like you can't wake up from pills. Go ahead. It's worth a try anyways."

"Cool," Beth said.

"Yeah, like you need my approval," Jay typed.

"Exactly," Beth said.

Jay then asked what else needed to be planned. "No Bobby obviously," he said. "Get her drunk before."

"You're making it more complicated than it needs to be," Beth said. "Of course she's gonna be pissed drunk. And no Bobby. Think!"

"Thanks," Jay typed.

"Sorry but human ignorance is starting to piss me off," Beth replied.

"Well I'm so much happier being the way I am," Jay snapped. "Rather than the way some people are. Sorry if that pisses you off or whatever."

"Just assumed common sense was applied by more people," Beth typed.

Jay told her it was common sense to have someone drunk before making their murder look like a suicide.

"Sure, let's go with that," Beth typed. She told him their plan for Friday, the night before they murdered their mother, was to smoke dope and get wasted with booze.

On January 14, at 3:54 p.m., Sandra discussed details about the plan with Jay online. She had chosen the next Saturday as the date. She also had a Plan B if something went wrong: everybody would get drunk and smoke some pot on Sunday. But if the plan worked there was no way they could get drunk. There would be way too much to do. They would have to deal with grieving relatives, and her mother's friends, and their father. For sure the police would have questions. But Sandra had everything worked out. She and Beth had rehearsed everything. There would be no time to party. That would have to wait at least for a few more days.

"We're planning on doing something this Saturday very hopefully," Sandra told Jay during their cyber chat.

"Yeah, well that's good I guess," Jay replied.

"No, I mean with my mom," Sandra said.

"I know," Jay answered.

"So we can't get drunk on Sunday," Sandra said. "I'm sorry. Unless it doesn't work out."

"Yeah, I probably couldn't anyways," Jay said.

"Oh yeah," Sandra replied. "You have school."

Jay asked when she was returning to school. (She had been skipping school on a regular basis.)

"I'm not," she said.

"Yeah, the rumour thing still hasn't spread," Jay told her.

"I'll just tell them, well today, I'm dropping out and keeping the kids," Sandra said.

"So I gotta be prepared then tomorrow?" Jay asked. "Practice my shock face."

"Yes," Sandra said.

During their online chat, Sandra pasted in a paragraph she had cut from a website:

"Be careful taking other medicines that also make you tired. The effect may be worse when taking these medicines with acetaminophen-codeine. Alcohol can increase possible drowsiness, dizziness, and confusion, and affect your breathing. Alcohol can increase possible damage to your liver. Avoid alcohol while taking acetaminophen-codeine."

Jay didn't understand why she sent the information. Then he clued in.

"Oh, I see, I'll keep that in mind," he said.

As their online chat continued, Jay learned more about Sandra's plan. He also wasn't shy about offering his own two cents' worth of advice.

"So we're gonna give my mom three Tylenol-3s or more," Sandra said.

"Yeah, ok," he replied. "Hahhhha and just leave her in the tub?"

"And go to Jack Astor's," Sandra said.

"Okay," he said.

"And come home partially drunk with good alibis," Sandra typed.

"Good luck with that then," Jay said.

Sandra was trying to figure out how many Tylenol-3s it took to overdose: "We don't wanna do that."

"No," Jay wrote, then asked if her boyfriend, Donny, knew what she and her sister were going to do.

"No," Sandra answered. "Fuck I really don't know what to do with him. Cuz I know he's never gonna understand me or anything. He's got his own sheltered life. He's happy. I probably should dump him. But I can't."

"But I thought you were happy?" Jay asked.

"Each time I think about it I want to cry," Sandra said. "I didn't talk to him yesterday. He said he dreams I'm dumping him. I don't know. I think the high you get from being with someone new wore off. And now I'm more depressed than ever. Fuck. He's too childish. Not immature. But in case you haven't noticed my life is falling apart. You actually think I'm going back to high school? After I get the $70,000 I'm gonna waste it on travelling, drugs, and a gun."

"Oh God, well, yeah, I thought you were a bit different than your sister," Jay told her. "Cuz it's not too late but I dunno what to say. It's always wrong or whatever."

Sandra seemed pissed with Jay for comparing her to Beth.

"What do you mean I'm the same as Beth?" she asked. "I might be a bartender in a resort and stuff for awhile in warm places."

"Yeah well you should at least try to do something like next year," Jay said. "Fuck, I dunno anymore. It's not like what I say makes any difference."

On January 15, 2003—three days before the murder—Sandra and Jay were online again. Sandra talked about what her life would be like afterwards. She also revealed how Jay was going to play a key role in helping the girls with an alibi, and that she was going to withdraw from school the next morning.

"Yeah, I'll believe it when I see it," Jay said.

"I have to," she replied. "I've been putting it off too long."

Sandra said she'd been sober only one day so far this year.

"It's Bobby's birthday today," she said. "My cousin Derek came over and got me so fucked. I'm pretty sure the stuff was laced with something cuz I was too happy."

Jay asked if she did anything special for her brother's birthday.

"Nope cuz we're planning to later cuz our mom didn't have no money," Sandra said. Then she returned to her murder plans: "I told you how we're gonna go to Jack Astor's on Saturday."

"Ok," he replied. "Yeah, I hope that works out really. Then the couple of days after are gonna be really hard or whatever."

"Me, like I'll just be a loner and stuff," Sandra typed. "And not talk to anyone."

Jay asked who else knew about the plan.

"Me and Beth and Justin and I'm guessing Ashley won't be surprised and will guess we did it," Sandra said. "Though I wouldn't be surprised if Justin told his best friend Jessie."

"Oh well, so long as they don't say something cuz I don't really know Justin or Jessie at all," Jay told her.

"Well, if they say stuff, they're going down too," Sandra said. "But Justin won't say anything cuz he's into this type of stuff I guess. I know his best friend is like him."

Sandra said they hoped to get three more people to move in with them in their townhouse after their mother was dead.

"I keep my room," she said.

"That's cool," Jay replied. "Wouldn't you need some kind of parent though?"

"Well no," she said. "I think I'll take the computer room."

"Like legally I mean?" Jay asked.

"Nope, legally you can at sixteen have a house if you're working," she said. "So I guess I'm gonna need a full-time job. Well if that doesn't work out, shit happens. But if it does, it's gonna be cool. You can legally move out and live on your own at sixteen. Wanna move in?"

"That would be pretty cool," Jay said. "But I don't think my mom would let me. Hahaha. I'm not a mommas boy I swear."

"Well we don't know what's gonna happen," Sandra said. "The whole living with people thing might not be possible."

"How much is rent?" Jay asked.

"Nine-hundred dollars a month but the rent might go up to fourteen-hundred dollars if the landlord considers them to be new tenants."

Sandra added that paying the old rent wouldn't be too bad if they had five people sharing the costs.

"There's also lights and heat and water and food and every-thing," she typed. "I think each person would just get a shelf in the fridge and buy their own munchies. And phone bills."

"Yeah that's gonna suck," Jay said. "That's like probably all the money you're gonna make."

Sandra asked if he knew if the government would give them anything. She added, "We'll figure out something. It's so cool. And then a minimum $70,000 when we turn eighteen."

Sandra warned Jay that he needed to delete his log files and their conversation. He told her not to worry: he'd already turned off the automatic save feature.

On January 16, 2003, Sandra revealed to Jay how many people knew about her plan. But that night, during another online chat, she caught Jay completely off guard with a chilling thought about her plans for Bobby. Sandra and Beth stood to inherit $70,000 each from their mother's life insurance. The other $70,000 would go to Bobby.

"[A]nd after that we do Bobby because we get another $35,000 each," Sandra typed, then added, "ha, ha, ha."

"I just didn't hear that," Jay replied.

"Don't worry, I'm not serious," Sandra quickly answered.

"Of course," he said.

Instead of dropping the subject, Sandra continued: "I'm just hoping for some natural selection thing to take him out— like getting hit by a car."

Later, Sandra told Jay she hoped Bobby's father would take him to Europe and raise him there.

CHAPTER 8
LET'S CELEBRATE

In the early hours of January 13, 2003, Beth and Justin chatted online. It was obvious they had already discussed the plot.

"Beth," Justin typed just after 1:27 a.m. "That doesn't work. Drowning is not asphyxiation."

"Well, there's back up stuff," Beth replied. "Yeah, well we weren't sure if it would work."

"You die very differently from a lack of oxygen than you do from drowning," Justin typed.

"Then just dragging her in the tub, making her hit her head and leaving her under water," Beth replied. "Either way. Just making sure she stays under for enough time."

Beth realized the problem with leaving the water running. The tub would overflow and damage their home, possibly even her basement bedroom.

"And flood the place," she typed. "She was so drunk she left the water running. Dammit. My poor basement. Where does water go? MY BASEMENT ... grr."

Beth asked Justin if he was still going to provide her and Sandra with an alibi.

"I'm thinking I can go buy movie tickets at Famous Players and tear them myself for like an hour before it happens," Justin replied. "Because it's a paper trail."

Beth initially didn't see any need to waste money but then liked his idea. "Oh yeah, I just always keep the other part of the ticket," she replied.

"Paper trails are purdy," Justin answered. "And so nicely irrefutable."

Beth discussed what she and Sandra would tell police if they were questioned.

"Where were you on Saturday evening?" Beth typed as she rehearsed for Justin. "Well, at 8:13 p.m. we were walking past Jack Astor's. You know the one by Square One. I remember that because as we passed by I looked at my watch and said, 'hey guys, it's 8:13 p.m.'"

Justin added a new wrinkle to the plan.

"Wanna go to Jack Astor's afterwards?" Justin typed. "That would be a nice celebration dinner."

Beth's thoughts turned to money.

"What happens with her account money?" she asked. "Where does that go? She did work for it. So it's legally hers. So would, like, the thousand dollars go to us? Or would they want to take it?"

Justin didn't know. "You're not eighteen so I don't think you can get it," he said. "Not sure though."

Beth figured there were other ways to gain access to the cash. "We can easily take $200 without people bitching about it missing," she typed.

Justin had a friend who was studying law. He would ask if they could legally get their hands on the loot. Beth decided it might be better for them to just take small amounts from their mother's bank account.

"That's why it's easy with like $200," she said. "Why the fuck would she give us over $1,000 if she has unpaid bills and shit? But I waaaaaaant it. I could buy that cute bondage dress for the semi."

"Yeah, well you can't have EVERYTHING," Justin replied.

"But you can try," she said.

"Sure can," Justin typed.

Beth told Justin what she and Sandra planned to do once their mom was out of their life.

"And then Sandra is going to get Aunt Martha, Derek's mom, to let us live there for a while," Beth said. "She can't say no if her sis just dies, and then it's constant stonerage, which isn't different from what we do anyways. Bet Derek is doing something right now. And he's one of those few great stoners."

Beth didn't think her father would want to move into their house. "If he did great," Beth said. "But he wouldn't be too keen on being somewhere where his ex-wife died."

Once more Justin told her not to worry and then suggested how she could convince her father to let them live in their townhouse.

"If you act distraught he might," Justin said. "Sandra is sixteen, right? She can legally own the house."

Beth had to cook up a believable story, something convincing, for her father. "I found my dead mom in a tub," Beth typed. "I don't mind staying though."

As soon as she typed the words she realized how lame the plan sounded.

"It would sound fucked up though if we don't mind staying," she typed.

She thought it might be better if Sandra took over the house so they could live there by themselves, without any parents. But there would still be problems.

"She could but we'd have to pay rent, dammit," Beth typed.

"Just say you can't deal with moving," Justin advised her, and suggested what she could say to her father. "My mom was my world," Justin suggested. "I loved her so much. I couldn't leave this house with all of its memories. It's all we have left of her. And my friends, I need them more than ever. I just can't leave—"

"Perfect thing for the Goth girl to say," Beth typed back.

Beth said she was going to call the cops when they found her. "Dammit. I'm gonna have to act all freaked out and shit," she said. "And like cry. Dammit."

"Don't worry, you can do it," Justin reassured, her and reminded her how much he wanted to help her.

"If there's one thing I can do is be extremely convincing," Justin boasted.

Beth immediately typed back: "Hey wanna see a dead body."

Justin offered some additional advice.

"Why not say we were headed back to your place," he typed. "I have a picture in my head of the three of us sitting huddled on the doorstep. It looks sooo convincing in my head. You two just sobbing. Me trying to act tough, eyes watering. Sorry, the dramatic side of me is coming through."

Beth told him they had to be drunk when they returned home.

"That's why we need to be tipsy," she insisted. "Dammit, crying. Fuck. Hysteria. Beautiful. I have to act ten again."

"Can you cry on a whim?" Justin asked. "I can."

"Just think about life," she told him.

"That's my secret," he replied.

"Or of Europe, or anything dammit," she said.

"Europe is a close second," Justin replied.

"Yeah, fuck it was great there," she said. "And then my brother goes to his dad's and they move back to Europe. And he lives there. Snazzy."

Beth reminded him there were other consequences. "But yeah the shittiest thing is our grandma finds out that our mom dies and that's like shit," Beth said. "I don't even know if she's gonna tell grandpa cause he has heart problems and shit. And then like in two to four years later she hears about me, and then a bit later about Sandra. Wow, that sounded gay."

Beth's thoughts turned to drugs. She told Justin she couldn't wait to get high in the school washroom the next day, then get drunk at lunch by drinking a pitcher of booze-laced lemonade in the cafeteria. Beth asked, "How fucked do you get after one vial?"

"Quite," Justin said. "'Cause if that's enough for a normal person, then will that be too much for me and my low tolerance to all substances? Especially if I've never tried it before."

"I heard it's easy to OD on that," Beth replied. "What's the worst that could happen? Last night a body was found in a ditch. It's outside fun then? Like the bitter cold."

Beth thought she could mooch money from her aunt or her father for drugs after her mother died. Justin was going to take $150 out of his bank account at lunch to buy drugs. Then Beth's thoughts returned to her mother.

"Dammit, she better get fucking wasted this weekend. This sucks," Beth typed. "I haven't slept well in a really, really long time and it's shitty."

As they chatted, it became clear that Justin knew of their murderous plans.

"Don't do the 'smother and put her in the tub' idea," Justin typed. "If anything, I'd just get her reaaaallly wasted. Then just put her in the tub. And hold her under for like ten minutes. Then leave her for an hour or two."

"One or two?" she asked "That's how long we're gonna be drunk."

"Yeah, I'd say leave her in there a good long time," Justin advised.

"That's not long," she said. "I was thinking like from six to ten."

"Oh yeah, the longer the better," he said.

"Wow, that's a very evil thing to do," Beth typed. "And I like to be proud the tub was my idea. Arrg it's gonna be fun dragging her into the tub. She bruises waaaay too easily. We're not gonna be able to touch her. It's gonna have to be like grabbing onto her clothes."

Justin again told her how much he really wanted to be part of their plan.

"Like I said, I'm involved this much," he reminded her. "I'm willing to help you with any of it Beth."

"Fucking whore makes everything so difficult," Beth typed. "That's all we need, finding your DNA on her body. Ours belongs there. Thanks though."

Justin wasn't concerned.

"Ummm, I really don't expect a DNA check," he said. "But yeah, I see your point."

"Aahhh, I already called her legs," Beth said. "Just grab her jeans and lift."

Justin had more ideas.

"Your mom gets Tylenol-3s right?" he asked.

"Probably," Beth answered.

"Seriously, you should include them in the game plan," Justin typed.

"Why though if they're not necessary?" Beth asked. "You

can't possibly make drowning into a suicide. But if she like ODS in the process."

"I'm not talking twenty here," Justin advised. "I mean like five. They knock you right out."

Justin said they needed to be prepared for anything that could happen, especially if their mother woke up while they were drowning her. Beth seemed appalled that he would think they hadn't thought their plan through.

"We're not just gonna be like—hmmm—she looks drunk—into the tub!" Beth typed. "We're gonna make sure she can't walk and can't possibly drink anymore. And doesn't react to water on her face at all. And besides, head first, easier to hold down. And then just turn her over or something."

Still, Justin wondered whether she had thought of everything.

"Not reacting to water on face and not reacting to lungs filling with water is very different," Justin warned. "Drowning is the single most painful way to die after burning to death slowly."

"Yeah, it would suck to drown," she said.

"You get water, instead of oxygen, pumped through your body," Justin typed.

"Either way she'll be shit-faced. She won't be able to get up," Beth replied.

"Then oxygen dissociates from the hydrogen into the capillaries," Justin typed.

"So holding her down won't be a problem," Beth said. "So she moves a bit. She still dies."

"At which point the hydrogen turns to acid and the capillaries bust," Justin typed.

"Beautiful," Beth answered, and added: "(wipes tears away)."

Justin reminded her they needed to be prepared for what they would see.

"It is not pretty," he said. "And then soaking for a while. My advice. If she wakes up partway through drag her out of the tub and pretend you were helping her. Even an inch of water in the bottom of your lungs and you'll die twitching in a few days."

"Aaaahhh it's great how you think we didn't think this through," Beth typed, mocking his suggestions. "That was discussed."

"I'm telling you things that I'm not sure you know them," Justin typed.

"It depends on how much she, like, fights back," Beth replied.

"An inch of water in the lungs will kill you in a few days," Justin repeated. "If medical attention is not sought. She'll think it's just a cold or something. A bit of a chest pain, and a bit of coughing. Dies slowly though and surely. Just so you know if she struggles a lot you don't have to keep her under to kill her."

"Yeah, I know," Beth replied. "It's not like she'll remember it anyway. Snazzy."

"Indeed," Justin said. "Well, I'm off to bed. Nites."

"Goodnight," Beth typed.

"Sweet dreams," Justin replied.

"Think about that one," Beth typed. "Someone who thinks the way I do, what are the chances of me having gooood dreams?"

"I didn't say good. I said sweet," Justin answered. "Those come in many forms."

"I suppose," Beth said.

The sisters' darker side had emerged in an earlier chat, on January 5, 2003, beginning at 12:13 a.m. Justin warned Beth about the danger of saying too much online.

"Sandra and I are planning something for, like, next week," Beth typed.

"Don't type things regarding that," he replied. "Just because, well, I'm paranoid. And now I'm gonna go and delete this chat log."

"Ahhhh, oh right, you told me about that," Beth replied. "But yeah, everyone that reads that is gonna know what 'that' and 'planning' means."

"Things make a lot of sense afterwards than before," Justin replied. "Circumstance and subjective shit. I figure why take the risk. It's not worth it."

Later Beth told Justin she was going to go to downtown Toronto and get stoned.

"It makes everything seem like a fairy tale," Beth typed. "All sooooo fake. Easier to think that way. So nice to be by yourself. You can think. And not give a shit and have no one telling you to feel better."

Beth then quoted from the song "Bleed" by Cold, a Jacksonville-based alternative rock band. The song was from an album titled *13 Ways to Bleed On Stage*.

I wanna bleed.
Show the whole world all I have inside.
I wanna scream.
Let the blood flow that keeps me alive.
I wanna scream.
I wanna feel.
I wanna scream.
I wanna bleed.

Beth told Justin she and Sandra would be spending the week at their aunt Martha's residence.

"With unlimited weed and donuts," she typed. She also told him how much she loved her bong. If her mother ever found it, she'd say it was a penis enlarger.

Then Beth typed: "Sandra is better keeping booze down. Doesn't get drunk after three shots." She also told Justin her mother gave her $10 for picking up Bobby and $10 for telling a friend she was at another person's house.

Six days before Linda's death, at 7:49 p.m. on January 12, Beth and Justin were online. Beth said she and her sister had set the date:

"Next weekend."

"Ahhhh," Justin answered.

"And so Friday we could still do stuff."

"Oh," Justin answered. He asked Beth why she wanted his friend Jessie to be in on their plan.

"He's funny," she replied.

"He's me," Justin answered.

Then Beth changed her mind: "I don't think there's any point in dragging anymore people."

"Yeah, that's what I was thinking," Justin typed. "Well, anyways, he's me so if you need the extra help. It won't be more people. I trust him with anything if that means anything."

"Well, always good to have friends," Beth said. "Real friends."

"So on Saturday then?" Justin asked.

"Jessie's coming or the other thing?" Beth asked.

"The other thing," Justin answered.

CHAPTER 9

SOME EXCUSES
ARE BETTER

On January 17, 2003, two days before the end of the semester, a day before Linda's murder, a group of students in Beth's careers class joked with their teacher about getting out of handing in their final class assignment.

"Do we have to hand it in if we break a leg?"

"What if we have the chicken pox?"

"What if we get into a car accident?"

Teacher Meredith McCarthy told her students she hoped none of those terrible things happened; she expected them to complete their final assignment.

Beth hadn't been attending many classes of late. Several teachers told her she was in jeopardy of failing the semester. McCarthy was pleased when Beth showed up.

As the laughter subsided, another question was posed from a student sitting at the back of the classroom.

"What if somebody close to me dies?"

The classroom fell silent.

It was Beth.

The students stared at their teacher. McCarthy didn't know

how to reply. There was something oddly disturbing in the tone of Beth's question.

The other questions had come from the usual class clowns but Beth wasn't one of them.

McCarthy couldn't help but smile, and even had a bit of chuckle when the other questions were asked. But Beth's question seemed different, even a bit eerie. McCarthy had been teaching for more than fifteen years. She had never heard a stranger question.

A few days earlier, Meredith McCarthy and the vice-principal had talked to Beth about attending classes and completing assignments. Beth, like Sandra, had been an extremely good and studious student, but had been skipping classes and ignoring assignments. She was in danger of failing a class she should have breezed through with ease. Beth was no dummy: she spoke four languages and was smarter than most students. Yet she acted as if she didn't care about school anymore. Her appearance and demeanour had dramatically changed. Instead of a bubbly young teen, she was a dark and brooding Goth girl.

It was just before Christmas when Sandra pulled her boyfriend, Donny, aside.

"What would you do if you ever found out I killed somebody?" she asked.

"Well, I guess I'd turn you in," Donny said. "Taking somebody's life is something you're not supposed to do."

"What if somebody was suffering?" she asked. "Isn't it your duty to take it away?"

"No," Donny said. "Absolutely not."

They had talked many times about life and death. Donny thought Sandra was having one of her deep-thinking moments. She talked about suicide a lot, especially that winter. She told Donny she never wanted to live to a natural old age. But Donny didn't believe she was serious. Sandra would change her mind about most things every other day. One day she wanted to kill herself; the next day she wanted to have children and write children's books. The day after that she'd insist she didn't want to live past her teens.

They had met the first day of the semester, in September 2002. Actually, Donny met Beth first. He was riding a Mississauga Transit bus with a female friend who knew Beth, and she introduced them. Beth was in Grade 10. Donny was eighteen, two years older than Sandra and three years older than Beth. He had graduated from high school the previous spring but decided to take a co-op course until he made up his mind about what college or university to attend. Within a few weeks, Donny dropped out of school and started working part-time at a construction job. One afternoon in November, he and a friend visited the high school and ran into Beth and Sandra in the cafeteria. Sandra invited Donny to her townhouse, and that night they smoked some dope, drank some peach schnapps, and listened to music. After that, they hung out every day, and before too long they started dating. Sandra wasn't the most beautiful girl in the world, but there was something about "the goofy kid," as Donny thought of her, that attracted him. Besides, Sandra was the one who initiated the physical contact.

Most days after school, they smoked dope; sometimes they drank. Sandra and Beth rarely went a day without smoking pot. Jay and Ashley usually joined them. Beth dressed in black clothes. Sandra enjoyed dressing like a bum, wearing raggedy clothes. At school, she got the nickname "Hobo." Donny didn't mind. They all were into the rocker scene and torn clothes.

Sandra and Beth could afford nicer clothes. Donny knew their mother gave them money to buy clothes, but they would buy dope instead. To them, pot was far more important.

"They might not have dressed great but it was nobody's fault but their own," Donny said.

Beth, Sandra, and Jay were much more into the rocker scene than Ashley. Donny thought Ashley was more a "cheerleader-type" girl who listened to rock music. He knew Sandra and Jay were best pals, but that didn't bother him. Donny said Jay was "one of the greatest guys you could ever meet." There was never any jealousy. The five of them would hang out into the early hours of the morning, always in Beth's room in the basement of the townhouse. Sandra's room was upstairs, and they never went there. Donny wasn't working. Most days, Sandra and Beth skipped their first few classes so they could hang out late and sleep in. Sometimes a few more friends would party with them, usually invited by Ashley, but mostly it was just the five of them. They would go outside to smoke their dope. In Beth's room, they watched television and talked about what they wanted to do with their lives.

Donny knew Sandra lived in a fantasy world and had pretty wild dreams. But so did he. He wanted to be an astronaut or a fighter pilot.

Donny and the others noticed that Linda was a drunk and often fell asleep on the couch watching A&E television. Sandra said Doug Landers—Bobby's father—made Linda drink. Sandra thought her mom was drinking herself to death. Donny never saw Linda smoke dope, but Sandra said Landers got Linda to try crack. Sandra hated Doug Landers and told Donny she wanted to kill him. She would find his drug dealer, get some crack, and then spike it with poison. Donny didn't think Sandra would ever kill him, though she hated him enough.

Sandra said she wished her mother was dead, or said she was going to kill her, but Donny never took her seriously. And he never knew there was an actual murder plan. Sandra told him how happy she and Beth used to be when they were younger, when alcohol didn't have such a tight reign on their mother. She said alcohol took all their fun times away.

Donny was sitting with Sandra, Beth, and Jay in the school cafeteria on Friday, January 17, when Sandra told him that he couldn't come with her and her friends for dinner at Jack Astor's.

"Why?" he asked.

"You just can't," she said. "You'll disapprove."

Donny looked at Jay, who avoided eye contact. Donny asked Sandra several more times why he couldn't go, but she refused to give him a straight answer. He dropped the subject but remained curious. They were all pretty tight. Why wasn't he included in their plans?

Maybe Sandra was going to do some harder drugs. Donny liked pot as much as everybody. He had tried "'shrooms"—hallucinogenic mushrooms— a few weeks earlier. He knew Sandra always wanted to try everything at least once. Maybe she was going to try something harder, and he wasn't invited because she knew he wouldn't approve.

On Saturday morning, Donny talked to Sandra a few times on the phone. He again asked why he couldn't meet them at Jack Astor's. But she still wouldn't tell him why. Finally, he gave up asking.

Sandra and Beth spent the first few weeks after their mother's death living with their aunt Martha in her nearby home. Eventually their father, Walter, moved into his ex-wife's townhouse so his daughters could return home. But things didn't work out, and by the middle of March the girls were again living with their aunt, who was their legal guardian.

Sandra and Beth quickly discovered life with Father wasn't for them. Walter was strict. He didn't drink, for one thing, and there was no way they could play him like they played their mother. Walter had very rigid rules. He gave them money but demanded to see receipts and movie stubs. He couldn't be conned. He demanded to meet their friends before he would allow them to come to the house. He scheduled regular mealtimes, which they mostly ignored. He instituted a curfew, which his daughters also ignored.

Their parties didn't stop when they were living with their father, but they had to make sure it looked as if nobody had been there. Everything needed to be cleaned before Walter returned home.

There were many disagreements, but Walter settled disputes by having his daughters write their concerns down on a piece of paper so they could discuss the issues.

Walter also wanted his daughters to start attending school. They had stopped going after their mother's death, and before that they had been skipping classes. Their marks were falling.

Walter felt it was time for them to get into a regular routine. The daughters were incensed when he tried to interfere with their lives. They sabotaged his efforts to get their education back on track.

He was unable to control his daughters. He held a family meeting, and it was decided the girls would live with Aunt

Martha. At her house, they each had a bedroom, and there was a common area in the basement with a computer. Compared to the townhouse, Martha's place—a modest two-story home—seemed like a mansion. For the girls, drugs and booze became more important. Aunt Martha's residence became party central for their friends and for the cousins who lived upstairs.

Sandra and Beth eventually resolved their issues with their father and resumed the relationship. Sandra had once thought her father was a great guy. He was involved in their lives; he phoned them and had weekend visits after the divorce. She loved how he made sure she had toys to play with. He played board games with the girls, and took them to the Woodbine Centre amusement park and to his gliding club. In Sandra's mind, he had always looked out for them and made sure they were fed.

But Walter remained oddly distant when it came to their mother's alcoholism. And Sandra never wanted to tell him all her concerns. She had fun when she was with him, and she didn't want to ruin it by talking about her mother's problems.

CHAPTER 10
MURDER MOST UNDERSTANDABLE

Ashley was a conflicted young teenager in the days immediately following the murder. She had known it was going to happen and all the details—the pills, the booze, the alibi—but didn't do anything to stop it. Had there been blood in the tub that night, Ashley knew it would have been on her hands too.

Ashley knew that what Sandra and Beth did was wrong, but she wasn't bothered that Linda was dead. Ashley didn't like Linda and Linda never liked her. Linda thought Ashley was a bad influence on Sandra.

Ashley wondered whether it was right for Sandra and Beth to get away with murder. She thought about going to the cops and telling them what she knew. But they might think she was just as bad as Sandra and Beth. She felt many different emotions, and irrational and illogical thoughts raced through her mind. She was scared and worried. What she knew might come back to bite her on her ass (as she put it). She might end up in jail if she didn't spill her guts. Her thought was, "If I don't go to the police, then I'm the person who has to live with it."

If she went to the cops and told them everything, could she be charged with something? Conspiracy? Accessory?

"I could have told somebody. I could have saved a life. I had the power to stop a murder. I could have walked the fifteen minutes from my house to their home after I chatted with Sandra online, after I knew that she was in the process of killing her mother . . . I could have saved a person's life."

Ashley wanted to believe she would have tried to stop her friends from killing their mother if she'd been there. Her conscience wouldn't have let her calmly stand by and watch Sandra push her mother's head under the water.

It's a lot harder to ignore when it's in your face. Not just on MSN. *You're looking at reality.*

But Ashley didn't stop Sandra. Sure, she tried to phone her several times after their online chat to tell her not to do it. At least she convinced herself that was the reason she kept calling. Or was she just curious?

I really wanted to stop her.

By the time Beth answered her phone call, it was far too late.

Maybe Ashley would have encouraged Sandra, offered her advice about how not to get caught. She had wished her good luck and reminded her to wear gloves. Ashley would live the rest of her life knowing she didn't do anything to prevent Linda's murder.

Others might think maybe she really shouldn't feel guilty because, after all, she was just sixteen. But who she was "trying to snow." She was smart. She was intelligent. Being sixteen was no excuse. There was no way she could justify not getting help.

We're all smart kids. We knew what was going on. We weren't helpless teenagers. All of us could have picked up a phone. The fact is, we didn't.

Ashley knew Sandra might not have listened to her, anyway. Ashley remembered the time Sandra decided to lose her virginity with one of Beth's former boyfriends. Sandra told Beth what she was going to do.

"Beth gave her blessing," Ashley remembered.

Sandra grabbed Larry one day and convinced him. They weren't romantically or sexually interested in each other. But Sandra was determined they were going to have sex so they could lose their virginity and get it out of the way. By the time of Linda's murder, Sandra had become fiercely independent and calling things her own way. No way Ashley could have talked her out of killing Linda.

Then Ashley wondered why she thought about going to the cops in the first place. She didn't care what happened to Beth. So what if she got caught?

Beth has no soul.

Beth throws tantrums if she doesn't get her way. She's so manipulative and cold.

Ashley thought the only thing that mattered to Beth was how Beth felt. She had no loyalty. But Sandra was different. Ashley cared for Sandra, although they arguably had a love-hate relationship in the months before the murder. She didn't care what happened to Beth, but she didn't want Sandra to go to jail. And she knew the sisters were a package in this mess. A deadly daily double for sure. She couldn't rat them out to the cops.

Ashley understood how Sandra and Beth felt:

If you've been abused your whole life, then maybe what they did was quite understandable. Linda was always drunk and always suffering and at least after death she wasn't suffering anymore. The people who are now suffering were the ones who had to pick up the pieces.

She understood why Sandra and Beth murdered their mother.

*But there's a huge difference between understanding why
something happened and justifying it. It's understandable because
of all the pain Sandra and Beth endured.*

The morning after the murder, Sandra called Ashley and
told her everything went off as planned, and that she was surprised the police didn't stay long at their townhouse.

Ashley said Linda's murder didn't seem real until she went
to the funeral home and saw her lying in an open casket.

"It was so creepy," Ashley recalled. "There really won't be
any Linda Andersen around anymore."

After the murder, Jay wondered how he could have been
nonchalant about such a horrific event. Sandra had provided
him with the final details of her plan about a month before
the killing. He learned details from Beth after he started
dating her in late December 2002. But he talked about the
plan more with Sandra. Beth told him they were going to
wear gloves to ensure they never left any fingerprints on their
mother's body.

By the night of the murder, Jay knew all the details. He knew
Sandra didn't intend to wait for the booze and pills to take effect.
She was going to hold her mother's head under the water.

Jay planned to help them with their alibi by having dinner
with them at Jack Astor's. But he changed his mind. He had
listened to all of the planning and had offered advice, and
then suddenly his conscience kicked in at the last minute.
Besides, they didn't need him. After all, Ashley and Justin
would be there.

Jay had known Ashley longer than he had known Sandra,
but he never spoke to Sandra about her murder plans when

Ashley was around. It was Sandra's decision to tell Ashley if she wanted to, he thought. Jay had never met Justin, but knew Beth had a crush on him.

Jay didn't know Sandra had committed murder until Ashley called the next morning. He was shocked. It finally hit home. Jay had never dealt with death. Nobody in his family had ever died, never mind been murdered. He felt unnerved, scared because of what he knew.

Sandra called him later that morning. She seemed upset and said she regretted what she had done. She told Jay her mother's skin had changed colour during death. She said Beth stood there while she was drowning their mother.

Sandra cried when she met Jay at the mall a few days later. She again told him she regretted what she had done. She had just learned that her mother was socking away money for her daughters' educations. Sandra said it was physically difficult to push Linda's head under the water and hold it there, but said it wasn't emotionally difficult.

Jay was concerned that the police might charge him with something. He had offered advice to Beth and Sandra, both in person and online. But had they taken his suggestions seriously?

He confessed, "They thought of me as a joke."

Like Ashley, he faced a moral dilemma and experienced a flurry of emotions. He felt extreme sadness and utter terror. He wondered if he was a decent person.

How in the hell had he become so involved? How had he become so caught up in a murder? He didn't see himself as a cold-hearted person.

But he had suggested that Sandra and Beth wear gloves to ensure they got away with the crime; to make sure they left no fingerprints or marks. He told Sandra he would practice his shock face to help keep their secret. But he didn't really mean to give them ideas.

It was their idea to kill Linda, not his. And he didn't help them kill their mother.

He had backed out of meeting them at Jack Astor's, despite assuring them he would be there to help them with their alibi.

Jay didn't tell anybody, not his parents, not the police. He was too scared. He was afraid of going away, of not being with his family.

Sandra had trusted him with the biggest secret of her life. How could he betray her by going to the police? Jay knew Sandra could see only one solution to her troubles: killing her mother. But he should have gone to the police. He should have told his parents. He should have told somebody. He knew he'd made a really bad mistake.

Yet he understood why he kept quiet.

Sometimes, the truth is hard to say.

Donny was so madly in love with Sandra that he overlooked the fact she murdered her mother. Even after he knew about it, he dated Sandra for several months. Like Ashley and Jay, he never went to the police.

Donny was not in on their secret. He became suspicious when Sandra called him the morning after the murder, just as he was about to go to church.

"My mother died last night," Sandra said. "She drowned in the bathtub."

Donny expressed his condolences during their brief conversation. When they talked on the phone later that afternoon, his suspicions were raised.

"Where was Bobby?" Donny asked.

"He was over at his father's," Sandra answered.

Donny thought it was odd coincidence that Bobby wasn't home. He also thought Linda's death was odd—nobody drowned in a bathtub.

On Monday, Donny visited Sandra at her aunt Martha's home and asked her about her mother's death. He also asked why she didn't want him at Jack Astor's. She refused to answer. He didn't want to believe Sandra had murdered her mother, but he needed to know the truth.

According to Donny, "Everything seemed too perfect. Sandra always talked about wanting her mom to die and then she did. And it was so convenient Bobby wasn't there. And that whole Jack Astor's thing was so weird."

On Tuesday, Sandra told him she had to see him. That's when he knew for certain that she killed her mother. He drove Sandra and Beth to the mall. Neither sister talked about their mother. Instead, they talked about living with their aunt and how they were going to drop out of school. Donny and Sandra sat in the food court after Beth wandered off with some friends.

"What would you do if you knew I had killed someone?" Sandra asked.

Oh God, Donny thought. He didn't want to have this conversation in the mall.

Before he could answer, his cellphone rang. His sister needed a ride. Donny told Sandra he had to go. She insisted going with him, but didn't say anything more about her mother's death. Later that afternoon, as they listened to music in her bedroom, Sandra finally opened up.

"I have to tell you something," Sandra said.

"I know what it is," Donny replied.

Sandra looked puzzled. "No you don't," she said.

"Yes, I do," Donny shot back.

"So why don't you just say it if you know what it is."

But before he could reply, Sandra blurted everything out.

"I got away with murder," she said.

She explained how her mother died, how she held Linda's head under the water for four minutes. She told him about the alcohol, the Tylenol-3s, and the rubber gloves. She explained why she didn't want him to join her at Jack Astor's.

"What went through your mind when you did it?" Donny asked.

All she thought about was that she needed to make sure she held her mother's head under the water long enough for her brain to suffocate so Linda wouldn't be a vegetable if she survived.

Sandra seemed proud that she had killed her mother; Beth had only been there for moral support, she said.

Donny felt sorry for Sandra because her life had been affected by her mother's drinking. He thought Sandra loved her mother, but she told him, "Some lives need to be taken." He knew he should tell somebody, perhaps even turn her in.

But he didn't.

"I'm in love with her. She's my friend. Her mother wasn't the best mother in the world. Not that I think what she did was right. But I kind of feel bad for her. Bad for Beth too. I know what they did was horrible. But I don't want to get her in trouble."

Donny continued to hang out with Sandra and frequently saw Beth, but he never spoke to Beth about the murder. Donny thought the sisters were best friends, although Sandra sometimes seemed jealous of Beth, who was a genius. Donny thought it bugged Sandra that Beth learned to read before she did. Sandra claimed her parents pushed Beth more.

"She's not smarter than me," Sandra would say. "It's not my fault. It's my parents' fault."

Donny thought everybody would think he was crazy if they knew about the murder. People would ask, "Why the fuck are you still with her?" He thought it would sound stupid if he said he didn't tell because he was blinded by love. Sandra had been his first real relationship. He was willing to conceal her secret. The only person he told was a friend in Europe. But the friend didn't believe him.

Instead of turning them in, Donny decided to end his relationship with Sandra. He figured it would soon run its course anyway. Sandra was distant after her confession. She drank more and smoked pot every day. Beth smoked dope every day, as well. Donny grew tired of the incessant drinking, so he decided to break up with her. It really had nothing to do with the murder. They rarely talked about the murder. Everybody in the inner circle knew it happened. Jay knew. Ashley knew. Justin knew. Nobody needed to talk about it.

Sandra often seemed sad in the weeks after the murder, but Donny never thought she regretted what happened. Both sisters insisted their mother's insurance money had nothing to do with killing her, although they often said it was a bonus.

After they drifted apart, Sandra often asked Donny if he was going to marry her. He always said no, but one day, when he was wasted on pot, he said yes. When he sobered up the next day he realized he'd been a complete idiot. He had no intention of marrying her. They broke up, then got back together about a week later and dated for another month. Sandra kept a journal. She described their breakup as "killing bunnies." She told Donny she wanted to write a book about a murder-suicide called *Dear Mother*, but she gave up on the idea. She never let him read any of the chapters.

CHAPTER 11
PERSONAL DEMONS & B.S.

Sandra and Beth returned to school a few weeks after their mother's death, but they continued to skip classes, and their grades continued to drop. Sandra was enrolled at Beth's high school. Records show that she missed thirty-five days and eighty-three classes that year; Beth missed twenty-four days and fifty-four classes.

They had achieved exactly what they wanted and gotten away with murder, but life didn't seem all that great. Things appeared fine on the surface, but Sandra was battling her own personal demons and often cried herself to sleep. She had frequent temper tantrums. She smashed her violin because she couldn't play a particular run of notes. She drank more and more.

Halfway through Grade 11, Ashley and Jay began to drift away from Sandra. They were all still friends, but didn't see each other as much. Sandra wanted to get stoned or drunk every chance she had. Ashley liked to toke but wanted to keep her pot smoking moderate, but that seemed to annoy Sandra.

When Ashley and Jay stopped hanging out with Sandra for good, both thought their once close friend was wasting her life on drugs and booze.

Ashley thought Sandra was always drunk. It was as if she had become her mother. One day, several months after the murder, Sandra showed up plastered for a math exam. "She was spitting on her desk," Ashley recalled. "I had to kick her ... to get her to stop."

Ashley knew Justin and Beth had shared ideas about how Linda should be killed. She also knew both had talked about committing suicide. From Sandra, she learned just how far Justin wanted to take things in that direction although as far as she was concerned it was just more bullshit.

"I was told his goal was to convince Sandra and Beth to commit suicide with him when they all turned eighteen at a Marilyn Manson concert, in the pit," Ashley said. "It was a big suicide pact but he never would have gone through with it. He's more of a Charlie Manson type. The guy who would run the cult and would never take the pill himself. He gets off more controlling their minds."

Another time, Beth and Sandra showed up at a soccer field where Ashley was coaching young children.

"They lit up a joint and started smoking it on the sidelines. I told them to get off of my field. You're not doing that here. But they just laughed." Ashley thought they got a thrill out of smoking a joint in front of the kids.

By April, Donny was also out of the picture. Who broke up with whom? It depends on to whom you talked. It would be almost eight months before Donny talked to Sandra again. One day she called him out of the blue and asked if he wanted to hang out. At first he didn't want any part of her. But then he agreed, and they smoked some pot. A few weeks later, Sandra called again and asked if he'd buy her a case of beer. They drank it together, but it was the last time they ever spoke to each other.

Knowing their secret was never a big deal for Donny, although it meant everything to Sandra.

In Donny's words: "She committed a great big murder and had gotten away with it."

But it didn't take long for the dark secret to make the rounds of the high school. Dozens of students soon either knew what happened, or heard rumours about what happened, from second- and third-, even fourth-hand sources. It seemed pretty crazy, but Donny understood why Sandra was obsessed with telling people, especially when she was drunk.

He says, "What's the point of getting away with something if nobody knows about it? She did something nobody else would ever think to do."

Billy wasn't among the close inner circle of friends who knew about Sandra and Beth's murderous secret. But he became suspicious when their mother died. He'd spent many nights at their home smoking pot and drinking. He'd seen Linda passed out. The sisters always complained about having no money. They told him many times how much better their life would be if their mother was dead.

After Linda died, he heard the rumours. He had to know if they were true. Did Sandra and Beth kill their mother?

Billy sensed that something, besides their mother's death, was troubling Beth. One day, about a month later, he confronted her.

"Did you kill your mother?"

Beth didn't answer. She shrugged her shoulders. Then suddenly nodded.

The rumours were true.

Beth gradually revealed details to him over time during

online talks. According to Billy, she also told him Justin had been involved. He thought Beth was remorseful.

Soon, Billy became a closer friend. Sandra and Beth would take him to Amsterdam as well. Billy liked the idea. But he still thought it was weird they'd be using their mother's life insurance. He also thought it was strange how happy they were.

Beth also told him they would use some of the life insurance money to take care of their little brother. They didn't like they way his father was raising Bobby.

On the whole, Billy was shocked. His mother had died from cancer.

How could anybody kill their own mother?

But he promised Beth he wouldn't say a word. Their secret was safe with him. He liked Beth. He had a crush on her.

But soon, he too distanced himself from the sisters.

Chad pretty much stumbled into Sandra's inner circle one cool morning in April, around the time Donny was slipping out of the picture. Sandra's drinking was out of hand, and the more she drank, the more she talked about the murder. Beth and Justin were concerned and warned her to stop talking. But she continued to blurt out details about the crime whenever she was drunk, particularly at parties.

Sandra had known Chad for several months; she met him a few weeks after Linda's death. Sandra had been standing outside her townhouse when Chad walked by, and they started to talk. Before long she told him her mother was dead and that she and Beth were moving to their aunt's home. He was twenty-four years older than Sandra, and Sandra immediately became obsessed with him. Donny had grown stale; Chad was Sandra's "new boy obsession," as she put it. It didn't matter that he had a girlfriend and was older. Minor details were not going to stop her from pursuing and catching him. Sandra told him that her mother had a drinking problem; that she was often verbally abusive (Linda said Sandra was useless); and that she often passed out on the floor. She hated her mother's alcoholism.

Chad found Sandra interesting and sometimes partied with her and her friends. Ashley, Jay, and Donny had drifted away; Justin was Sandra's only close confederate.

That changed on the April morning Chad went to see Sandra at school. His shift at a nearby Zeller's department store didn't begin for a few hours, so he decided to drop by the high school to say hi. It was early in the morning but Sandra was already drunk. (She had a water bottle full of vodka.) Sandra insisted on walking to Zeller's with Chad, and they took a shortcut through a wooded area.

"I need to tell you something big," Sandra said, and started sobbing uncontrollably. Then she said, "I killed my mother," and "I drowned her in the bathtub."

Chad was stunned.

Had she killed her mother out of "blind anger?"

"It had nothing to do with anger," she said, and then explained how miserable her life had been. Her mother had been "really drunk" when she "pushed her head under the water."

Chad literally had to drag her from the street and into the wooded area where he sat her down on a log, and she passed out. Chad believed he and Beth were the only people in the world who knew Sandra's secret.

He felt sad for his new friend.

I need to save her.

But he was in a bind. He had to get to work, yet he didn't

want to leave Sandra in the woods, especially in her condition. In the end, he left her there. At work, he told his boss he needed to take care of a personal matter, and returned to the woods. He found Sandra exactly where he left her. In the next several hours Sandra provided details, for example, that Beth had been with her when she started to drown her mother but suddenly left to answer the phone. Beth left the bathroom "right when she was helping her." Beth had abandoned her.

Sandra's infatuation with Chad grew over the next several months although his interest never amounted to anything. She always craved attention. She admitted she always needed to impress people to be accepted by them. At one point Chad even thought she'd made up the whole story just to impress him.

But with Chad now the sixth member of their inner circle Sandra felt comfortable enough to tell him about the murder during online chats.

On November 24, 2003, at 11:54 p.m., ten months after Linda's murder, Sandra and Chad were online. Sandra said her aunt was taking her shopping, and that she was going to start taking violin lessons. Then she asked Chad if he felt like doing some cocaine. Chad asked her if she'd done any lines yet.

"A bit so I don't think I'm gonna sleep tonight," Sandra typed.

"Why are you doing it?" Chad asked.

"Cause it makes you feel better for a bit," she replied.

Chad was concerned. A few days earlier, she had been so stoned he didn't want her to go home alone. Sandra apologized for that day.

"When you were trying to walk home you were really out of it," he typed. "It kind of freaked me out. It was just like you didn't give a fuck about anything. You just kept mumbling shit. And telling us you hate us and shit."

"When I'm on drugs I give millions of meaning to anything," Sandra said. "I say none of it makes any sense except to
me in my altered state. I won't do 'shrooms around you. I think
I get a bit crazy sometimes, so I've heard anyways. I'm sorry."

She didn't need to apologize, Chad told her. Then he typed,
"We were just looking out for you. That's why we didn't want
you to walk."

Sandra said it was nice that people cared about her.

"I'm used to people letting me leave whenever 'cause
nobody gives a shit," she wrote.

Sandra didn't remember much about that day except how
she was drinking rum and beer and doing "'shrooms." She was
"an idiot" because she hadn't slept for hours.

"You kind of seem different lately," Chad replied. "Like
you're trying not to think. That freaks me out."

"All I ever do is lie to everyone, every day, about everything
almost. It sucks. I sorta fucked myself up too much."

"What do you mean you feel like you're lying about everything?" he asked.

"You know my past," Sandra answered. "I see my aunt and
uncle, cousins, brother, friends, people. All the time. I don't
think I should let them all know."

Chad understood because he already knew her secret.

"Like going to the cemetery. Heart to heart talks with my
grandma. My life's bullshit. Ah well, it's my fault. I'm venting
a bit."

Chad said he wanted her to confide in him more. "I wish
you would more often, obviously not to everyone, but to those
who wouldn't judge you. Me, for example. It's like, I don't really
think you did the wrong thing. I would have in your situation
too. But you feel all kinds of guilt. Because it's done. And can't
be changed. Do you think you can ever forgive yourself?"

"I don't have it against myself," Sandra answered. "I just miss my childhood and how things used to be. And hate how fucked the world is and how stupid people can be. So much ignorance. Plus my dreams fuck me up sometimes. And it never works properly. I just need some time. It hasn't even been a year yet."

"It's not something I would forget," Chad wrote. "But also remember how you felt and what led up to it. Don't let yourself get lost in guilt. It's definitely going to take you a very long time to start feeling good again. But please don't destroy yourself in the process. The more you try and avoid it, the more it's going to haunt your subconscious."

"I don't feel guilty for the actual act," Sandra said. "It just made me realize a shitload of things about life. I'd rather have a shorter, more interesting ride, than a crappy long sad one."

Then she told him how she felt when she murdered her mother.

"It takes four minutes of water inhalation into the lungs before death is irreversible," she typed. "So it was four minutes of crap. Beth left then too."

"She probably just didn't wanna get into it," Chad wrote.

"No, she was into it," Sandra answered. "The phone rang and she felt she had to answer it. Anyways, it's probably better to talk about this in person. I'm gonna burden you."

Chad told her she was never burdening him. He encouraged her to talk to him.

"I don't really think honesty and talking [will] fix me," she said. "But talking's good."

CHAPTER 12

YOU DID WHAT?

Nearly a year had gone by when Sandra emailed a friend. David was twenty-one, attended university, and kept in touch with Sandra and Beth sporadically. When Sandra and Beth were small, Linda had moved them from Holland to an apartment building in Rexdale, a community in northwest Toronto. David's mother lived in the same building and babysat the girls, then befriended the family. When Bobby was born, David's mother babysat him for a few years while Linda worked.

David's mother kept in touch with Linda, who invited David's family to their home just before Christmas 2002. David and Sandra began exchanging emails and talking online once or twice a month.

David wasn't close to either sister, but he felt sorry for them, and he worried about Bobby, who had to cope without his mother. David had always liked Linda and thought she was a good mother. He thought it was odd that neither of her daughters cried at the funeral. They had to be hurting even if they didn't show it.

Almost a year later, during an online chat, Sandra wrote, "I need to speak to you in person. I'm a good person. But I've done something that could send me to prison for twenty-five years." Sandra refused to tell him more online.

David agreed to meet her and went to her aunt's home on November 30. He and Sandra took Bobby to a playground. As the child played on the swings, Sandra talked to David.

"Do you know what's the worst thing I've ever done?" she asked. "You don't really know me at all."

"No, but if you want to tell me, okay," David said.

Sandra told him her mother didn't accidentally drown in the bathtub.

"I killed her. I murdered her. Somebody was going to die that night, either me or her."

She said she "fooled" the police.

David was so shocked he didn't know what to say. The more Sandra talked, the more concerned he became. He and his mother had visited Linda's home just before Christmas last year, and Sandra had seemed obsessed with suicide. She never wanted to grow old, she said, and would find a way to end her miserable life long before that ever happened. Then she said she wouldn't take her life until her grandmother died. Sandra's death would be too much for the grandmother to endure.

David never took Sandra's suicide rant seriously. It was just "teenage talk." All teenagers thought about suicide at one time or another. Sandra also told David that her life wasn't what it seemed. Her mother's alcoholism was ruining her life. David said he'd never seen any signs that Linda had a drinking problem.

"She's just putting on an act for your mother," Sandra told him. "She's an alcoholic. She's drunk all the time."

Her mother even "soiled herself" when she was drunk.

Their house had seemed a bit messy, David recalled, even a bit dilapidated, and dirty, especially with all the crayon marks on the walls, which David knew must have been Bobby's doing. But Linda always seemed coherent and in control. Still, he remembered thinking Sandra and Beth were thin. Had they been eating properly?

After their mother's death, he saw Sandra and Beth two or three times in person. They'd hang out in their basement rooms but they never talked about their mother's death anymore. But Sandra still often talked about suicide. How she never wanted to live to an old age like her grandparents. How she didn't want to die from an incurable and horrible disease. Those past suicidal thoughts now took on a different meaning for him.

In the park, Sandra told David that her mother had been drunk when Sandra held her head under the water. She said she had worn gloves. She said Beth had nothing to do with it. Sandra repeatedly stressed how Beth didn't want to go through with the murder.

Sandra never told him that she deliberately got her mother drunk that day. David figured if her mother was sober, then she probably would have fought back, so it made sense for Sandra to make sure her mother was drunk before she pushed her head under the water.

She told him they took a bus to Square One Shopping Centre afterwards and went to Jack Astor's restaurant where they met friends for dinner about 7:30 p.m. She thought she killed her mother sometime between 6:30 p.m. and 6:45 p.m. They went to the restaurant because they needed an alibi for where they would be for several hours.

Sandra had told many people what she had done over the past year. But this was the first time she confessed sober.

"Why do you think I drink and do drugs?"

David had no idea what to say. How many people had a

friend who confessed to a murder? He tried to comfort her, and suggested she see a priest David knew and trusted. He advised her to turn herself in to the police. Sandra said she might see a priest, but she wasn't going to the police. She made David promise not to tell anyone about the murder.

As they walked back to her aunt's home, David couldn't even look at her. Sandra hadn't told him why she killed her mother. But she had admitted her biggest fear: that she was going to hell.

They went down to Sandra's basement room and listened to music until Aunt Martha came home about 4:00 p.m. She asked her niece why they never went bowling and what became of the $30 she gave her. Sandra said they spent the money on a taxi, which David knew was a lie. When her aunt left the room Sandra told him that she was going to use the cash to buy drugs. Before he left, Sandra again made him promise not to tell anyone. He promised he wouldn't. Her secret was safe with him.

But David feared Sandra might kill herself.

David, a deeply religious young man, was extremely troubled. He needed to tell somebody, talk to someone. That night he went to his friend Mario's house, and they both went to evening Mass. But he never told Mario what had happened. Just being in church gave him some comfort, although he remained tormented by what Sandra had told him. The next day, David had trouble concentrating at school.

David kept her secret to himself for about a week; then he couldn't carry the burden any longer. He called Mario and told him about Sandra's confession. He said he was worried that she might kill herself. David also told a friend and a co-worker. Eventually his mother knew. Mario urged David to contact their former high school and a guidance counsellor, who was also an auxiliary officer with the Ontario Provincial Police. David agreed.

He spoke with the guidance counsellor but said he didn't want to talk over the phone. The counsellor asked him to answer yes or no to a few questions.

"Is it about you?" the teacher asked.

"No," David replied. "It's the worst thing you could do."

"Is it murder?"

"Yes."

"Does it involve parents? Were the parents murdered?"

"Yes," David answered.

The guidance counsellor set up a meeting with David.

In his struggle to betray Sandra, or keep her awful secret hidden, David's conscience won. He went to the meeting with the guidance counsellor, then contacted Toronto Police, then Peel Regional Police, because the murder occurred in Peel region.

David admittedly had a bit of crush on Sandra. Had he spilled his guts to police because she "rejected" his "amourous advances" as defence lawyers would later allege?

Sandra had placed him in an extraordinary position.

"I care. Sandra might be suicidal."

He believed going to the police might be the only way to save Sandra.

CHAPTER 13

SECRET AGENT MAN

Peel Constable Ken Wright had just been transferred to homicide. On the morning of December 17, 2003, he was at 12 Division, where Homicide Inspector Mike MacMullen was about to brief officers on a domestic murder that had occurred overnight in Mississauga. Before the meeting started, Wright's phone rang. A Toronto high school guidance counsellor had a young man with information about a young woman who admitted drowning her mother in a bathtub.

Wright spoke to David, who gave him Linda Andersen's name, a date and location, and the names of the two girls he believed were involved in a murder. Wright immediately talked to MacMullen.

A check of police records indicated that the death had been ruled an accidental drowning due to alcohol consumption. MacMullen gave Wright the green light to bring David in for an interview. Wright and Constable Karl Layne picked David for a formal interview. David provided a written statement and a formal videotaped statement. It was clear he had vital information.

MacMullen decided to split up the homicide team he'd assigned to the domestic killing. He put Detective Brent

Magnus in charge of the new murder investigation, informally called the Bathtub Girls murder. Magnus asked Wright and Layne to find out why, after a whole year, David had come forward. The two detectives listened to David and thought his motives were genuine and truthful. He was obviously concerned that Sandra Andersen, a young woman he had known and liked for many years, might be suicidal. Police began to gather information, and David was asked to help with their investigation.

David didn't have specific details, but he believed a murder had occurred. Investigators needed corroborating evidence, as well as information from Sandra and Beth. They needed confessions.

The police wanted to wire David and use him as an agent.

Constable Dan Johnstone was David's handler. He would make sure David could perform the undercover assignment. David had to get the sisters to talk about their crime. After several meetings, Johnstone was certain that David could do the job.

"We felt David also wanted to know the truth and he wanted us to help find the truth, no matter if that truth meant Sandra and Beth murdered their mother," Johnstone said.

The decision to use David as police agent evolved over several days. David had to be on the same page as police for the sting to work. In the end it came down to one simple fact; David realized the police, just like him, were only interested in finding the truth, no matter what that truth was. If his friends got arrested, David believed they would at least get the necessary psychological help they needed to help them deal with the terrible and "heinous" crime they had committed.

"It was the moral decision and the right decision," David later told me in an interview. He said he had had grave concerns about Bobby. In his heart, he thought he needed to protect him from his sisters, too. Something told him Bobby might be in danger, that if Sandra and Beth were capable of killing their mother they were capable of doing just about anything.

Acting as a police agent is different than being a police informant, or to use the vernacular, a snitch. An informant sometimes is paid for their information, and information often is obtained under dangerous situations. Informants usually have some criminal ties and often agree to provide information in return for favours such as lighter sentences. An informant acts on their own with no direction from police. Sometimes informants might be required to testify in court. But a police agent is different. They're told what to do and how they're to obtain information. They act on behalf of police and are given certain guidelines and parameters under which they're to obtain information needed for the specific case. Money sometimes changes hands, but David wasn't paid a cent for his help.

Johnstone said, "David was pure as the driven snow. He was the kid next door."

In a plan dubbed "Project Andersen," David agreed to be wired with a hidden taping device. He drove a special car equipped with a hidden video surveillance camera and a recording device. David met Sandra once in late December 2003; he met Beth twice in early January 2004. Eventually he obtained enough information to provide Peel homicide investigators with probable cause to arrest them for killing their mother.

To snare his friends, David was asked to follow a three-stage plan. He would first see if either girl brought up the topic of murder. If they didn't, stage two called for him to ask about their feelings so they might talk about the crime. Stage three called for him to ask how they murdered their mother.

Johnstone said, "David was well-rehearsed and knew what needed to be done. We did our job in preparing him. Every day we met and went over the game plan and different scenarios. We wouldn't have put him in that position if we didn't think he was capable."

Magnus said it was understandable David was a bit shocked about what he heard because even seasoned investigators were shocked by what Sandra and Beth told him. "It's not every day somebody tells you they committed a murder. I think he was more shocked when he learned just how much Beth was involved and I think Beth was shocked Sandra told him so much stuff. At the end of the day David did everything right, legally and morally. If the girls had more friends like him their mother might still be alive today."

Without David's role, police likely wouldn't have even known about the murder, at least not at that point.

"I think eventually one of the other kids would have come forward but none had the abilities David showed. He was our star witness," Johnstone said.

On December 20, 2003, eleven months after the murder, Peel Police conducted the first of three "electronic intercepts" (secret tapings) involving Sandra, Beth, and David. Constable Johnstone met David that afternoon and went over the strategy. He hoped Sandra would admit she and Beth murdered their mother. David showed up unannounced at Aunt Martha's home, driving a wired Ford Focus rented by Peel Detective Heather Andrews. The car was essential because police needed David to speak with Sandra alone.

When David picked Sandra up she was wearing her pyjamas

underneath her winter coat. David told her he needed to talk to her because he was extremely bothered by her confession. Sandra giggled and laughed as she talked about the crime and described her life in general and her use of drugs and alcohol. Johnstone phoned David several times on his cell, and each time David pretended he was talking with a friend. At the beginning of the tape, Sandra accused David of thinking she was weird because she wore pyjamas. Later she told him she was tired. David said it was natural for teenagers to be tired; Sandra said, "I'm a kid. I'm not a teenager. I don't want to be responsible for anything."

Sandra said she didn't drink coffee. Was he going to buy her booze?

Later she said she was going to buy pot and was getting a good deal, but she expected it to only last two days instead of a week because she intended to give half of it to her friends for Christmas. "So I have to remember I can't smoke it," she said, then added, "I can't wait until I get my own weed farm. That's like my ultimate goal. Well, just like having my own land and my own supply." She told David she needed a cellphone so she could deal pot, and that she could earn $400 a day by dealing. Then she said, "You don't need to be involved in coke or anything, but . . . if you're dealing coke, then the penalties are a lot stiffer." She denied being a regular coke user and admitted she tried it once. "I am like a natural-born cokehead," she said. "I still have all my good coke trips ahead of me, which is something to look forward to."

When David brought up Linda's death, Sandra joked about the car being bugged. David told her he had been bothered by what she told him in the park. Sandra asked what she could say to make him feel better.

"Like what do you want to hear from me?" Sandra asked. "What can you expect from me, like I dunno?"

David said he felt scared.

"Um, I won't do it again if that's what you want to know. Unless I was put into that same situation again. It was purely situational."

David said he was confused and wanted to know what happened. "You actually drowned her, right?" he asked.

"Well, I sort of, I guess—yeah," Sandra replied.

"I don't know how you could have done that. She was pretty big, you know."

"She was filled with, like, so much booze and so many Tylenol-3s," Sandra said.

"Who put them in there?" David asked. "Did she take them?"

"Well she was just like taking them or that's what happens when she gets drunk," Sandra said. "Like, sometimes she'd go through like bottles of pills, like, in a day and not remember it or anything and be like, holy shit."

"Man, that's been bothering me for two weeks now," David said.

Sandra told him that her mother's death hadn't bothered her for two weeks, ever.

"Okay, honestly. It really was at such a point where it was either me or her," Sandra said. "And I'm younger. And like, I saw myself as having more potential."

David asked how she managed to get her mother, a fairly large woman, into the tub.

"She was like fat, and that was from all the drinking," Sandra said. "She was gaining so much weight really fast. How many times have you [been] around drunk people? How many in your life? Because drunks act a certain way. There are, like, distinguishable stages.

"And like when somebody is really drunk, honestly, doing

something like that, you could drown somebody in like a puddle on the street. Easy, if they're too drunk. That's how people drown in their own vomit all the time when they're too drunk."

David said he never heard of people drowning in their own vomit. "All the drunks I know are still alive."

"That's one, like a huge way of drunks dying from getting too drunk," she replied. "You haven't heard people puking up and drowning in their own vomit?"

"Well all the drunks I know are still alive," David said.

"That's, like, a pretty high cause for death," Sandra said. She told David he only knew social drinkers, not alcoholics. "If you, like, choke on your puke, you die, right?" she said. "Like, there's a way you can puke if you're a drinker. Have any of them ever woke up with puke in their bed? Because that's never happened to me. But that's happened to some people I know. So that's really a big warning sign that you can kill yourself really, really easy. Like lying on your back is bad and lying on your stomach's bad because both ways you can drown."

David told her the thought of her killing Linda was hurting him.

"Life's not all peaches and cream," Sandra replied. She said she probably shouldn't have told him, because he wasn't handling it too well.

"You think I would?" he asked.

"Well, some people have a completely different reaction," she said.

David asked who else knew.

"This is something that's, like, pretty hard to deal with, right?" Sandra said. "Like, sometimes I do get really, really depressed. And it's really, really good for me to sit down with friends because I have some amazing friends. That I can talk to about anything. And so a couple of people know, yeah. Don't worry other people, well not too many, like three or four other people. But only people, like, I trusted and stuff."

Sandra said she told a boy named Chad when she was drunk, but she had always intended to tell him. "Except he thinks, like, I'm insane," Sandra said. "The thing is, like, I'm not completely sane."

"Everybody is a little crazy, you know," David answered. "Everyone has their flaws."

"Some people are crazier than others, trust me," Sandra said.

"Everyone has their flaws," David repeated.

"Yeah, I know, but I'd rather know what mine are," she said. "So, like, I can be aware of them and control them, possibly." Sandra wanted to talk about Chad and her plans to get him to fall in love with her. She planned to ask her aunt Martha for money so she and Chad could go to Europe.

"I'm going to ask her for ten thousand dollars," Sandra said. "Because it's gonna be my whole summer vacation. I'm gonna say I want to go around Europe and I want to enjoy myself."

Sandra said her cousin got a thousand dollars from Martha for a weekend in Montreal.

"Like fuck, I'm going to Europe and I want ten thousand dollars," she said. "Yeah, one weekend for a thousand dollars. So I want like two months. Ten thousand dollars, all over Europe. Well, I'll say it's all over Europe. But it's only going to be in Amsterdam."

Sandra said Chad was twenty-one, and that she wanted to rape him in a forest and go skinny-dipping with him. She told David that she and Beth went skinny-dipping in Europe and twenty older guys wanted to screw them. "Yeah, we were like basically throwing them off of us," she said.

She said she was obsessed with Chad, that he had a girl-friend, and that if he didn't want to have a relationship with Sandra it would shatter her.

"It would be like my heart shattering for, like, the billionth time into like a billion pieces. But if I'm going to work my ass off to make him fall in love with me, I'm going to pull anything I can think of," she said. "Anything and everything I can think of."

Sandra told David he could ask questions: "You have to get it off your chest or the rest is just going to keep eating away at you," she explained.

"That's always going to eat off of me," David said. "Yeah, like I still don't know how you could have done it. You just, like, dropped her in?"

"No, she was taking a bath and I told her to turn around and she did," Sandra said. "And I held her head like under, like okay, when someone is that drunk, like honestly, nothing is being registered in their mind or memory."

"Your sister wasn't in the room, was she?" David asked.

"Uhmm, nope," she replied. "Beth was in the house. And then we went to Jack Astor's after that."

David said he felt sorry for her.

"But like, my mom's life was really, really bad," Sandra told him. "And she kept going downhill and downhill and downhill."

David asked how Bobby was doing without his mother.

"Well, what would have happened if he would have stayed with our mom?" Sandra asked. "That's the thing you don't know, what our life was like with her. And it was really, really horrible. Like, it wasn't our mom anymore. It was just a drunk. Especially when you come to a point where you miss, like, three out of four weeks per month of work because you're at home, piss-assed drunk. And you keep losing your jobs and then like that other week, you're like semi-sober.

"Like, that's not a person anymore. And like, she was going to kill herself. And like, she's fallen off the stairs. Broken shit a couple of times."

Sandra told David not to worry about her or Beth or Bobby.

"Honestly, he's like, probably better off now no matter how much it really, really hurts me to say that he is better off now," Sandra said. "And me and Beth have never ever been better off than we are right now. Well, except for when, you know, we were really small kids in Europe."

Sandra told David she and Beth had been raising Bobby, who suffered from ADD or ADHD; his condition had never been medically diagnosed because his father never took him to see a doctor. Then she told David it was nice to know he was concerned about her, but she said the stress would harm him.

"Hey, ninety per cent of the shit you worry about won't even happen, and the other ten per cent you can't do shit about anyways, so don't waste your time worrying," she said. "All that's gonna do is like stress. Stress kills. It really does kill. And like, you're not suppose to be in a state of stress for more than two weeks 'cause you know that's critical. And like, it's the same with depression or whatever."

Sandra told him the only effect her mother's death had on her was that she felt as if she was playing God.

"Not like, actually God, all powerful." Sandra laughed. "But the way I see it is like if I'm faced with any real problems so far I've proven I can get myself out of them. Then again, I'm constantly proving how horribly possible it is to screw up relationships. Like, I don't know for one success, there's like billions of failures. I have to remember that too, so it's okay. Basically, it just made me like a rational, sober individual that doesn't act rationally. I'm an optimistic pessimist. People call me an optimist, like, rationalist. But no, I'm a pessimist. I'm so fucking pessimistic about everything, except I might as well enjoy whatever I get left of life and stuff. It sort of made me open my eyes a lot 'cause like, if I was put in the same situation with my mindset now, I don't know what I would have done or how I would have done what differently or whatever.

"Like, 'cause, especially then, like it was just a lot of like hate. And everything against my mom that I had too since after that. Like you realize how many people like cared and loved your mom and stuff. And it's like, oh, and especially since I had to call a lot of people and tell them. That she was dead. So like I had to deal with a lot of people crying on the phone. So I don't know if it like changed me a lot. But I think it changed me for the better. Except for making all my bad habits worse."

Sandra told David she drank too much but if she stopped she might wind up killing herself.

"And then I'll like slit my wrists from like getting too depressed in like three weeks," she said. "Trust me, it's like my stress relief, not being coherent in like chunks of time."

"Don't slit your wrists," David told her.

"Well, no, I won't when I'm like, but it will be in a couple of years, 'cause, okay, when I've accomplished everything I want to. But the thing is I do want kids, 'cause I can raise them. But probably, well no. But I would rather be in charge of when I die than letting old age take care of it or some freak accident.

"But the thing is, like, I want do to everything I want to do in my life first. Then, if I had my own weed farm and my own ranch and everything, like fuck, I'm just chillaxing and sticking around for as long as I can. And I have to think of something 'cause on average, if you drink three alcoholic drinks a day for ten years, you get liver cirrhosis. That's like an average, right, obviously there's some individuals that drink like motherfuckers their whole life, right.

"They're fine. There's some that drink a lot less and die or whatever. Then pot and everything obviously makes everything worse and happen faster. But then again, there are hippies that are, like, still alive, right. And like, I qualify as a hippie, especially since the second I turn eighteen, I'm going to like start doing shit for the marijuana legalization thing."

David asked Sandra if she thought about turning herself in to the police.

"Nope," she replied. "'Cause, like, if I did, that would destroy my life and . . . affect a lot of people's lives around me. Plus, like, how am I supposed to help raise my little brother if I'm not here?" As soon as she was living on her own and had a job, she intended to have Bobby live with her instead of with his father.

"So, like, I have—that's why I actually have to stay coherent in the next couple of years do something with myself to earn money," she said.

Sandra told David she and Beth got through each day because they were so good at lying.

"Well, overall, like, I think I'm doing pretty okay for some-body like that, A, has planned everything that I planned and, B, gone through with it. And, like, I don't know, just like my aunt's like sort of noticed that I have very little trouble lying. I have to lie every day. I have to, like, even when I'm caught unaware, I have to lie. I have to lie on the spot so much. And like honestly, each time I lie, I hate it. It's so horrible. And like, but I'm pretty good at lying." Sandra laughed.

"And like I'll do it like without even realizing it," she added.

"And yeah, I'll get caught in lies. But then sometimes I'll say, like the most retarded thing and people, like, believe me, right. So I learned to lie. Well, I don't know since last year I learned a lot of stuff."

"Like?" David asked.

"Well, how to lie," she said.

Sandra said she didn't have anything specific to "get off her chest" but she thought he might, especially because she knew how religious he was.

David said he'd been having trouble sleeping since she told him her secret.

"You planned it too, that's just, wow," David said.

"'Cause it was really, like, it was a solution to, ah, the worst problem I was ever faced with," Sandra said. "And it was the worst solution I could ever possibly come up with, I guess, besides for me slitting my own, like, veins, which would have been, like, worse I think. 'Cause then I would have wasted my whole life . . . and my mom would have continued to waste her life."

David asked how she planned it.

"My original plan was really, really, like, gruesome and

horrible. I was going to ... get her really, really drunk and like have her pass out on her bed and, like, light her bed on fire," Sandra said.

"Arson's not good," David said.

"Yeah but I was like, hmm, well, not that it would have been pretty easy," she said. "Then you just spill wine on her and make it look like she was smoking."

"Smoking?" David asked.

"A cigarette," she replied. "But then I was, like, yeah, fuck that. I don't want to do that, right. That would have been so much waste. And this [drowning] was a lot less messy. And only four minutes."

"Four minutes?" David asked. "That's how long it took? Or that's how long you were in there for?"

"That's how long, like, I held her head under water for," Sandra explained. "'Cause, like, you have an inch of water or something in your lungs you could survive, go to the hospital or something. And, like, yeah, you have to wait for four minutes to make sure, like, it happens completely. After that she just kept convulsing and stayed in the water and kept twitching. It's really hard to meet another person that knows how it feels to have a body twitching and convulsing."

"I don't think you're going to find a person like that," David said.

"You'd be surprised how many people have killed other people," Sandra replied. "Like, if I, like, confided in some people, some of the shit they'd tell me, holy shit.

"Okay, the world, honestly, there's so many layers of it. There's so much undetected crime. So many murders of like, honestly, people just get away with. The best way to, like, get away with anything is to be like random, well, not random but like, yeah, and being unpredictable is obviously really, really good. That increases your chances of success. Like, dramatically. It's just that you have to make sure, like, that everything is pretty unpredictable, and not just like a crime.

"Then the way you get out of place or whatever as long as I don't know depends on yeah, I've developed like this criminal psychology, honestly."

"You'd be good in criminology," David said.

"No, honestly, I would," she said. "But the thing is I wouldn't want to turn people in. And I can't really write a book about everything I've done and stuff.

"'Cause like that'd be like horrible. My aunt, like reads it, oh my God."

"So that's the thing then again. I wouldn't want to write a book 'cause, fuck, like the masses . . . nobody would care. They just like criminals. Yeah, just be retarded. And people would hate me for what I did."

"It could be a bestseller," David said.

"Yeah, but people would hate my guts," she said.

"I don't hate you," David reassured her.

"Really, thank you, I guess," she replied. "I don't know, saying you hate somebody doesn't mean shit, though, 'cause, like, I told the people I love the most that I hate them, whatever, I'm drunk without realizing it."

"Yeah, but I don't hate you," David repeated.

"Hey, like honestly, if you were a druggie, you would know how, like, meaningless our emotions are," Sandra said. "Well, no, I can't say meaningless, 'cause they do rule your life, right?"

Sandra said she was thinking about writing a diary, recording her thoughts. "And my diary is going to be fucking interesting, I think. I'd have to lie in it too in case somebody finds it," she said. "But I'd already wrote in it. I'm like, yes, I'm lying in this shit."

"Geez, you didn't write one?" David asked.

"Nope," she said.

Sandra said her book would be filled with "interesting stuff'" and her "own philosophies" because she would want to call herself "a philosopher."

Then she again told him she was sorry he'd been losing sleep over what she did.

David said, "It's like I said before, I don't understand how she was so big and you were able to . . ."

"Well, all I had to do was hold her head under water," Sandra said. "She was in a bathtub filled with water. It's not hard. It's a lot easier to kill a person than you think. I don't know how easy it is to get away with it. But I planned it pretty well. And like there's all this stuff you have to remember. Like when you're giving your statement to the cops or whatever. You have to remember, like, you know things that people do when they're lying. Like, start off with something big, and then get more and more into details. Like, that's obviously a major sign that you're lying. Or just like, just your whole body thing. And then, like, what people would react, like trauma. Like you know, having to remove, basically, getting away with a crime is like overanalyzing all possible, like, predictable outcomes. And, like, I don't know, movies teach you what could possibly go wrong. They give you a really, really good grasp of imagination, which you can easily expand on. And you sort of change [it] so it applies to real life, not movie land. But the ideas and stuff are pretty good."

David asked Sandra if Bobby knew anything.

"Well, obviously he doesn't know anything," Sandra shot back. "I don't think I'll ever be able to tell him. It depends on who he becomes later in life. If he's a rational sober individual I can talk to. Then, like, you know, I don't really have too much of a right to keep this hidden from him. But I'd have to wait until he's an adult, for sure. He should be okay."

Later David introduced the topic of the Tylenol.

"Like, wow, who knew you could knock somebody out with that?" he said.

"I don't know. Well, no, she didn't get knocked out," Sandra said. "She was just, like, fucked. Yeah, I don't know. How am I supposed to know she'd go through a bottle of any pills you gave her?"

"Yes, like, it was horrible. It was like really, really bad. Like, that's what she was. Honestly, every month. Like, she'd get visibly fatter."

David said he remembered her mother was getting really fat.

"She just kept getting worse and worse—everything was getting worse," Sandra said. "It was my way to heal her. But also to end everything. But it was a really efficient way to heal her—it just finished it. But an alcoholic, if they want to quit they can't ever go back drinking. It's just not possible for alcoholic[s] to moderate their drinking once they're really bad. She'd need all this willpower and support to get anywhere."

"So you wanted to end her life?" David asked.

"Yeah, with our current situation," she said.

"The only way out you saw was by killing her?" David asked.

"Well, I guess," Sandra replied. "She would have needed clinical treatment but that would have meant losing her job and everything. It was so fucked."

"Still, I never knew you could drown somebody in only four minutes," he told her.

"Well, I know, actually, technically, I'm guessing. I could have probably pushed her head down and left her there alone, and she wouldn't have moved," Sandra said.

"But you wanted to make sure?" David asked.

"Yeah, 'cause it would have been horrible if she survived that," she said. "I couldn't take any chances."

"Yeah, and like, there is a degree at like, you know obviously there's no such thing as the perfect crime, as you said before, right? But there is a degree that once you get to it's perfect enough. And [that] happens a lot more than people expect."

Sandra told David she'd been suicidal for years.

"I know how to deal with myself, which is always to tell myself to go to sleep," she said.

"Like, if I've been awake for like, er, I mean alive for this long, then I might as well, like, sleep and, like, be awake, alive for another day. And if I really, really want to blow my brains out or whatever, I'll do it later."

David told her he didn't want her to kill herself, and she said she had no intention of committing suicide—at the moment.

"Well, I will but like honestly, in a bunch of years," she said. "Give me forty or fifty years, if I can manage. I would hate to die from old age. That'd be so horrible. I've seen so many people die like that. And like there's so many people I know will die from old age."

"Did you want your mom to go through that old age thing?" David asked.

"I didn't even consider it, honestly," she said. "'Cause she was at a point where she was physically deteriorating really badly in front of our eyes. I don't know how bad her liver would have been or anything. She always was a drinker and always had alcoholic tendencies. They just got out of hand. Completely out of hand."

"But how did you feel doing that?" David pressed.

"Like peaches 'n cream, like what do you mean," Sandra answered sarcastically.

"No, like what was going through your mind when you were doing it?" he asked. "I remember you told me you couldn't eat after that."

"Well, I'm not going to go to a restaurant and like chow down man," she said. "I worked up an appetite, yeah. Like, it was horrible. Like okay. Like, the thing is like, some of the happiest memories I have are me spooning with my mom when I was a little kid. And I loved her so much. It's just like, I couldn't see her as my mom anymore. 'Cause like, the things, like her whole persona, everything about her changed—even when she was sober. Even if she'd be sober for a couple of days. She was just at a point where it was bad."

"You just wanted to end it?" David asked.

"Okay, this sounds really selfish and horrible but that was the only real cure I saw," Sandra said. "Besides us winning a couple of million dollars and her going to a really good rehab. You have to know, I was only sixteen and a little kid still. It's debatable if I did the right or wrong thing, but I did it anyways."

Then Sandra told David, "Whenever you want to talk about it, I'm here, honestly. It's a really, really big thing, telling somebody else that you did this. It does sort of mess up everything about life."

"You just turned her over and she let you?" David asked.

"No, I asked her to turn over," Sandra said. Then she told him there were people going through a lot worse than she was.

"Me and Beth only had to deal with booze, and there's so many completely druggie parents," Sandra said. "Well, our mom did crack too, but that was on the side. Crack on the side is pretty bad. Coke isn't physically addictive but the psychological addictiveness of it is enough to result in many physical effects."

Sandra said Bobby's father got their mother into cocaine.

"He got our mom into crack. He got her into smoking cigarettes again. And he got her drinking a lot more."

She told David that Bobby was the sacrifice in what she and Beth had done.

"It's so horrible," she said. "And our aunt [tries] to talk to me about her theories on everything. I'm the worst person in the world for her to talk to. She gave me this book to read and talked about how you can communicate with dead spirits because they're always with you. So you just have to put yourself into this state. Like a Ouija board."

David still didn't understand how she felt when she was planning her mother's death or how she felt when she killed Linda.

Sandra told David she and her sister watched their mother "slowly kill herself" with booze at every family gathering, but nobody did anything to help them.

"Every single family get-together, Christmas, Thanksgiving, Easter, New Year's," Sandra told him. "Anything. Sometimes she'd be like drunk for a week before they even started and like she'd show up already completely plastered and drink more and fall asleep at the table. Or be awake and drunk. So many stupid arguments and stuff. Like, basically, all Christmases in the past. And there's one I remember when she wasn't drunk, when I was really, really small. But all other major holidays. It just got bad. It was completely out of control."

David asked how Beth was dealing with her mother's death.

"I don't know how's she supposed to deal with it," Sandra said. "I don't know how much at liberty I am to disclose her emotions. The way she saw this situation was the way I saw it, too—it was really horrible. We were suffering so much. I took the initiative. And I went through all the plans and everything. She didn't do anything to stop me. We're both in a better situation now than we were before. Even though it was horrible to get there. But don't worry. She cries a lot about it."

"I just don't know how you can plan something like that," David said.

"Well, how were we supposed to continue living the way we were?" Sandra asked. "It was so bad." She started to cry.

David apologized for upsetting her.

"It was years and years, day in and day out," Sandra said. "It was a completely natural occurrence at our house. Like an adventura." (Adventura means a yelling match or a fight.) "We'd go through three or four of those a day sometimes. Me and Beth were raised with screaming, violent fighting matches. Now, our aunt and uncle are completely calm. We have to adjust."

"Did your aunt and uncle know about the drinking?" David asked.

"Yes, our whole family knew," she said. "That's the thing— our family wasn't doing shit. [Our aunt] took our mom to church once and they prayed a bit and that was supposed to be her on the road to quitting drinking. We should have sat down with our aunt and told her that our mom was drinking herself to death. And [she needed] to go to a clinic, and like for me and Beth and our little stepbrother live with our aunt."

"Like an intervention?" David asked.

"Yeah, but the thing is, I thought about this like months after everything," Sandra said. "I don't think there was any way for me to think about this before. And obviously this might have worked or [it] might not have worked. The person that signs up for rehab has to be sober when they sign the commitment, and once they sign it, they can't leave. But, like, our mom, even though she'd drink for weeks at a time, she'd still deny being an alcoholic. Sometimes she said she'd try to control her drinking a bit because it was getting a tiny bit out of hand. But you knew how much denial she'd go through. That's what made everything worse. All the denials. She'd be drunk one day and we'd say, 'Mom, you've been drinking,' and she'd say, 'no I haven't. What do you mean? I haven't been drinking.' She'd hide alcohol everywhere, It was normal for me and Beth to go around and we'd find a bottle or two. Our mom wasted hundreds of dollars weekly on booze. I'd say probably two to three hundred a week on the average, which is a lot. And it kept going up. That's the thing. At first there was just wine. And then it got to vodka and whiskey. And other alcohol, too.

"We tried to get her to quit in so many ways. But talking to her about it when she was sober was impossible. [She'd say] 'Fine, I'll stop.' And she wouldn't want to talk about it at all. She'd say, 'I don't have a problem,' or [she'd] just get all defensive and start yelling. You can't have a conversation with somebody that's in denial about it. We wasted so many days, so many years, so much effort. It was so bad. It was really, really horrible. It was making me really fucked up, too. I'd get really violent and I'd smash mirrors and throw shit. I'm still violent because of it. I can't help it. But sometimes...I get too violent when I'm drunk."

At one point, Sandra told David, "I regret everything about my life. Me and Beth had this seemingly picture perfect childhood from our point of view. But if you look at it logically, it wasn't nearly close to picture perfect—everything our mom must have been going through would have been really horrible: a single parent, new immigrant, and she had to do all her shit again, like getting any licences to get a better job. And like, looking from her point of view, she did a lot of work. But she destroyed everything she worked for and accomplished. [She] butchered it so badly.

"That's the thing. Our life was so good and amazing, our family loved each other so much. And then it just fell apart into the worst possible situation. It's like it went from the best to the worst. And everything that we loved and held dear got switched around and then destroyed. And now our life's like all good again. Our materialistic needs are being met."

"But you still have that on your conscience," David said.

"Yeah, but then again, like, I'm pretty sure it made me a lot smarter," Sandra said. "Like I see the world completely different. A lot more like well, but then again I see it only from my point of view. I try to incorporate other people's point of view but I'm really only interested in my view of the world. 'Cause then again, I'm me, right?"

Sandra told David she thought children should be taught religion. "Most kids grow up watching TV and that's where all their values come from," she said, then added that most people didn't want to believe their minds could be warped by television.

"But especially if you grow up watching TV your mindset is based on whatever programs are on when you're growing up," she said. "Our generation—Simpsons humour."

If she had children, she added, she'd let them watch *The Simpsons* because it "teaches you the right sense of honour, especially the old episodes," which "were hilarious but they had good messages in them. The new ones are shit. The old ones had good messages in them like the 'shoplifting is wrong' show. But I want my kids to watch every fuckin' episode of *Bill Nye the Science Guy.*"

David pressed Sandra about the murder.

"It's just alcohol, pills, flip her over, blip, four minutes?" he asked.

Sandra nodded.

"That's it?"

"Yep," she replied.

"She got drunk and you just went in and flipped her and that's it?"

"Well, she flipped herself," Sandra said. "I asked her to do it and she did it."

"You just held her?" David asked.

"No, I pushed her head in a tiny bit," Sandra replied. "She was putting herself in, basically."

Then Sandra described a few family drives.

"There [were] times there's been me and Beth and Bobby, and our mom driving us somewhere piss-assed drunk. Sometimes, we'd get mad and [say] let's just go home. Then she'd start yelling—'You want to drive this car off this bridge!' One time it was just me and her driving around. I was trying to give her instructions to go home, like, 'turn right here for the love of God!' So she would go left without realizing she went left. [Or she would] stop in the middle of the highway. Or that time we were driving and she hit the car beside us. Her mirror flew right in front of my face. That could have easily hit me. There's been so many bad things, so many horrible memories. And there's also a lot of repressed memories too. Like, I developed a selective memory when arguments get really, really bad and you remember the next day you had an argument but you can't say what it was about or who said what. You just kill your memory. Some people say that's not possible. It is. Trust me. I can't turn it off but I can turn it on. It takes a lot of work to get back at them. You have to go step by step."

"Everybody has repressed memories, you know," David told her.

"Yeah, but some people have a lot more than others," she said.

David told her he wanted to help her and apologized for having to put her through the torment.

"Well, I'm through it," she said. "I really don't mind. And I'm not going through anything right now emotionally. I don't know if it's just turned off or if I'm really desensitized to it by now."

David asked where she obtained the Tylenol-3s.

Sandra said her mom had them because she worked in a hospital.

"I know you told me something about gloves, too," David said.

"Yeah, I didn't want to leave my fingerprints on her head," Sandra said. "I'm not a dumb-ass. And so I had gloves."

"Wouldn't the cops search the house and see them?" David asked.

"That's why we threw them out," Sandra told him. "We walked around the restaurant and threw them out. I didn't want to get caught. What evidence would there be against me? We went to Square One and threw [them] out there. Obviously my fingerprints and traces of me are going to be around my house.

But it's different if your hand print is on a person. I didn't want to leave any bruises or anything."

"You worked it out?" David asked.

"Every detail," she said. "It's horrible, like, how do you think I feel? What am I supposed to do with myself? Like, I'm a person and like, I'm here and I have nothing to do."

"Didn't she have insurance, life insurance?" David asked.

"Yeah. Me and Beth got sixty thousand each," she said.

"Sixty thousand?" David asked.

"But it's in the bank," she said. "That's nothing. Our friend gets half a million when his dad dies. There's four kids [and] they each get half a million. We should have been getting two hundred fifty thousand each but our mom cancelled that one a month or something before. There would have been a huge difference. But our aunt wants to save that for university. But I'm not going to university. I'm going to try to get it for my vacation. Our aunt is using the money now. You know how we got four hundred dollars Christmas money each? So by the time I'm eighteen, there's probably going to be around forty thousand left."

"That's still a lot of money," David said.

"No, that's not much, trust me," she said. "A kilogram of coke is a hundred thousand, right there."

"Phew, never mind that shit," David told her.

"And that's only one kilogram," she said.

"You really didn't have an intent to cash in, did you?" David asked. "Like, I hope not."

"The money, no, the money had nothing to do with it," she told him. "The money is just what happens. Don't worry, the money had nothing to do with it."

David said he was glad she hadn't killed her mother for the money. He asked how she and Beth were holding up.

"Well, we're both good as we're going to get," Sandra said. "She's doing good. She has an amazing relationship with Justin. They really go so well together. I can easily see them getting married. He knows so much about her, and like, he knows, like, all her moods and stuff. And you can tell, they just love each other. Well, they're in love with each other. There's a huge difference. I love all my friends but I'm only in love with one of them. Beth suffers from depression and has a lot of stress on her, but she's doing pretty okay. We're both doing amazingly okay for our circumstances."

David then asked if she and Beth had followed their mother into the bathroom?

"Well, no, I'd suggested she take a bath," Sandra said. "And I drew her a bath, and like, she'd be so drunk."

Sandra said her mom was often so drunk she took her clothes off in front of her daughters' friends and masturbated in front of Sandra and Beth.

"That's one of the worst images you can have, but like I've seen it happen more than once," Sandra said.

"I don't want to think about that," David replied.

"Well, I dream about that, honestly," she said. "My childhood has so many images that people don't even want to imagine. I've got multiple versions of these different situations. With different people around. I've had a bunch of friends that have seen our mom naked more than once. I don't get what's with drunks and getting naked."

"That sounds weird," David said.

"You haven't been raised by a drunk," Sandra said. "Trust me, if you were raised by a drunk, you'd see the world differently."

"I remember you told me you had to drag her up the stairs once," David said.

"Once?" Sandra replied. "I've had to drag her ass around like so many times. Sometimes, she's naked. Sometimes, she's clothed. Sometimes it was to pay bills, like in the city. She'd be like, leaning against me and I'd like, say sign here, do this. The whole situation was horrible. It was as bad as it could get."

"So you just saw it as a relief for her," David said. "I'm guessing your sister saw it the same way."

"Yeah, sure it was a release," Sandra said. "Even though it was the end of everything. It was the only real efficient cure. But it was horrible."

Sandra said Beth was doing better than she was. "She doesn't have that substance abuse going on in her life. Plus she has Justin and I still have to strive to get Chad."

David decided to ask Sandra point blank about Beth's role.

"Well, she didn't do anything," Sandra replied. "She was just there for me to talk to and stuff. She was aware of everything that was going on but no input."

Sandra later told David that she was never afraid to leave her house, even in the dead of night.

"I'm always aware of the possibility that every time I leave my house I might never come back to it 'cause there's like so many accidents that happen. And I don't know how happy God is with me. He might like, you know, squish me at any moment." Later, Sandra told David that he worried too much about things.

"You waste your life being too worried about shit," she said. "Like the second I turn eighteen I'm going skydiving for my birthday. So far only my cousin wants to go with me."

CHAPTER 14
"I LOVE 'SHROOMS"

On January 11, 2004, David picked Beth up at her aunt's residence at about 10:50 a.m. in the police-supplied Ford Focus for the first of two secretly recorded videotaped conversations.

David asked Beth how long it had been since her mother's death.

"On the eighteenth it's gonna be a year," Beth said. "Two days after Bobby's birthday."

He asked if she and Sandra and Bobby were going to lay flowers at their mother's grave.

"Probably, I know our aunt is going to want to," she said.

"What about you?" David asked.

"It doesn't matter where I am because either way you can still think the same thoughts," Beth said. "I don't feel any more special being by her grave. But it calms our aunt down so I go with her so I can make her feel better."

Beth said they usually only visited the grave on holidays and when their aunt wanted to go. David told Beth he'd been worried about her and Sandra.

"We're too pampered now," Beth said.

"Sandra told me something she shouldn't have," David said.

Beth asked what her sister told him. David didn't hold back. "She said she did it. She killed her mom."

"Oh," Beth replied.

"Is it true?" David asked.

"Everyone feels guilty," she replied.

"I know, but still, she even kinda described it in detail and it's kinda worrying me." Then, not wanting to seem curious, David changed subject and asked Beth if she wanted to get a coffee. She told him coffee was poison. The conversation turned to drugs. David asked Beth if she ever tried coke.

"Not yet," Beth said. She said she knew people who felt like God after doing cocaine. She thought she'd never be able to do enough lines to get really high because she'd never be able to afford it. But she admitted to doing magic mushrooms several times with her friend Justin.

"For us, it usually takes ten to fifteen minutes and already you're buzzing," she said. The buzz lasted longer if she also smoked dope, and it felt like being drunk.

"Sometimes on 'shrooms people get paranoid and they have too much energy." She told David about a time five or six people were at her house, all doing 'shrooms.

"Someone starts having a bad trip," she said. "And a bad trip is like you can't tell whether your eyes are open or closed. You can't feel your tongue. You wouldn't be able to chew. The thing is you don't know where your tongue is. You feel there's something in your mouth." She didn't think 'shrooms were dangerous because "it's not like you'll overdose and die."

When David finally got the conversation back on track, he asked if Sandra was telling the truth about how their mother died.

"Well, you don't have a lot of the background information so it's kinda hard to understand," Beth said.

David said he knew her mother was an alcoholic.

"Everyone did," Beth said. "Everyone knew and nobody did anything."

David asked about Bobby and said he looked a bit undernourished. Beth said Bobby was anemic but he was healthier now that he was playing sports. They were going to sign him up for soccer so he could learn sportsmanship and get lots of exercise.

"And I'm giving him an allowance," Beth said. "Five bucks a week."

David asked how Sandra was handling their mother's death, and said he was concerned Sandra might be having mental problems.

"Depends on your definition," Beth said. "Anyone can pull a disorder out of their ass. I think her problem is she's too sane. Like, you see everything too much for how it really is. And it's just so depressing. I just try to block it out. But I still have crying fits and stuff too."

"You weren't part of it, were you?" David asked.

"Yeah," Beth replied.

"You were?" David asked again.

"Yeah," she replied.

"But did you actually—?" David shot back.

"Yeah," Beth replied.

"You did?" David asked.

"Yeah," she said.

"You were in the room while she was doing it?" David asked.

"Yeah," she replied.

"Wow," David said.

"Right behind her," Beth told him. "I was the one who mixed our mom's drinks that day."

"Oh fuck, she didn't tell me that," David said.

"Like uhmm, if you think about it, she just wouldn't randomly tell people everyone that was involved, right?" Beth said.

David said Sandra protected her by saying Beth had nothing to do with their mother's death, then asked if insurance money played any role in Linda's death.

"It wasn't to gain good things," Beth said. "It was to lose bad things. Being sensitized as a kid, that's the consequences, I guess. We're learning to hate things. I mean, shit in one hand and hope in the other. And see which fills up first."

David started talking about a book Beth was reading, and her thoughts suddenly turned morbid.

"It takes one bullet to kill the whole world 'cause it's all in your head," Beth said.

"You're not doing that?" David asked, concerned she might take her own life.

"No, I wouldn't use a gun," she said.

"Well, what would you use then?" David asked.

"I don't know, probably something that just makes you drift off and sleep and not notice," she said.

"Don't do that," David told her. "You're too special to do that."

"I'd just like something quick," she said.

"You're not planning to?" David asked.

"Well, no," she answered.

"Jump off a balcony or something?" he asked.

"No, I'd hate to fall," she said.

"Well, you know what I mean, commit suicide. You're not planning to do that, are you?"

"Yeah, I do," Beth said. "I hate to slowly get old and see my mind decaying."

David said his grandma still had all her senses well into her eighties.

"Most people don't stay healthy in their old age," she said. "Like my grandparents. They were really respected engineers and they had connections in Europe. But you could see their minds decaying. It's sad what happens to you."

David's initial intercept with Beth created questions that needed answers. So he talked to her again on January 17, 2004, when he took Bobby, Beth, and Sandra to an arcade. Johnstone, decided David should tell Beth he was so bothered by what happened he was having trouble concentrating.

"You're going to have to flat-out tell her it was bothering you, that your university career is on the line," Johnstone told David. "And I want some assurances. You know, 'What do you mean, you were standing behind her? Did you actually watch Sandra put your mom's head under the water? Okay, you said you mixed the drinks. How did you mix them and how does somebody not taste something in their drink? How many pills did you put in there?' Those kinds of questions. We're worried about how did the pills get into the glass."

The intercept took place a day before the one-year anniversary of Linda's murder.

David told Beth he felt as if he was an accomplice. He knew what they did. He felt just as guilty. He was also worried about them and Bobby. Beth told him he worried too much. Bobby "obviously didn't know." He should "chillax" and "smoke a doobie."

David then asked Beth straight up if she and Sandra planned the murder.

"Yeah, we're not stupid," Beth said. "If we were stupid we would have gotten caught. We used her weak point against her."

David said he didn't understand why Linda didn't taste the drugs in her booze.

"We didn't put anything in there—she took them herself," Beth said.

"I thought you ground them up and put them in," David said.

"No," Beth replied. "They were Tylenol-3s and she just took a bunch. We told her to," Beth said. "She was like already way too drunk to notice something was wrong."

"So you didn't grind up anything?" he asked.

"No," Beth replied.

David asked Beth if she saw her mother die.

"Yes," Beth answered.

"Did you do it?" David asked.

"I was part of it," she replied.

"I know, but did you actually put her head down?" David asked.

"No," Beth answered. "Think about it, how our washroom was. If someone is standing by the tub, there just isn't enough room for another person. So, I was two feet behind."

"Wow, it just freaks me out," David said. "How many people did you tell?"

Beth admitted she told one person, her boyfriend.

"He was the one that supplied the Tylenol-3s," she said. "You need a prescription to get those 'cause they're so strong." Then she told David, "Sandra and I are realistic people. We know how other people will react to certain things we do and we use that to our advantage. And we don't make fucked-up decisions [or] stupid mistakes."

"How long were you guys planning it?" David asked.

"Well, it was kind of like a building rage," Beth told him.

"About not being able to control things. It was mounting our whole life."

Beth told him that she and her sister had been planning their mother's death months before David and his mother visited them at Christmas.

"Months?" David then asked. "Like, how do you feel about that?"

"You can't feel one way about something like that," Beth said. "Like if you look at it one way, I don't regret it. 'Cause now Bobby has like—"

"A better life?" David said.

"Yeah, well it was shitty with his dad," Beth said. "But like, she was spoiling him and ruining him horribly and stuff. And like, if you look at it another way, I'm like completely devastated about it."

"Would you do it again?" David asked.

"Feel horrible," she replied.

"Would you do it again?" David asked her once more.

"I don't know," Beth replied. "If there were the exact circumstances then I would be the exact person that I was back then. I would have done it again. But like you can't expect a straight answer for something like that."

David said he was still going to worry about her and her sister because he'd known them for most of his life. But Beth said he shouldn't be so concerned about them.

"Like honestly, we know how to take care of ourselves," Beth said. "Honestly, Sandra and I do know how people react to, like, different things or, like, anything we do. As a whole, we're like more realistic than a lot of people.

"You can't understand unless you've known, like, our whole life. And there'd be, like, hours and hours of like explaining, like you know. Just, like, years of seeing shit that you know is wrong but not being able to change it 'cause you're, like, just a kid."

"So no one will listen to you even if you tried to say anything or no one even takes you seriously. Being ever so powerless like makes you bitter on the inside."

David said it was hard to imagine what she went through. Beth admitted they were still depressed.

"We'll have screaming fits and crying rages," she said. "But no one knows about it so we're not going to start talking to random people. We know how to act very, very well."

Beth told him that she neither she nor her sister regretted what they had done. She said Bobby's life was now better. "She was spoiling him and ruining him horribly," Beth said. On the other hand, she felt "completely devastated."

David asked how they managed to fool the police.

"What do you mean?" Beth asked.

"Like your statement," David said.

"It just looked like she drowned in the tub from drinking too much."

David asked her which boyfriend gave her the Tylenol-3s.

"His name is Justin," Beth said.

"Then you just told the cops a lie?" David asked.

"Yeah," she replied.

The videotaped intercepts provided police with a wealth of incriminating evidence against Sandra and Beth—information explaining the lack of fingerprints, about the insurance money, the girls' state of mind at the time of the murder, and the Tylenol-3s. The police hadn't known about the drugs because no toxicology tests had been done when Linda died. And now they had a problem: Sandra told David the pills belonged to her mother. Beth said the pills came from Justin.

Sandra and Beth had been under surveillance since January 7. Police began to collect information about their close friends. Detective Magnus secured a copy of Andersen's post mortem report. Dr. Tim Feltis had checked her blood only for alcohol, so there was no mention of codeine in her system. But some blood samples had been frozen and stored at the Centre for Forensic Sciences in Toronto. Constable Mike Pulley requested toxicological tests for the presence of codeine or any drug associated with extra-strength Tylenol. When the results came in, they showed that Linda had acetaminophen and codeine in her system—the main ingredients for Tylenol-3s—as well as five times the legal limit of alcohol. These were potentially deadly levels of codeine. Investigators did extensive background checks on the sisters' close friends. They checked school records and Linda Andersen's bank accounts, credit cards, and life-insurance policies. Police also listened to the 911 tape.

To make sure the sisters didn't know they were prime suspects in their mother's murder, the police didn't interview a single person until the day of the arrests.

After all this research, Detective Magnus had probable cause, and Peel Crown attorney Mark Saltmarsh authorized the arrests of Sandra and Beth. He also provided the search warrants investigators requested for residences and school lockers.

Magnus assembled a team of fifty Peel homicide officers, and they met at about 5:00 a.m. January 21, 2004. Officers would grab the sisters, all their known friends, and anybody who might have information about Linda Andersen's death. More than twenty-five cruisers and unmarked cars rolled out of the parking lot at about 6:30 a.m. Arrests would occur roughly at 7:00 a.m.—a time most of the people police wanted to speak to would be at home.

One team of officers went to Justin's residence. (At this stage, he was considered a witness, not a suspect.) Other teams went to the homes of Walter Andersen, Doug Landers, Ashley, Jay, and several more friends. Officers also went to the girls' high schools, searched their lockers, and retrieved their school records. The officers were empowered to collect computers and other electronic gadgets from homes and schools. Later in the day, Chad and Donny were brought in for questioning.

Sergeant Rick De Facendis headed the team of eight who went to Martha Kronwall's residence to arrest Sandra and Beth. Martha was stunned when police told her why they were there. Beth was in her pyjamas, sitting on her bed reading a magazine, when Constable Olga Skok entered her room. The sisters lived in the basement; Sandra's bedroom was an actual room, and part of the recreation room had been turned into a bedroom for Beth. A large wall divider gave her some privacy. Beth had just dyed her hair, which was covered by a plastic bag.

"Are you Beth Andersen?" Skok asked.

Beth looked up. "Yes."

Skok thought Beth seemed unconcerned that a police officer was in her room. "I'm Constable Skok and I'm here to arrest you for murder."

Beth said nothing.

Skok read her her rights. Beth didn't seem shocked.

"You have to get dressed," Skok said.

"No, I'm fine with what I'm wearing," Beth answered.

"Okay, but you're going to need to put shoes on and a coat," Skok said.

Beth grabbed her winter coat from a nearby hanger and put

on winter boots. She asked Skok if she could rinse her hair. Skok said she could do that at the police station. She handcuffed Beth, who asked if she could take a swig of mouthwash. Skok agreed. Beth then asked if she would be able to go to school to take an exam.

"Not today," Skok said.

Sandra's room was in darkness. Once Rita Late flipped the light switch, it was another few seconds before Sandra woke. When Late told her that she was being arrested for the first-degree murder of her mother, Sandra nodded calmly. Late told Sandra to get dressed, and Sandra insisted on wearing pyjamas. The sisters were taken to the division in separate cars so they couldn't discuss what they would tell investigators.

"I've got a party to go to," Sandra said in the car. "Do you know how long this is going to take?"

Inside Skok's cruiser, Beth was read her rights again.

"You've been arrested for murder," Skok said.

"For who?" Beth asked.

"Your mother," Skok answered.

"Oh," Beth replied.

At the homicide bureau Beth took a shower. She was offered street clothes but preferred to wear her pyjamas.

Skok and Late, both veterans, found it remarkable how calm the sisters were. Skok said Beth had fallen asleep in the cruiser.

Other officers executed a search warrant at their aunt's home and removed computers, books, and clothing. Police also canvassed the sisters' previous townhouse complex asking if anybody could provide information about the girls or about the night Andersen drowned.

CHAPTER 15
NO DEATH PENALTY, HOORAY!

Sandra was placed in a polygraph room at about 7:30 a.m. Detective Blaise Doherty, an interrogator with more than twenty years of experience, advised her of her rights under the Charter of Rights and Freedoms and the Youth Criminal Justice Act (YCJA). He asked her if she wanted an adult present, and to speak with a lawyer, but she declined both offers several times. Doherty began to collect personal information from her. They talked about life and alcoholism, and he tried to build a friendly rapport. Sandra told him her philosophies on life, religion, and the world in general, then told him about her musical interests and her dreams. They discussed everything except Linda Andersen's murder.

Sandra seemed far more worried about missing her brother's birthday party that Sunday.

"So am I going to be in custody? Because his dad doesn't know how to have a birthday party. What's the earliest I can get out? Am I gonna have a trial?"

Sandra wanted to call a friend to tell him she wouldn't be coming to his house to watch movies. Doherty asked if there was anything more serious than being charged with murder,

and Sandra replied, "Genocide." He asked if she wanted anything from McDonald's, and she said McDonald's served "pure
crap food" and asked for steak and lobster instead. She didn't
want coffee ("black death") or tea ("mild poison").

Sandra told Doherty she once thought about becoming a
forensic pathologist but changed her mind because she wanted
an easier life. She was going to go to bartending school after she
graduated from high school, and then become a flight attendant. Eventually, she hoped to be a paramedic.

"You're seeing real things, saving people, and even though
some people might die, you're still going to help some," Sandra
said. "I want to be a paramedic but I want to get other life experiences first. I want to be a rock star. That's why I need to learn
to play an instrument. I'm trying to enjoy my youth before it
fades away forever."

She said she was learning to play the violin but thought it
would be at least five years before she could play "Flight of the
Bumblebee." Then she said, "Dream as if you'll live forever and
live as if you'll die today."

Doherty asked how she had become so mature for her age.

"I guess I suffered a lot," she said. She told him she used to
go to church but then her views on religion changed.

"You grow up watching Disney movies where there are
always happy perfect endings but then you realize life isn't like
that. I'm trying to decide if there is faith or destiny. I'm still
very much confused as to what life is all about. I'm sorting
things out."

Asked for her views on death, Sandra said, "Whatever happens, happens, [and] you have to die sometime." She said it
would be cool if she didn't die in a car crash or from some horrible disease. She said her family drank booze a lot, especially her

alcoholic mom. "She would sometimes get drunk, pass out, and go to sleep." She added, "The worst things are drunks in denial."

She also asked Doherty if it was illegal for her to get drunk or just illegal for her to buy booze because of her age.

Eventually Doherty asked her to tell him about the day her mother died.

"It was a pretty bad day," she said. "My mom started getting drunk so I got money off of her and we went to Jack Astor's and then came back and found her. So, the last thing I ever said to her was [about] getting money off of her, which is pretty bad."

Around 10:00 a.m., Doherty's line of questioning changed. He said he knew she caused her mother's death and asked why she did it. Sandra denied having anything to do with it.

"You have to understand we just don't go out and grab people for serious offences like this, right?" Doherty said. Sandra told him she saw her mother's death coming because she often fell down stairs when she was drunk.

"It was getting to the point where I really wasn't surprised at anything happening to her," she said.

Doherty asked if she "still loved her mom" whereupon Sandra replied, "Well, it's sort of hard to love a dead person, isn't it? I love the memory of her."

Sandra knew police had "theories" of why she and Beth went to Jack Astor's the night of her mother's death, because of the many rumours at school, including her pregnancy. She also denied crying at Jack Astor's, getting Tylenol-3s from Justin, and discussing over dinner how they were going to make the 911 emergency call.

As the interview continued, Sandra again denied she killed her mother. Doherty told her it would be disturbing if she had killed her mother for $60,000 in life insurance.

Doherty refused to accept her denials; Sandra dug in. She would let the justice system decide her fate. She asserted her right to silence at least seventeen times in the next several hours.

Then she said her mom would sometimes spend weeks in her room drunk, and how depressing it was for her.

"Did you think ending your mother's life would change things for the better?" Doherty asked.

"I didn't know what would happen afterwards," Sandra said. She didn't seem to realize she had admitted involvement. "I just wanted everything to stop."

"What have you learned since?" Doherty asked.

"That I'm a dumb-ass," she said.

"Do you think it was a mistake?" Doherty asked.

Sandra started to cry. "I know it was a mistake," she said. "I didn't realize how many lives I would ruin."

Doherty then played a portion of her conversation with David where she confessed to killing her mother.

"Okay," he said. "Let's try to understand why this happened."

"I'm not answering any questions," Sandra shot back. "I'm just giving you a warning right now. But you can ask them if you want."

Doherty tried to get Sandra to reveal more. He said he didn't think she was a "bad person" and didn't want her to think he thought "poorly" of her but that she needed to take responsibility for her actions. He said he believed she thought she was doing the right thing for her brother.

Sandra ignored him, then asked, "How long until I get to go to Brampton [court] or whatever? How many hours do I have to sit here?"

"I don't know, but I do know it's important for me to try and understand you," Doherty said.

"I don't have anything to say," Sandra snapped. Doherty insisted that needed to understand why it happened.

Then she asked if she was going to have a cell to herself. She added, "How long until I get to see somebody?"

Doherty told her she wouldn't be talking to anyone but him. Sandra insisted she wasn't going to tell him anything. Doherty wanted to know whether she was just a young girl, who had made a bad mistake, or a young adult, who made a conscious decision to do something evil.

"I'll write some books when I'm in jail," Sandra answered.

"Try and imagine what people are thinking?" Doherty said.

"I don't care," Sandra said.

"You don't care what people are thinking?" Doherty asked.

"No," she said.

"Everybody cares what other people think."

"Well I'm not everybody," Sandra said.

Doherty didn't believe her. She had heart because she cared about her sister and her brother. He understood the person in the tub that night wasn't the person who raised her. "But she was still your mother. And it must have taken a tremendous amount of either emotion or courage on your part to do what you did. It wasn't an easy decision. But I don't think you did it for yourself. I think you did it for one of two reasons."

Sandra didn't care what he thought.

"But do you think it's fair that you don't tell your side of the story?"

"Who cares if it's fair?" Sandra replied.

"Death isn't fair either," Doherty said.

"I know that," she said.

Doherty reminded her that she and her sister had revealed how their mother really died in the videotape with David.

"Well, I only said it on the tape," she replied.

Later, she asked, "When can I have my cell to crawl into? I'm not gonna say anything else. I don't care. I'll go to jail for like twenty-five years or whatever. But I'm not saying anything else."

Doherty said the biggest problem people have is keeping a secret. She had already shared her's with several people. What was missing was why their mother had to die? He kept prodding her, trying to get answers. Then he asked if she was going to tell her brother. "Some day, sooner or later, he's gonna come and he's gonna say, 'Sandra, what happened to our mom?'" Doherty said. "And you'll need an answer for him."

"And I'll answer," Sandra said.

Doherty asked if it was "fair" for her to have taken Bobby's mother away? Sandra, again, refused to give him a straight answer. Doherty asked more questions, but Sandra was adamant. "I told you I'm not saying anything else."

"He doesn't have a mother and you know why?" Doherty said. "You took her away from him."

"I'm not answering anything else," Sandra defiantly told him. "So you're wasting your breath."

"I've got lots of it," Doherty said. "But your mother doesn't. Someone has to speak for her because she's not here to speak for herself."

Doherty then told her he wondered whether the killing had been more cold and calculated.

"Maybe," Sandra replied.

"Maybe," Doherty said. "But I would hate to think that about such a young girl."

"Once again, what you think, does it matter?" Sandra asked.

At one point, she asked, "Is your education paid if you're in jail by the province or something?"

"Probably, I don't know. I've never been in jail," Doherty said.

"You're sort of associated with criminals," Sandra replied. "So shouldn't you be current about like, I don't know, criminal punishment?"

"I know where we put them," Doherty said. "I don't really know what happens once we put them there. Just from reading the newspapers, you see people like Karla Homolka."

Sandra didn't know who she was, but then Doherty explained she was the wife of Paul Bernardo, one of Canada's most notorious killers, and a sexual predator.

"I didn't rape my mom," Sandra said.

Doherty didn't think she was selfish.

"I'm a greedy bitch," Sandra replied.

"Who said that?" Doherty asked.

"I just did," she said, and then told him she wanted to be a millionaire.

Doherty then asked if she cared about Beth "a little or a lot?"

"A lot," she answered.

"She's up to her eyeballs in this," Doherty told her.

Later, she asked, "Can you wake me up when you're done? I'll talk to my lawyer. But there really isn't anything I'm gonna discuss, just general knowledge."

Doherty told her the best time for her to talk about what happened was right then.

"I don't think you understand," Sandra said. "I don't have any hope. I really don't care who believes what or whatever. Like, I'll just let the justice system do whatever.

"I don't care who believes me. Hopefully I won't be dead by the time I get out of jail. I'll get an education. I don't have any hope. I'm guessing I won't be put to death. I'm just going to try to make the best of whatever happens."

Sandra didn't think her dreams about her mother were going to go away any time soon.

Despite her refusing to talk, Doherty insisted he wasn't going to leave the room.

"This is a reality you have to face," Doherty said. "And you knew back then this day may happen. You had to know that."

"Yeah," she replied.

"You're an intelligent woman," Doherty said.

"I'm not a woman," she replied. "I'm a little kid."

"But you've done something," Doherty said. "That's an adult situation you've found yourself in. If in fact it was a bad decision of a little kid compared to the cold calculating strategy of a young woman, that's important for me to know. But I don't know at this point. And I don't know what you were like a year ago. You may have matured greatly over this year. I bet since this has happened, you've changed a lot. I'm sure you've probably changed since that day. Nobody can take a life and not be changed by it. But I wonder if the young girl in the bathroom back in January of 2003 is the same girl sitting here today. Was it a young girl who made a bad mistake that she now feels bad about or is it someone who as an adult made a conscious decision to do something very evil? I don't know. I don't think you're this person. I don't. But it makes a difference in my mind."

"So I'll write a book when I'm in jail," Sandra told him.

"What do you think should happen to you?" Doherty asked.

"I don't know. I'm guessing I won't be put to death."

"No, you won't," Doherty replied. "What do you think should happen to your sister?"

"Nothing should happen to her," Sandra answered.

"Why?" Doherty asked.

"Because she didn't do anything," Sandra replied. "She's not responsible for anything."

"That's not the evidence we have before us," Doherty said. "What about Justin?"

"What about Justin?" Sandra asked.

"Is he as responsible as you?" Doherty asked.

"No," Sandra replied. "Nobody is as responsible."

Doherty told Sandra that Beth was being interviewed in another room.

"Did she play a big role in it?" he asked.

"I told you, no, she didn't." Sandra said.

"What role did she play?" Doherty asked.

"I'm not explaining anything."

Doherty then asked—in percentage—what role she had played in her mother's death.

"Five or something," Sandra answered.

"Five per cent?" Doherty asked. "Does it rest solely with you?"

"I guess, yeah," she replied.

"Does some of it go to Justin?"

"He didn't do anything," Sandra said.

"But he supplied some stuff that played a part in it?" Doherty asked.

Later, Sandra refused to answer when Doherty asked if her sister had tried to stop her.

"I'm just trying to understand in my mind what role Beth played," Doherty said. "What should happen to your sister? Unless you tell us otherwise, we will consider her as much responsible as you are."

Doherty knew he'd finally found Sandra's breaking point.

Her sister would go to jail if she didn't convince police otherwise. Sandra broke down. She admitted she used gloves when she murdered her mother, that she threw them away and that her mother never struggled.

"She was falling asleep," she said. "She did most of it herself. There wasn't any fighting." Sandra insisted Beth didn't know she was going to kill her mother until she started to drown her. She hated Ashley and David. "I've never had a friend who hasn't backstabbed me," Sandra said.

Doherty said David didn't help police because he wanted to "hurt" her. But Sandra insisted David had helped police for his own selfish reasons.

She asked Doherty if "convicts could have successful lives" after prison.

"There are some examples of that," he said.

"Well, I guess I have to be one of the best," she said.

Later, she said her mother only worked one or two weeks out of two months during the summer before she died. Her friends saw her naked many times when she was drunk.

Sandra then accused Doherty of only pretending to care for her.

"How many murderers do you keep in touch with?" she asked. "Like, I know I'm completely fucked."

Sandra understood she would be locked up for many years. Her biggest concern was how her family would react. She was upset that she wouldn't be able to help with Bobby's birthday.

"His Dad is incapable of even ordering pizza," she said. "The only reason I haven't blown my brains out is 'cause that would completely destroy Bobby. That's why I'm still alive."

Later, she said she never understood the pressures her mother dealt with every day as a nurse. Her mother often had to take care of battered babies, who were brought to the hospital by abusing parents.

"I didn't know alcoholism was a disease," she said. "I just thought my mother didn't care and was hurting us on purpose. But now I know she didn't even know what she was doing. I was a stupid kid. It was so bad. Everybody else had a normal life. Even if their parents were alcoholics, it wasn't as bad as our mom. I was just suffering so much. I couldn't take it anymore. I was still a kid. I was self-centered. I wasn't thinking how it would affect others."

She told Doherty that she didn't want her family to attend her trial because she didn't want them to hear the testimony. She felt ashamed and didn't think she'd ever be able to face her aunt Martha or her uncle Fred again. "I don't think my family will ever trust me again," she said. "She (mother) needed help but I didn't know how to get it for her and so I just had to ruin everything."

Later, Sandra refused to tell Doherty if she had told anybody she had caused her mother's death. He assumed she had.

"You can assume what you like but when you assume you make an ass out of you and me," Sandra shot back.

Near the end of the interview, Doherty thanked her for sharing her secret.

"I didn't share it," Sandra snapped. "You stole it."

At about 3:00 p.m. Doherty left the room, and Sandra lay on the floor and took a nap.

While Sandra was confessing, Beth steadfastly denied any involvement in her mother's death and refused to speak with Detective Magdi Younan. Beth asked to see her aunt Martha, but her aunt was being interviewed in another room. Three hours later, Martha spoke to her niece and requested that defence attorney Michael Bury be contacted. No one could reach Bury, so Beth spoke briefly to a duty counsel over the phone.

Unlike the United States, where police have to immediately stop questioning a suspect once they ask to speak to a lawyer, Canadian law is less clear in that matter and Younan continued to try to obtain information from Beth when he resumed the interview about 1:40 p.m. But Beth completely shut down when Younan asked her specific questions about the crime. Younan told her that he knew she was guilty. He wanted to know why she did it.

"I have nothing to confess about it," Beth snapped. "I didn't do anything. I'm not saying anything more."

Younan asked a lot of questions. He also played a portion of the incriminating videotape with David. Beth refused to talk. She asserted her right to silence at least twenty-five times.

CHAPTER 16
HE'S SUCH A FOOL

Detective Magnus, hoping the sisters might incriminate each other, let them speak alone for ten minutes. They were told their conversation would be monitored and recorded.

The girls thought they had a clever strategy. They spoke to each other in Danish. On the surface, it seemed as if despite their intelligence, it never donned on them that police could have their conversations translated. It seemed inconceivable that they didn't know police would eventually know what they were talking about.

Beth urged Sandra not to say anything to the police and not to give away their tactics. She said David was a fool to believe them when they told him they killed their mother.

"So here we are," Beth said. "If we wouldn't have wanted to scare him like that we wouldn't have had to lie to him like that."

"What?" Sandra asked, not initially realizing the ruse her sister was playing.

"We didn't have to scare him like that," Beth said, laughing. "We didn't have to lie to him."

Sandra still wasn't certain what her sister was up to.

"I didn't think he would do something so stupid as to hand over this tape," Beth said, again laughing. "Because he's such a faggot. He had to be scared like that. Okay?"

Sandra became emotional.

"Well, you know that I did it ... all my fault," Sandra mumbled. "Not you, remember? What am I going to do?"

"Don't tell them anything," Beth snapped. "Don't say anything. No talking without an attorney."

"But did you hear what they're telling me?" Sandra asked. "Scary."

Beth then assured Sandra "it's easy to lie" to a person.

"It's too late, isn't it?" Sandra asked.

"So you tell them now that you were more and more scared and thought you had to tell," Beth said. "I'm telling you nothing. Everything I say is nothing without a lawyer. Don't answer any questions without a lawyer." Beth then warned her sister that the police would try to trip her up.

"Auntie is trying really hard to help us," Beth said. "She wants to see you. I told her we wanted to scare ... David it was a lie. And we wanted to scare him."

By now Sandra had composed herself and had figured out what Beth was up to.

"They are taping everything we say," Sandra reminded her sister.

"I know but David was simply irritating," Beth said. "We wanted to scare him."

Again Beth laughed. "I didn't think he would tape something because I would not have said anything like that if he would have reacted that way. Because you know how many people love to scare people. And tells all kinds of things but not everyone takes it and tapes it and gives it to the police."

She said the police told her that she would be in the station for hours unless she talked to them.

"Well, we have to sit it out," Beth said. "I have been sitting alone for hours in the same position. Have to make it through."

Sandra said police told her their friends talked.

"But that's not true," Sandra said. "They always said they'd be quiet."

Sandra asked Beth what Aunt Martha would think of her. "How am I going to look her in the face?"

"She believes me," Beth said. "She believes we didn't do a thing. Simply stick to that. Simply say that's the truth. Because it is."

"And don't take a lie detector test."

"I know," Sandra said.

"Did you talk to this guy on the phone? Don't get sucked in. Don't say anything. No conversation, because even though they start gently, little by little, they add things on and then it's not true."

"But you know the tape," Sandra said. "It looks so true. And nobody will believe me that it's not the truth."

"But it is the truth," Beth said, laughing again. "David is so stupid."

"But nobody will believe, nobody will believe," Sandra said.

"I know but you have to stick with it," Beth said.

Beth then laughed again at the thought of missing her exam because of where she was.

"I don't think you will get penalized for it," Sandra said.

Sandra told Beth she wanted to go home, but her sister said they needed to remain strong.

"I heard that with murder, it's weeks in a junior place," Beth said. "Simply have to wait for a hearing and this is a few weeks or a few months. Simply have to sit it out."

"I hate David," Sandra said. "And he took us to the arcade after that."

She reminded her sister that the doctor, who examined their mother, said it was a drowning.

"Because she was drunk," Beth said.

"I said she fell herself," Sandra said.

"And I said I don't even know," Beth said.

"I was saying you don't know nothing about it," Sandra said.

"On the tape I was telling David about the bathroom and it was so small that I had to stay behind you and David believed it all of course," Beth said. "It's stupid. Because they think this is their strongest point. The whole thing we told. That he believed it."

Sandra then asked Beth why David would believe what they were telling him was the truth when he never believed it when she told people she was pregnant.

"You and your lies," Beth said, laughing again. "But simply don't say anything to them because that's the truth."

"I'm sorry," Sandra said.

"And don't say things like that," Beth shot back.

"My head hurts," Sandra said. "It doesn't seem real."

"It's just a bad dream," Beth said. She told Sandra the police would send them to different places so they couldn't see each other.

"Oh well, maybe it's time to tell the whole truth," Sandra said.

"The lawyer was saying not to tell them anything, anymore," Beth said. "Everything you say they will try to tangle us and use against us. Simply say it was a shock. They get you out of bed at 7 a.m. and that this is not making any sense."

Sandra told Beth they needed to call Bobby's father and explain what happened. But Beth told her police were already talking to family members, including their dad.

"Dad?" Sandra asked.

"Interrogated him," Beth said. "They were saying they were going to call the school and talk to teachers about our character and who are friends are."

When Sandra returned to her interview room a few minutes later, she immediately changed her story.

"How serious is it to lie to cops?" Sandra asked Doherty.

"Why?" Doherty asked.

"Just wondering," she replied. "I guess the fact I'm a compulsive liar...use it in my defence, right?"

Doherty said the evidence against her was "compelling."

"Well that's interesting because I still consider myself innocent," Sandra told him.

"Innocent of what?" Doherty asked.

"Of committing the crime," she said.

"How so?" Doherty asked.

"Because I didn't do it," she said.

"Too late," Doherty said.

"I don't think so because that's what I believe and that's what I know happened," she said. "I'll get in trouble for lying."

"You're not in trouble for lying," Doherty said. "You're in trouble for causing the death of your mother."

"I didn't do it," Sandra said.

Doherty reminded her how she cried earlier. How sad she was when she confessed to killing her mother. All of the emotional anguish she'd experienced.

"Well basically it was like me and my sister knowing my mother was drunk, we left the house and went to a restaurant without making sure nothing happened," Sandra said.

"Nobody is going to believe you killed her that way," Doherty said.

"I feel bad about my mom's death but if the justice system works, like, I'm innocent," Sandra said. "I didn't actually kill her. I might have not been there for her."

"Well, you understand the problem we have believing that," Doherty told her.

"Well people have always have trouble believing me," Sandra said. "People can't tell if I'm lying or telling the truth. The evidence will show the truth."

Doherty assured her the evidence indicated that she and her sister discussed murdering their mother with Justin and that he provided the pills. The evidence would also show Beth mixed her mother's drinks and they knew their mother was already dead in the tub when they went to Jack Astor's.

"It's pretty straight forward," Doherty said. "It's not a mystery."

"Well, I still claim I'm innocent," Sandra said.

"You understand there's a point where you need to accept responsibility for what you've done." Doherty said.

"Which is why I decided to stop lying," Sandra countered. "I know I should really stop lying completely. I think because this day doesn't seem real at all."

"Oh it's real," Doherty said. "When you wake up in the morning in jail, it's very real."

"I did nothing," she replied.

Doherty told her for that to be true it meant all of her friends, who were being interviewed by police, were lying.

"Well, I guess they were lying under pressure or something," Sandra said. "I don't know. It's pretty easy to scare a little kid if you're a big cop. You just keep asking the same questions over and over again.

"All I wanted to do was to get out of here, to see my lawyer. If I just talked, I'd be able to leave sooner and then tell the truth."

Doherty asked her where she thought she was going to go.

"Anywhere, hopefully somewhere with a window," Sandra told him.

Doherty said she'd totally convinced him earlier that she wasn't a cold-blooded killer. That she really did care about her dead mother and felt pretty bad for what she'd done.

"Well you changed my mind," Doherty said.

"I'm a liar," Sandra said. "I have to cut back on that. 'Cause it really messes up your life."

Sandra and Beth were interviewed for nearly eleven hours. They were kept overnight in a police jail cell and didn't appear before a Justice of the Peace until the following day.

They were still wearing their pyjamas.

CHAPTER 17
THE PYJAMA GIRLS

On the morning of January 22, 2004, Sandra, seventeen, and Beth, sixteen, appeared in Courtroom 104 at the A. Grenville & William Davis Courthouse in Brampton, Ontario.

Reporters knew only that the sisters were charged with killing their mother, forty-three, who had drowned in her own bathtub on January 18, 2003. Her death had been ruled accidental; it appeared she had died as a result of excessive alcohol consumption.

The story took on a circus atmosphere when the two young sisters appeared in court wearing pyjamas underneath their open winter coats.

Michael Bury, the lawyer acting for Sandra, spoke to a news reporter before entering the courtroom: "I guess you're here for the Bathtub Girls." The nickname stuck.

After their brief appearance outside the courtroom, Bury criticized the police for the way they had treated the "frightened" young girls. "They didn't have the decency to let them change into their street clothes," Bury said. "They weren't even allowed to take their teddy bears with them."

"The case is simple. Their mother got drunk, took a bath, and drowned."

Newspapers printed several letters condemning the way police had treated these young, innocent girls. The truth behind why they were still in their pyjamas had yet to be revealed.

Bury and Robert Jagielski, who appeared for Beth, told the media their clients were shocked and upset. They insisted the girls were innocent.

"They are two very young girls who were getting ready to go to school when they were arrested and now they're facing first-degree murder charges," Bury said. "They're still grieving the loss of their mother. This comes as an incredible blow to them. They're anxious to clear their names. Their position is they're one hundred per cent not guilty." He also told reporters the teens had been forced to sleep on a cold slab in a police jail cell.

Jagielski said Beth told him they slept "on a piece of toilet paper" covered with a piece of plastic. "They don't understand why this has happened," Jagielski said. "Everybody is just shocked by all of this."

During their brief appearance, both lawyers raised their concerns about the way the girls had been treated. Justice of the Peace Maurice Hudson ordered medical attention be given when they arrived back at the Vanier Women's Detention Centre. Bury asked the court for painkillers to be given to the girls. How ironic that request would later become, considering the role Tylenol-3s played.

Bury also told reporters that police had removed clothing, computers, and books from the girls' residence.

"They're average young teenagers," Bury said. "They've been doing very well in school. There is nothing unusual about them. Imagine what they're now going through. They feel quite alone but their family is standing behind them."

Neither lawyer knew what information had caused police to investigate Linda's accidental drowning.

"There has been some inkling of a tipster out there but they're a dime a dozen," Bury said. "Police rejected foul play a year ago. I'm anxious to see what this great tip is."

Peel homicide inspector Mike MacMullen told the press the teens had been treated no differently than anyone else.

"They were wearing pyjamas when they were arrested," he said.

MacMullen provided very little else, except the teens called 911 and emergency workers found their mother lying face down in the bathtub.

"Her death was considered unusual in the sense that it's rare to find an adult drowned in a bathtub," MacMullen said. "Based on that alone, it was considered a suspicious death. The initial investigation, including post mortem and forensic examination failed to show any foul play."

He wouldn't say what new information resulted in the reopening of the case. He described what happened as a "tragic set of circumstances." He said their mother suffered from alcoholism for years. "Their mother's alcoholism was the major contributing factor in the decision and the actions we're alleging the girls took," MacMullen said.

Detective Magnus and prosecutors Mike Cantlon and Brian McGuire knew their case wasn't airtight. They needed more evidence and they hoped to find it in the sisters' computers. Crime-fighting software programs would help them retrieve evidence from deleted or hidden files. Personal online chats could be recovered and used by police and prosecutors.

They turned to Peel constable Joseph Coltson. He was one of Canada's foremost forensic data specialists, and was certified by the International Association of Computer Specialists as a forensic computer examiner and an electronic evidence expert. He had been with Peel's tech crime unit less than two years.

Coltson discovered a series of chilling and disturbing MSN instant messages, emails, and websites that had been accessed by the girls and their friends. He essentially conducted a hi-tech autopsy. The information became the cornerstone of the prosecution's case. Sandra and Beth had left very little in the way of a paper trail. But they left a mountain of incriminating evidence inside their computer.

"A lot of things were confirmed by these chats," Coltson said. "There were so many specific details. You learned what was in these kids' minds."

He and tech-crime analyst Constable John So went to Martha Kronwall's home on the day of the arrests. In the basement, just outside the girls' bedrooms, they found a disconnected clone computer tower on a bookshelf.

Coltson and So found information on its hard drive that provided prosecutors with almost everything they needed to secure a conviction. They also seized several other computers, including a Toshiba laptop. No information connected to the homicide was found on the other computers. The tower became Exhibit 200.

Coltson examined the computer and noticed the time stamp was about seventy-five minutes ahead of real time, and that the machine had last been used on October 22, 2003, ten months after Andersen died. He knew his data retrieval had to be flawless so that defence attorneys could not challenge the integrity of their case. To retrieve the data, he used two tools. First he used a "write blocking" device, so nothing could be added or erased from the hard drive during the copying process. Then he used a software program called Encase, which allowed him to make an exact copy of the computer's hard drive, including all deleted files and emails. He could also see which websites had been accessed.

Coltson began his data analysis on March 17, 2004. To search the hard drive, he used more than thirty key words, including "bathtub," "drown," "Tylenol," "Jack Astor's," "alcohol," "insurance," and "drunk." The data extraction was completed on March 23; the software had found 14,680 hits on the word "drown" and 247 hits on the word "Tylenol."

Coltson was stunned by the information retrieved over the next several days.

"This was one of those cases every police officer dreams about," Coltson said. "You're finding hundreds and hundreds of hits. You have this mountain of evidence in front of you. Then suddenly, this very first chat is opened and you realize you've found the needle in the haystack. The words just jumped out of the page."

In the next several weeks he found numerous other online conversations between Sandra, Beth, and their inner circle of friends. The chats revealed specific details about the plan to murder Linda and about the alibi. The conversations were dotted with chat lingo symbols, such as happy faces, and abbreviations, such as "LOL," which stands for "Laugh Out Loud."

Coltson found a PDF document entitled "The Inhalation of Water—The Drowning Process," which described what happens when a person drowns. This document had been accessed at

5:58 p.m. on January 14, 2003, four days before Linda Andersen drowned. He also found a paragraph taken from a website that described what happened when a person took alcohol and Tylenol-3 and codeine. It was one of several sites visited in January 2003. Another document, called "Good In Moderate Doses," said a person would be relaxed, mellow, and not likely to care about anything if they mixed alcohol with Tylenol-3s.

Coltson concluded the web searches had been done by someone looking for information on the effects of mixing Tylenol-3s and alcohol. He thought that most of the chats among the teens were logged inadvertently, and he found no evidence that the retrieved data had ever been tampered with. Nothing had compromised the data.

The emails and chats matched everything Sandra and Beth told David.

Coltson knew the Internet service provider account had been opened and paid for by Linda Andersen. He could not be certain which individuals had searched the various websites. But apparently only three people had used the computer— Linda, Sandra, and Beth.

Coltson found no evidence that someone stole the girls' identities and pretended to be them. He knew people often lied, fabricated, and exaggerated when they chatted online. But everything he retrieved appeared to be true and factual. He also found some chats that described events that had not yet occurred. The people involved had intimate knowledge of events, including the pending murder, and a familiarity with Andersen. Coltson told prosecutors he was certain Sandra, Beth, and their close friends were the people involved in the chats.

Coltson also examined Justin's computer. The original hard drive had been removed. The new hard drive contained no information related to the murder. The old hard drive was never located.

"The chats were ... the crux of the case," Coltson said. Every time he discovered a chat, he sent the information to Magnus. For Coltson, the Bathtub Girls case was like "looking at a window" into a homicide: "No [other case] had the smoking gun that this one had."

The next step was to find some hard medical evidence to show that Sandra and Beth were telling the truth in their taped conversations with David.

On January 23, 2004, forensic toxicologist Dr. Robert Langille examined Linda Andersen's stored blood and urine samples and found overdose levels of codeine. He concluded that Andersen had consumed a deadly combination of alcohol and codeine. Langille also found a substantial amount of acetaminophen, the main ingredient in Tylenol.

Her urine contained blood alcohol levels of 510 millilitres, more than six times the legal limit. Langille thought Andersen consumed her last drink about thirty minutes before she died. He found elevated levels of codeine—0.07 milligrams in 100 millilitres of blood, more than double the range for therapeutic usage. He estimated that she had consumed four to five pills. He also found traces of Benadryl or Gravol. There was no indication of barbiturates, cocaine, or marijuana.

Dr. Langille thought Linda would have been light-headed and disoriented. By itself, the combination of codeine and alcohol could have been deadly.

Ashley told police she never believed Sandra or Beth murdered their mother although she knew they hated her and told her many times they wanted to kill her.

"They used to say stuff all the time about how they wished their mother was dead," Ashley said when she was initially interviewed by police. She didn't think her friends were serious. And she didn't know much about Linda's death, just that she had drowned in her bathtub. She denied being part of their alibi dinner at Jack Astor's.

Ashley told police she hadn't thought about Linda's death for many months.

But Ashley wasn't being truthful.

In fact, she was extremely worried. Her heart was racing because of what she really knew and the role she had really played.

Soon after the murder, Ashley had convinced herself to go to the police. But she kept putting it off. The next day turned into the next week and the next month. Before she knew it, an entire year had passed.

When police woke her up, she didn't care what happened to her. Police were going to ask what she knew about the murder. And when she knew it. *If I'm in jail, then I'm in jail, so fuck it. I did it. It happened.* She'd become totally disillusioned with everything in general in her "soap-opera filled life."

When she was interviewed, police had yet to discover any of the disturbing chats. They also didn't have any hard evidence that she knew about the murder beforehand. But Ashley knew she could be charged.

Jay also didn't tell police the exact truth when he was initially interviewed. He said he didn't know much about the murder, that he never thought they would actually kill their mother. But he lied. He was intentionally distancing himself from his friends so he wouldn't be implicated.

Four days later, Ashley and Jay chatted online.

She was concerned police were going to find out about a book she had been going to write. In the book, tentatively titled *The Average Teen,* there would be a chapter about the murder. Written in large letters across the top of a list of potential chapters were the words "WHAT HAPPENED IN THE MALL." Another chapter would be entitled "TALKING ABOUT HOLDING MOM'S HEAD UNDER WATER."

"I remembered today that last year I was starting to write a book," Ashley typed just before midnight on January 25, 2004. "I included the stuff about Sandra killing her mom and it's dated. This could be very beneficial to police. But will it hurt me in any way?"

"I think it won't do any good for you," Jay typed. "The police already know you knew. So it probably can't hurt too much."

"'Cause it would eventually help them," Ashley wrote. "I just don't want it to be good circumstantial evidence and you're under arrest."

Jay asked if she knew any good lawyers.

"I was trying to figure out someone who would know a lot that I could talk to," Ashley said. "The only person I could think of was my aunt's brother who is a cop. But I think he would find that a conflict of interest since he works with Peel."

She wondered if she should show her book to the police. And she was worried because the police had confiscated Sandra's computer.

"I didn't tell them I was talking to Sandra the day she did it," Ashley typed. "I'm fucked if I don't tell."

Ashley couldn't remember every word she had typed in the online chat. But she knew she had encouraged Sandra and warned her to wear gloves. She felt better when Jay said Sandra and Beth had been using a new computer for the past several months. He believed it was the new computer the police took. He didn't think they had confiscated the old computer, the one with the incriminating chats.

"Oh nice," Ashley typed. "Well then that is less worrying. Did they toss the old one?"

Jay thought it was still at their old house.

"So it's at their dad's house?" Ashley asked. "I don't think I'll mention that one."

"Yeah, best not," Jay replied. Ashley said she felt guilty. She didn't want them to "get away with it" just because she hadn't said anything to police.

"Yeah I know," Jay said. "I'm kind of wishing I said something, not only cause my ass is on the line."

"I know, me too," Ashley said. "I don't know why I didn't. I can't justify it. It really comes down to laziness, which is pathetic. And it's really bad that it doesn't bug me more. I'm emotionless with things like this," she said. "Not good."

The murder didn't affect Jay much either. "They were telling me to go [to counselling] but really I was fine," he said.

Ashley said she thought she needed therapy to make her feel "not fine."

"I think it's because we knew all along," Jay said. "And we're dealing with this in our own way since we knew." His mother was "flipping" and was trying to speak with a lawyer. She was worried he was going to be arrested. "So my mom isn't doing too good," Jay said.

Ashley then asked Jay if his mother could see if their lawyer would talk to her as well. But she insisted that his mother couldn't tell her parents.

"Like, my parents cannot know," Ashley typed.

"I thought they knew."

"Only the fact I got questioned about the murder," Ashley said. "Not that I'm involved."

CHAPTER 18
EVERYBODY'S
GOT A STORY

Aunt Martha's sons, Derek and Hans, told police the allegations against their cousins were preposterous.

"My aunt was always drunk," Derek said. "The girls complained about their mother getting drunk. She wouldn't listen. She wasn't a good parent." His cousins often complained their mother would drink and drive. They said their mother often called in sick for work because she'd been drinking all day.

"Sandra and Beth reached out to us but we didn't know what to do. She [Linda] didn't want to go into rehab. The family knew she was an alcoholic."

Derek said Beth's grades fell once she started hanging out with Justin.

His cousins had nightmares after their mother died.

"They dreamed a lot about Bobby. They dreamed about falling. Being in a dense jungle. Can't get out. They also had dreams about their mother. They cried a lot the night of their mother's death. They didn't get out of bed for the first day. But they slowly got back into their routine. But they've been depressed since their mother died."

Derek continued, "They told me they came back from Jack Astor's. They were with Justin. They came home in the evening. Just the two of them. They called around and got no answer. They found her."

Aunt Linda gave his cousins "a lot of cash," he said, but he didn't know if they had access to her bank card or credit cards.

Hans told police his cousins were sneaky and rebellious and that they tended to lie to get out of situations: "They'd go out drinking but make excuses and cover it up and their parents bought their excuses."

His cousins' demeanor changed after their mother's death, he recalled. "They coped well. My mom was crying. They were not crying or depressed. They kept their emotions to themselves." They didn't pay too much attention when their mother's funeral service was conducted.

Sandra often cried in the morning and had trouble sleeping, he said. "She missed a lot of school. She would sleep during the day. She also swore a lot. She would snap at people. Beth also had trouble sleeping."

Hans said one day Sandra smashed her violin. He heard a bang. When he asked her if she was okay, she replied, "I'm never okay."

Neither cousin ever told him they had murdered their mother, then added, "She [Sandra] said she did something really, really bad. But she never made any reference to her mother. She was in an angry mood but it never struck me that she was talking about her mother."

Martha Kronwall was shocked when police suddenly showed up to arrest her nieces. Other than about six weeks in February and March, Sandra and Beth had spent the entire year in her home.

"It's impossible to believe. I don't believe they could do that. They loved their mother. I don't have one reason why they would kill her."

She insisted her sister had died because of alcohol. She knew Linda had a drinking problem. "She was somebody else [when she was drinking]. She would go to sleep and be in a different world. She didn't remember a thing."

When her sister woke, she would be afraid and nervous. "She thought something had happened to her children. She would even be afraid of me. She would say, 'don't touch me.'"

Her nieces once called to tell her that their mother wouldn't go to work. "They knew she was drunk and they were afraid to be with her. The next day, everything would be all right. She would promise to stop but she wouldn't. When she was drunk, she was bad. But when she wasn't, she was the greatest mother. They [Beth and Sandra] loved her a lot. She would never hurt her kids but when she was drinking she would tell people to leave her alone."

Her nieces were upset and crying when police brought them to her home the night of the drowning. "They told me they'd been at a movie. They called 911. They were devastated. They were shaking and crying. They almost couldn't speak. I was crying so much. I took care of them."

Her nieces were "gifted and intelligent" students but their schoolwork declined following their mother's death. They didn't want to attend classes, she said. "But I could understand that. Then they started to go a little more."

After their mother's death, Martha said Sandra couldn't sleep many nights. She also had trouble concentrating at school.

She sent her niece to a psychologist. She told her nieces they would receive the insurance money when they went to college.

"I told them I have their money to manage. Life is not easy but I can't think this could happen. I cannot understand that this is not an accident." She said her nieces visited their mother's grave many times. "I think they loved their mother a lot."

Billy said Beth had told him that "she, Sandra, and Justin" got their mother drunk and it was Beth and Justin, who planned the murder and Jack Astor's alibi.

Guidance teacher Randy Langois told police he spoke to Sandra in the fall of 2002 because of her declining marks and attendance. They also discussed her difficulties at home.

"She said there was a drinking problem with her mom but she never said it was out of control or causing problems to make it unlivable. The conversation never reached the point where I could do an intervention."

Sandra's fall attendance became extremely erratic, he said. She'd been a good student and was in French immersion but then there was a dramatic change in her academic achievements.

"She decided it didn't satisfy her anymore. She knew what her goals were. She wanted to get out and experience the world."

Sandra's appearance also changed along with her hair colour and she became more outgoing, he said. "I knew drugs and alcohol were in her environment."

Sandra's father came to talk to him with Sandra and Beth after the death, he said.

"He wanted to know what they could do to salvage their

year. I was going to help them with their assignments and get teachers to help them. But both girls became animated and angry that their father was coming back into their lives. He wanted to get the back on a regular schedule with curfews and establish responsibility in their house. But the girls said they didn't want their father back in their lives."

The girls attended a few counselling sessions and one session involved an exercise where they would buy groceries.

"The father took it seriously and came up with a list of items and agreed to give the girls the list and money. They just took the money and threw away the list. They didn't buy what they agreed. They did it on their terms. Their father said he was frustrated and being roadblocked by simple things like a regular scheduled mealtime, keeping the house neat, and cleaning rooms."

Chad sympathized with Sandra and discussed the murder with her.

"She's not a bad person," he told police. "Not a cold person. She's just a person who needs a lot of help."

He was never sure Sandra was telling him the truth. "I asked her what was running through her mind and she said she had a lot on her heart. She said, 'Whatever I've done can't be changed.' She was hiding from herself."

He didn't know how to handle the situation. "It was a big burden to unload on me. I didn't know how to react. I sort of distanced myself from the conversation."

Teacher Betty Haines, who taught Sandra law, described her to police as being "strong academically, but quiet, nervous, and polite." She never had any problems with her. She said her closest friends were Ashley and Jay. "Ashley always seemed to know what was going on with Sandra," she said. Haines, however, disliked Ashley because "there was an evil undercurrent within that class that was more applicable to her." In her last year, Sandra took history and law, including the Charter, Canadian law with topics such as the elements of offence, the Young Offenders Act and the Youth Criminal Justice Act, and defences involving battered wife syndrome, temporary insanity, provocation, duress as well as the rights upon arrest. Records show Sandra received 67 per cent for her presentation on the Youth Criminal Justice Act the same month she murdered her mother.

When Sandra and Beth returned briefly to school on the Monday following their mother's death, Justin passed a sympathy card around for fellow students to sign and offer their condolences.

Police gleaned snippets of information from many of their classmates, although most information came from second- and third-hand sources.

Most of what Mary knew came from Billy although there was one glaring difference. Billy told her Sandra "didn't have anything to do with the murder," and Beth and Justin were in the bathroom and they held Linda's head under the water. She said Beth and Sandra often got drunk and bragged about getting "$50,000" from their mother's life insurance when they turned eighteen. They were going to take their friends to Amsterdam.

Beth told Tommy in March 2003 that their mother fell in the bathtub and hit her head and drowned. In September 2003, Beth told him she was getting $1,000 each month from the government and would soon be selling magic mushrooms to earn more money. At a New Year's Eve party Sandra admitted to him that she was doing cocaine and both sisters were doing drugs.

Steve, a close friend of Chad, told police that Sandra confessed she had murdered her mother when they spoke during a July 1, 2003 holiday weekend party. "Beth walked in on her when she was in the process of killing her mother," he said. "Sandra drugged her mother before killing her but she was already drunk. Sandra was always smashed at these parties but Beth was the responsible one."

Jordan, another of Chad's friends, told police that Sandra often "propositioned her friends for sex" when she was drunk or high. Sandra was always smashed and would take whatever drugs were available.

Donny's view of Sandra and Beth and their lives had changed by the time of their arrests. He now had a very different take on the sisters. "Before I learned some of the crazy things I kind of felt bad for them," Donny said. "I was their friend. But my knowledge of their life really came from them."

"Sure their mother was an alcoholic. But they still had a roof over their head. They had food in their fridge. For me, they were spoiled. They just felt they deserved more."

Months after the arrests and before their trial, Donny had to write a short story for his college English class. He chose the title *Four Minutes* and while it was a piece of fiction, nobody knew how close the story was to the real-life drama, which he had first-hand knowledge. His story included pills, vodka, a drunken mother, a bus ride, a little brother, two sisters' hatred of their stepfather, and a bathtub drowning. There sisters argued when they were drowning their mother. They story revealed how rubber gloves had been used. In the story, the older girl drowned the mother while the younger one stood in the doorway. In Donny's story, the sisters jumped off a bridge and died.

The short story was worth 30 per cent. Donny received a 25.5 mark for his efforts. "Excellent story," his teacher wrote at the end of the 1,800 word composition. "With confident, creepy writing. Well done."

Donny was glad Sandra had never asked him for advice on how to kill her mother. He was relieved when someone went to the police. "Finally, somebody did the right thing," Donny said. "I'm just glad it didn't have to be me."

CHAPTER 19
ABSOLUTELY PREPOSTEROUS

Immediately after the death, Sandra transferred to Beth's high school where she enrolled in several Grade 11 classes and completed Grade 10 with an 88 per cent average. But she had difficulty concentrating and attending classes so she was moved into a special class where students were given more time to complete their assignments and tests. Beth was halfway through Grade 11 when she was arrested.

Sandra and Beth spent two months in custody in separate youth facilities.

Before being granted bail, Sandra was at the Invictus Youth Centre in Brampton. She continued her education there and by all accounts was a model inmate. She participated in regular Narcotics Anonymous and Alcoholics Anonymous programs, Sandra completed her Ontario Secondary School Diploma and took several courses designed to get her into university.

Randy Dickinson, head educator at Invictus, was impressed. He thought she was a superior student, highly intelligent and intuitive, and a powerful writer; as a student, she liked structure but could learn without it. He believed she would continue to learn for the rest of her life. She had good manners and supported other inmates. "Although she can be a leader, she can also be led," Dickinson said. "She is drawn to power."

Sherril Morris, a social worker at Invictus, also described Sandra as a model inmate and said she participated in regular programs and went to church on Sundays.

In February 2006, Sandra was transferred to the Cecil Facer Youth Centre in Sudbury for two weeks of assessment, then was returned to Invictus.

Beth spent her entire time in custody at the Syl Apps Youth Centre in Oakville, Ontario. She taught yoga to other inmates and tutored them in math. They called her "the Dictionary" because she knew so many words. She took courses in food, nutrition, fashion, math, and leadership, and achieved a ninety-five per cent average.

On April 8, 2004, both sisters were granted bail and placed under house arrest in the home of their aunt Martha. It was a rare decision to grant bail to anyone charged with first-degree murder.

At times, their bail hearing turned into a comedy show. Their father and other relatives, including their cousin Derek, laughed at the allegations. Giggles especially were heard when an officer revealed drug paraphernalia had been found in their bedrooms with empty liquor bottles under their beds.

Martha, who was also Beth's Godmother, was certain police had made a terrible mistake. It was absolutely preposterous they had killed their mother.

Prosecutor Mike Cantlon insisted they were flight risk because they spoke four different languages. Despite their being charged with killing her sister, Martha told the judge she had no problems allowing her nieces to live with her.

Beth's attorneys Robert Jagielski and Jack McCulligh, who now represented Sandra, knew prosecutors believed Sandra and Beth might have been driven to murder to collect the life insurance money. Under questioning from the defence, Martha said she didn't know the policy even existed until a broker contacted her a few days after her sister's funeral. She never told Sandra and Beth about it until at least a month or two later.

"The children wanted to know how they were going to live," Martha said. "They didn't want to be a burden on us. They knew there were costs involved. I told them not to worry. There were certain funds, which we'll use for their education. And for the moment, we will just have to manage."

Jagielski asked if she feared for her life.

"Absolutely not," she said.

"Do any of your family fear for their lives?" Jagielski asked.

"No," Martha replied.

Martha told McCulligh that her nieces stood to receive $120,000 but she'd already spent some of the money.

"How much is left?" McCulligh asked.

"$50,000," she replied.

Martha was prepared to hand over the "the whole amount" to be held in trust by lawyers to ensure her nieces couldn't use it to flee the country.

Cantlon suggested the girls had moved in with her because they refused to obey their father's rules. "They would go out at night and not abide by a curfew," Cantlon said. Martha denied knowing anything about her nieces' problems with their father .She said her nieces often didn't attend school because they were still dealing with their mother's death.

Martha told Cantlon she never saw her nieces take drugs. She also wasn't worried Sandra might harm herself.

Cantlon asked about the insurance money.

"I understood the girls came to you with a concern about a financial burden and you told them not to worry about it, that we have money for your education, and we'll provide for you," Cantlon said.

"I told them about the insurance money," Martha said. "It's not that they came to me and said 'Auntie, we've got insurance money.' That didn't happen."

Martha paid funeral expenses with some of the $120,000 set aside for her nieces. She also paid Linda Andersen's $740 Visa bill.

"What happened to the other $70,000?" Cantlon asked.

"New beds, new clothing," Martha, said. "The winter clothing was purchased. Computers. Everything they needed for school."

Cantlon asked if there were any friends she was particularly concerned about her nieces associating with if they were released into her custody and if she believed her nieces were innocent.

"Yes," Martha replied. "Of course, one hundred per cent."

"I'm going to suggest you've heard new information that suggests the girls planned, in some detail, talked about it with their friends, talked about it with each other on how to kill your sister. You didn't know that before, correct?" Cantlon told her.

"I never heard," Martha said.

"Having heard that for the first time, does that raise any concerns for you with regards to you being able to control, or act as a surety for them in the community?" Cantlon asked.

"I don't have any concerns," she said.

"I'm going to suggest unless you actually saw them do it, you would think they're innocent?" Cantlon said.

"Yes, because I know them," Martha replied.

Justice of the Peace Ford Clements imposed strict conditions for their house arrest. Sandra and Beth were prohibited from having any contact with Bobby or their close friends. The only people their age they could see were their cousins, and then only because the cousins and the sisters lived in the same house.

Martha was one of five different sureties who posted their bail of $100,000.

The sisters had to remain indoors between 10 p.m. and 6 a.m. They had to stay in Ontario and turn over their passports. They could go outside only for school or work, or for medical or legal appointments. They were prohibited from possessing any weapons, ammunition, or explosives. They were forbidden from consuming any drugs or alcohol other than prescription medication. Should they need to be out of their aunt's home for any reason other than school or work, they had to be accompanied by one of their sureties. The court froze the remainder of their mother's life insurance policy.

"I've not made your lives any easier by releasing you," Justice Clements said as they sat beside each other, handcuffed, in the prisoner's box. "The matter is really in your hands now." He warned them that they would be back in custody if they breached any of their conditions. Police would be monitoring them closely.

He said they were "fortunate" to be living in a country which takes a "liberal view" of pre-trial custody for youthful offenders.

"You are being given an opportunity of going home to your father, your aunt, and your family," he said. "Good luck to both of you."

After her release, Sandra volunteered at a local church once a week. Most of her time was spent in her basement room, studying and reading, watching television, and searching the Internet. She taught herself how to play the guitar. And she wrote in her journal. She told probation officer Suzie Martin that she felt a sense of freedom when she was writing.

She and Beth became closer during the house arrest. They had a good relationship with their aunt, uncle, and cousins. Derek often purchased groceries for the sisters, and went with them to their various appointments and for walks. Few people came to visit. The sisters lived in their pyjamas. Sandra worked briefly at a liquor store, then at an Italian bakery.

Despite being granted bail, the girls were not allowed to attend their high school, and no other school in Peel would accept them. They took courses through the Temporary External Learning Link program and from the Independent Learning Centre. Sandra's grades dramatically improved. She completed the credits for Grade 11.

The sisters followed their father's strict diet regimen, which involved preparing and eating meals based on specific amount of carbohydrates, fats, and proteins.

By August 2004, police had enough evidence to arrest Justin for conspiracy to commit murder. But first, on August 8, 2004, they interviewed Ashley again. She told them she never deliberately lied or tried to deceive them, and insisted she had blocked the incident from her mind. In fact, she said she had forgotten about the online chat she had with Sandra on the afternoon of Linda Andersen's death.

Eventually, she admitted she was wrong not to have told the police everything she knew. "I was looking out for my friend but I was one hundred per cent completely wrong."

She admitted to police that she logged the incriminating chat with Sandra in case she ever needed proof that her friend had murdered her mother. She felt tremendous guilt about not trying to stop Sandra from killing her mother and for not going to police. She knew her actions could have prevented a death.

In the months leading up to this police interview, Ashley had been re-examining herself, trying to self-analyze what was in her mind at the time of Linda's death. Her views on why Sandra had killed her mother had also dramatically changed. She was now certain there were more important reasons why Sandra felt she had to kill her mother.

If she was really feeling so guilty, so filled with regret, then why was her mother's death so often a party topic?

Sandra often talked about how she'd "gotten away with murder" when she was partying hard. Sandra told her many times how they had no choice but to kill her mother. Her alcoholism was ruining their lives. Sandra believed Bobby's life would be so much better if his mother was dead.

She no longer believed Sandra and Beth had killed their mother because they wanted to raise Bobby. In fact, Sandra often told her Bobby was an "annoying little kid."

Ashley thought Sandra had been fooling everybody. She now believed money and Sandra's craving need for attention and her driving desire to prove she was smarter than everybody else might just have been the real reasons behind the murder.

Thank God she never included me in her plans of using her mother's insurance money to take her friends to Europe. She always wanted to be the best, and killing her mother might have been a way to prove ... that she could outsmart everybody, including the police.

Sandra often told Ashley how bad her life was; how they never had any food; how her mother hated her and treated her with contempt. Ashley asked Sandra to come live with her. But Sandra said no.

Sandra just didn't like having to be anywhere at any certain time. She didn't want to have a curfew. She didn't want somebody to be her supervisor. She didn't want anybody to bug her about doing her homework. She didn't like her life at home but she didn't think my option was any better.

Sandra had told Ashley that she wished she had a normal family life with a mom and dad, but then in the next breath said she couldn't live any other way than the way she was currently living because she'd gotten use to the freedom. She could drink and smoke dope and come and go as she pleased. She didn't want to throw that away. So even if her mother passed out on her couch, then all the better it was for her and Beth. Ashley thought Sandra always felt she deserved more than anybody else.

It had always been very important for Sandra and Beth to be smarter than everybody else, Ashley said. Sandra took an enrichment test in elementary school five times. Sandra missed the cut by a couple of points and that made her very upset, Ashley said. Beth was already in the top enrichment class while Sandra had to be satisfied with just being with the above average students, like her, Ashley said.

"That's why she always needed to work harder and study harder than Beth," she told me. "If she or Beth were ever beaten on a test, or found out somebody knew more than they did, then Sandra and Beth would become really angry. It was a real problem for them."

Ashley was also shocked with how many people knew the truth.

Still, even during her second interview with police, Ashley kept her real feelings for Sandra to herself.

"It [Linda's murder] was almost like a game for them," she told me. "They saw a plan that would give them money and absolute freedom to go around the world. They saw it as a plan to prove they were smarter than everybody else. Money was a big part but just knowing they could get away with it might have been more important. How could they prove they were smarter than anybody else? Why, they needed to get away with it. So they killed their mother for the attention. It might have been bad attention but bad attention is better than no attention."

In her August interview with police, Ashley said she thought she was telling the truth about Justin giving the girls the Tylenol-3s. When the girls got arrested, she told police that Sandra had told her she got the pills from her mother.

Because police had discovered the chats, Ashley knew police might charge her with being an accessory.

"I know this sounds irrational, but I was so sick of it, that I really didn't care what happened to me," she told me. "I just wanted it to go away."

Police did not charged Ashley with any crime, and she agreed to testify against her former friends at their trial. So did Jay, Chad, and Billy.

CHAPTER 20
FUHGEDABOUTIT!

On the eve of their sensational eight-week murder trial, Judge Bruce Duncan ruled that Sandra's police interview, her confession, and her recanting on the day of her arrest were inadmissible for trial. He would decide whether the sisters were guilty of first-degree murder—based solely on the evidence presented during the trial.

In ruling Sandra's confession inadmissible, Judge Duncan decided Peel Police had violated her right to silence under Canada's Charter of Rights and Freedoms. (Police had also violated both sisters' rights by not bringing them to court within twenty-four hours of their arrest.) As well, he ruled that Sandra's confession had been involuntary.

Judge Duncan also ruled that a conversation between the two sisters videotaped in a police interview room couldn't be used against the sisters in their trial.

The girls had decided they wanted to be tried by judge alone, without a jury. In an interview later, Judge Duncan said he didn't have any trouble separating what he knew from what he was about to know. He said, "It was no big deal. As judges we're supposed to be able to put information out of our mind. It's routinely done. Breath tests are often excluded in impaired driving cases. We throw them out. Put them out of our mind. Of course, a jury would never have heard this. That's why what happens in *voire dires* [evidence presented outside of the jury] never gets presented to juries."

Because the case was being tried by judge alone there was no need for a publication ban. The media could not reveal the identities of the sisters, their friends, or the name of their dead mother, but they could report everything else.

Before the trial began, defence attorneys Jack McCulligh, Eugene Bhattacharya, and Robert Jagielski sought a stay of all charges. Bhattacharya argued police deliberately kept the teens in interrogation, then put them together, to gain incriminating evidence. The tactic forced the girls to spend another night in a police station cell because court was closed before their interrogation ended. McCulligh said an investigating officer ignored Sandra's repeated requests to end her interview and thereby breached her rights to silence under the Charter.

Prosecutor Brian McGuire denied both points.

Judge Duncan found that Peel Police had arbitrarily denied the girls their right to appear before a JP within twenty-four hours of their arrest and had also denied Sandra's right to silence under the Charter. The conversation in Danish between the two sisters was also ruled inadmissible because that conversation arose from the earlier interrogation. Judge Duncan agreed, as McCulligh had argued, that Sandra's confession had been obtained in an "atmosphere of oppression." He said young persons are particularly vulnerable to coercive efforts.

He explained that much of the law regarding an accused person's right to silence under Section 7 of the Charter involves adults, and that it was important to remember this case involved young people; the imbalance of power, which existed in any custodial interrogation, was magnified when the accused person was young.

Under Canadian law, an accused person has the fundamental right to choose whether to speak to police and may refuse to do so without any consequences. In the United States, Judge Duncan said, the law clearly states all questioning must end when a right to silence is invoked under the infamous case of Miranda versus Arizona where the court ruled "if, after warnings have been given, an accused indicates he wishes to discontinue questioning and asserts his right to remain silent, the questioning must cease."

But "no such line of rule" has ever been "authoritatively declared" in Canada, Judge Duncan said, "[The Supreme Court of Canada] has never dealt with the issue of whether or to what extent the police may continue to question and attempt to elicit evidence after a detainee has asserted his right to remain silent in the course of an interrogation." He said, "police persuasion, short of denying the suspect the right to choose or depriving him of an operating mind, does not breach his right to silence."

In his view, police had exceeded their limits of persuasion, and Sandra's right to silence had been violated. He considered all of the circumstances, including the "gross imbalance of power" between the young offender and the police.

"Sandra's seventeen assertions of her right to silence do not stand alone. They occurred within the context of her prolonged detention and after hours of denials that are ignored or dismissed as being lies or unacceptable. No doubt her will and freedom of choice were overridden by the superior powers of the police."

He described Sandra's interrogation as being one where the power of the state, combined with the experience, skill, planning, and cunning on the part of the officer, was pitted against a single, unassisted detained youth, who although obviously very smart, was inexperienced, and unprepared and "no match" for her opponent. He said, "The interrogation delivered an unmistakable message to Sandra: 'We know you are guilty. Your denials will not be accepted no matter how often they are repeated. Your repeated [assertion] of right to silence will be ignored. Your detention and interrogation will continue as long as we want, and we want it to continue until we hear what we know to be the truth—that you are guilty.'"

Even before police raised the subject of Beth's degree of responsibility, police had "created an atmosphere of oppression" and offered her a quid pro quo inducement to her to confess, Judge Duncan said. When Doherty asked her what she thought should happen to her sister, it implied a clear message—that a lesser degree of responsibility is "obviously a good thing" when it comes to crime and punishment and therefore things will be better for her if she accepted all or most of the responsibility.

He also ruled the girls were deliberately not taken to court so police could extend their interrogation and get a confession. Prosecutors argued the interrogation of the girls wasn't completed until after 5 p.m. when court was finished for the day. They couldn't find a JP to do an "after hours remand" and they didn't think it was "an emergency" situation so the twenty-four-hour time period didn't apply. But Judge Duncan found there was no evidence police ever had any intention of bringing the girls before a JP during normal court hours. He didn't believe they couldn't locate any JP to do an after hours remand.

"At the highest, the Justice wasn't available when the crown and police were ready to take them. Police told the girls they were being interrogated for one purpose—to find out why they did it—not if they did it. He added, "Once the girls asserted their right to silence, police had reasonable time to get them to change their mind and any further delay in getting them before a [Justice of the Peace] was unreasonable. Police knew from early afternoon that continuing their interrogation would take them beyond the reasonable compliance of getting the girls before court within twenty-four hours of their arrests. A delay cannot be reasonable if its consequence is breaking the law. In my view, the reasonable period for interrogation ended at the point where the rights to silence had to be respected."

Although he found police had violated the girls rights to be brought before a JP within twenty-four hours, a serious infraction that could have resulted in a stay of proceedings, he denied the defence bid for a stay, indicating that would have resulted in a "windfall" for the accused—and be "grossly disproportionate to the breach."

Prosecutors insisted because the girls were charged with murder they weren't going to be released in any event after their first court appearance. But Judge Duncan said compliance of the twenty-four-hour rule wasn't the only factor to consider in this case.

"The unreasonable delay in getting the girls to court provided the opportunity for police to gather evidence that otherwise would not have existed."

Of all the witnesses, nobody was more bizarre than Justin.

Testifying as a reluctant Crown witness, he not only put a different spin on his involvement and what he knew or didn't know, but even denied being the person chatting online with Beth five days before the murder.

Described by one newspaper columnist covering the trial as having a striking resemblance to the "Dylan" character from television's *Beverly Hills 90210*, Justin also accused Detective Mark Armstrong of "painting memories" in his mind, making him believe he knew far more, than he actually did, about the murder.

When the seasoned homicide investigator took the stand, he denied feeding crucial information to Justin.

"It's his evidence we wanted to hear, not my evidence," Armstrong said. "I didn't want to taint the witness."

Justin, however, insisted Armstrong "painted his memory" by giving him information about Linda's murder during his interview of January 21, 2004, the same day Sandra and Beth were arrested. He denied knowing anything beforehand about the crime. Justin claimed Armstrong told him about the incriminating online chats, which the police said he had participated in. He claimed the veteran interrogator threatened to charge him with murder unless he repeated the story he'd just been told.

Justin said Armstrong spent fifty minutes to two hours giving him details about which he had no prior knowledge. Armstrong insisted he only spent twenty minutes with Justin— the time between leaving his residence at 7:29 a.m. and the time their four-hour interview began about 7:50 a.m.

"Did you follow him into the bathroom and whisper into his ear, say this, say that, say the other thing?" McGuire asked Armstrong at trial. "Did you coerce or intimidate or threaten him in any way that unless he co-operated he would be charged with first degree murder?"

"No I didn't," Armstrong said.

Cantlon told the court it would have been impossible for Justin, then sixteen, to have been told everything about the case, and then repeat it back to the officer in an interview that spanned a hundred pages of transcripts.

Armstrong said that when he questioned Justin, the police thought Justin knew the girls murdered their mother. The police also thought Justin supplied the Tylenol-3s. "Justin was treated strictly as a witness, not a suspect," Armstrong insisted. "He was being interviewed for his knowledge in the death of the girls' mother."

On the stand, Justin steadfastly maintained his version of events. When he was presented with a transcript of a chilling Internet conversation, he vehemently denied he was the person chatting online.

"I can guarantee you it's not me," Justin said after Cantlon read several disturbing passages. "I'm a lifeguard. My mother's father died from drowning and as a lifeguard I can tell you that's not how somebody drowns."

Cantlon shot back, "Oh, so you know a lot about drowning do you?"

"Yes I do," Justin replied.

The police videotaped interview was played in court. In it, Justin admitted knowing essential details about the crime. He tried to talk the sisters out of burning their mother alive. He met Sandra and Beth for dinner at Jack Astor's afterwards but denied it was part of any well-planned alibi.

On the stand, Justin told a different story. He also vehemently denied giving the girls any pills.

Like the other friends, Justin never went to police. In his initial interview on the day of their arrests, he played down his role. He admitted he had discussions with the sisters about various ways of killing their mother. He convinced them not to burn their mother. "That would have been a barbaric and inhumane thing to do to a loved one," he told police.

Yet on the stand, he denied everything. He insisted it was the police, who told him everything, including that his friends had confessed and implicated him.

"They might have said something like, 'oh, I wish my mother was dead' but it never came close to any plan," Justin told the court. "I never took them serious. It was just a joke. Beth might have mentioned something about being 'mad' with her mother and how she 'wished she would die in a house fire.'"

In his interview, Justin initially told Armstrong the girls never said anything specific about their plans. They thought their mother could get drunk one night and they'd burn their house down. "Everything would be done in one shot," he told Armstrong.

He told Armstrong they mixed lemonade with vodka for their mother before drowning her. How they reacted when they met for dinner at Jack Astor's. He knew the girls were going to kill their mother, and that he decided not to stop them. "I didn't think it was my place to get involved," Justin told Armstrong. "They were so utterly convinced it was the right thing to do. I didn't think it was right for me to do anything either way. I don't know if even the police had talked to them if that would have changed their mind.

"They confided in me. I pride myself in being trustworthy. One thing I pride myself is my trust. I don't break people's trust. I felt it wasn't my decision to make. I guess I could have called police but I don't think it was my phone call to make. Their mother had put them through hell. It's what it all came down to for them."

Justin denied telling the girls it would be better for them to drown their mother than kill her in a fire.

"I told them it was a terrible way for someone to die. I

didn't make any suggestions. I told them it was a bad idea. I told them they should consider something else. I told them drowning was probably a more painful way to die than in a fire. You don't just take in water and drown. Your blood cells explode. It's a slow death. They were completely convinced that was the only way to get away from what they were dealing with but I still think it would have been a terrible way of dying in a fire."

"I didn't mean to say they needed to find a better idea," Justin told Armstrong. "I pretty much told them it was a bad idea [fire] and they should consider something else. If they were going to do it they should consider something else because fire wasn't an appropriate way."

Justin also told Armstrong the girls "mentioned they planned it together," but he insisted it wasn't like they sat down and "drew up plans."

Even though on the stand he denied providing the Tylenol-3s, in his police interview, he told Armstrong he did. But he denied knowing they were going to be used to help them knock out their mother before they drowned her. Later, in the same interview, he admitted he had assumed they would use the pills on their mother.

"But they didn't paint a picture for me," he said.

Justin told Armstrong the sisters always planned to get their mother drunk. "That would have been insanely easy because she's probably always very drunk," Justin said. Justin thought he had given them four or five pills—medication left over from an ear infection.

"I wasn't gonna use them," Justin told Armstrong. "They said they wanted them. I said if they wanted them, they could have them. I guess it wasn't a good decision on my part."

He told Armstrong the girls believed they had no choice but to kill their mother because her alcoholism was ruining their lives by being in a constant state of drunkenness and continually out of work.

Justin said it was Sandra's idea to drown their mother in the bathtub. He met Sandra and Beth at Jack Astor's for dinner, but he denied knowing the dinner was arranged as an alibi. "About a week before, Beth called me and asked me to meet them. It sounds arrogant but Beth felt safe when I was with her. I made her feel better. She had a crush on me all through Grade 9. Her father was never around. I was somebody she could hold onto. Somebody to comfort her."

Justin told Armstrong that knew he wasn't going to be able to stop them from killing their mother. He basically met them "to let them know I was still there for them." Neither he nor Ashley knew many details.

At dinner, Justin told Armstrong that Sandra seemed somewhat normal—"maybe a little edgy"—but Beth looked "utterly distraught" and she had "a cold expression." She cried a few times. At one point the sisters argued. He said Sandra seemed to get more upset as the dinner went on. "She mentioned she was concerned her mother bruised easily and she might have left fingerprints or marks on her body. She said her mother didn't struggle." Beth told him that she mixed her mother's drink of lemonade and vodka.

Justin told Armstrong that he offered to go back with them to their townhouse but Beth didn't want to get him involved.

"I just wanted them to know that after they had made their choice, whatever, they were going to do, that I was still there for them," Justin said.

He knew the sisters stood to inherit some insurance money

but insisted it didn't play any role. Their aunt was holding the funds for their university education.

"They were going to get seventy thousand dollars," Justin said. "If they didn't go to university they weren't going to get any of it." Sandra mentioned she planned to take their friends on a cruise when she turned eighteen and got her share of the life insurance cash. "And just spend it all and buy as much drugs as she can," Justin said.

Sandra and Beth told him later "they had gotten away with it," but while Beth rarely spoke about her mother's death, Sandra told many people how she and her sister killed their mother.

"Sandra told everybody," Justin said. "I told her she should leave Beth's name out of it when she was telling people."

On the stand, Justin insisted neither Sandra nor Beth ever discussed the murder with him during their dinner at Jack Astor's.

"Police told me what happened," Justin testified. "I was trying to remember what was said to me. Seriously, I couldn't ever remember it being said to me. Sandra told a lot of people. I thought it was a joke. I never provided them with Tylenol-3s. I was never actually involved."

Armstrong, however, told the court that Justin knew everything.

"He told me about a murder," Armstrong said. "He didn't tell me about an accident."

In his police interview, Justin described Beth as being "somewhat of a nerd" who did all of her "homework religiously. She always sat at the back of the room and worked quietly on her schoolwork."

"Friends used to tease her. That's how I met her," Justin said. "She used to draw pictures of turtles and used the word 'snazzy' a lot." They became closer friends in Grade 10. He initially thought Beth was "cutesy" and "happy" but then she started dressing in Goth clothing and became "sullen" and "quiet" as well as "tearful, sad, and upset," and was always concerned about her brother Bobby.

"She had brown long brown hair, halfway down her back, fairly long past her shoulders," Justin said. "She used to put it in pigtails and used to wear blue jeans with T-shirts with funny little sayings, all very colourful, all the time." She often wore a T-shirt with a picture of a "little turtle." Beth was often "so happy" it was "overbearing sometimes."

Beth volunteered at a local vet because she was "into animals all the time," he said. When Beth started to change she began wearing everything in black such as black pants, black shirts and she cut her hair, dyed it and spiked it.

"It was a definite huge change for her," Justin told Armstrong. "She got body piercings, probably a month or two before her mom's death. She used to always be happy but then got more and more depressed. Before she was a little over the edge with happiness. Then she went to the other extreme. She became quiet, sullen all the time and underwent a personality change. She didn't like the person she used to be and how that person wasn't her anymore." After the murder, Justin said Beth was often "inconsolable" and got upset "about three times a week," but was mainly upset because of what they had done to Bobby.

Justin told Armstrong that Sandra used to always wear baggy pants and baggy sweaters. "She always had her hair done immaculately, always took care of her appearance," Justin said. "She was fairly straight edged but people called her 'Hobo' because she started to wear ratty clothes all the time and this plaid jacket she found." Justin said Sandra drank a lot. "Whatever she could get her hands on," Justin said. "She does everything to excess." Justin claimed Sandra also took cocaine, marijuana, magic mushrooms, and hashish—"anything she could get her hands on"—and how after her mother's death she "completely lost control" of herself. "She just kept getting more and more out of control and violent even," Justin said. "Like around school, she was talking about wanting to get into fights with people and wanting to smash things. She wasn't like that before. She didn't take care of herself. She had an edge to her. Her alcohol drinking got so out of hand that her aunt and uncle wanted to send her into rehab."

Linda was a "habitual alcoholic" who would be "completely drunk and pass out" every time he saw her, he said. She'd buy alcohol for Sandra and Beth. "She would make deals with them. If they bought her a pack of cigarettes, she would buy them a two-four of Corona provided they paid for it of course. She just never seemed to be around for them. Just passed out all the time on the living room couch. And there would be people over sitting in the kitchen making Kraft Dinner and she'd be passed out ten feet away, half naked, and mumbling something who knows what."

Linda never really had much to do with Bobby, he said.

"Sandra and Beth would take him to school and they went to his parent teacher interviews so they basically raised him because their mother was habitually drunk," Justin said. "She also blamed them for everything that went wrong with her life. She used to say it was their fault she was drinking and their fault she didn't have any friends. It was their fault she had to stay home and look after them so she couldn't go to parties. Their mother often blamed them for injuries she sustained during one of her many drunken falls."

"I don't think she abused them physically," Justin said. "I remember a few odd stories. Beth told me when she was younger she was coming down the stairs, really angry about something, and slipped and fell on the concrete floor and like split her back of her head open—bleeding all over the floor. They called the ambulance. And her mom told the doctor her children had done it." The girls told him their mother often told her friends they had been "beating her." They also told him their mother often bought pot from them and had used crack cocaine in their home. "She would scream at them even though they were down in their rooms in the basement," he said.

Beth also told him about the various men her mother slept with for favours. "There was this one old guy in his sixties or seventies," Justin said. "Not for money but he used to buy her things and food. She also slept with a taxi driver to get free rides."

Justin insisted he was only told about what was going to happen a few days before they actually killed their mother. It was Sandra's idea, but Beth was on board. Sandra said, "don't worry. I'm not stupid. I researched it on the Internet." He told Armstrong the girls never thought they would ever get caught.

Judge Duncan ruled that Justin's interview of January 21, 2004, was admissible against the sisters. But first he criticized Justin's performance on the stand. Duncan was frustrated. He didn't want to waste court time to determine the truthfulness of Justin's statement.

"Because this guy makes blanket statements—'oh the police put it into my head,' I can't imagine we should take our marching orders from this witness" Judge Duncan told the court. "He is not a very trustworthy chap. What air of reality is there, really, to his assertions, after viewing four hours of this videotape? Obviously, he's either lying here or lying there."

The chilling online chats discovered by Constable Coltson were the centrepiece of the prosecution's case, especially the January 13, 2003, conversation between Beth and Justin. They hardly needed anything else.

Ashley, Jay, Billy, Chad, and Justin all testified for the prosecutors, and all added to the evidence against Sandra and Beth.

Ashley admitted she had been scared during her police interviews.

"My thoughts were going a mile a minute," she testified. "I was frightened in August when they told me there was a possibility I could be charged."

Billy told police after Justin's arrest that he thought Beth had told him that Justin and her were in the house when the murder occurred. But on the stand, Billy never mentioned anything about Justin being so closely connected to the crime.

Defence attorneys saved some of their best techniques for David, questioning his religious beliefs and attacking his reasons for turning against his friends. Beth's lawyer, Robert Jagielski, accused David of being a "big man on campus" and a "celebrity" for his portrayal as "secret agent" in his relentless bid to get the girls to incriminate themselves. He wondered whether David had already cashed in his "thirty pieces of silver."

The sisters had broken the most precious of the Ten Commandments, David countered: "Thou shalt not kill."

Defence attorneys said Linda might have accidentally drowned, because there were no signs of any struggle in the bathroom and because even the pathologist, Dr. Timothy Feltis, couldn't find any signs of foul play.

"Believe me, we looked very carefully at her hands, at her feet, at her legs for any sign of bruising, scrapes, or abrasions," Dr. Feltis testified, "It just wasn't there."

As well, defence attorneys said, the officers and medics had different memories of how Linda was found.

Teacher Meredith McCarthy said the sisters' arrests hit her like a ton of bricks because of that strange question Beth had posed a year earlier in her career's class.

CHAPTER 21
SHE'S ALIVE

The evidence against Sandra and Beth was overwhelming. By the time Ricky Rodriguez testified on December 4, 2005, there was little doubt they had murdered their mother. Rodriguez was the first and only defence witness, and when he was on the stand the bizarre trial took a startling turn.

According to Rodriguez, Sandra and Beth couldn't possibly have drowned their mother. She was alive, although very drunk, long after her daughters left their townhouse to dine with friends at Jack Astor's restaurant, he claimed.

Rodriguez, forty-six, lived in the same townhouse complex as Linda and her children. He spoke to Linda about 9 p.m. January 18, 2003—two to three hours after the time prosecutors claimed she was dead in the tub. She had tried to bum cigarettes and booze from him. His testimony completely contradicted more than seven weeks of prosecution evidence.

"Her speech was slurred," Rodriguez testified.

He had seen Linda from an upstairs kitchen window.

"She was leaning against the wall. She couldn't stand up very well. She was losing her balance." He opened the window, threw two cigarettes down to her, and told her to get her own booze because he didn't have any.

"She left and that was the last I ever saw of her."

Jack McCulligh, however, insisted Rodriguez "may have been the last person to see," Linda Andersen "alive." He said the "central issue" of the trial was "what happened in the bathroom" the night of her death. Yet a forensic pathologist said rigor mortis had already appeared when Linda's body was removed from the bathtub, at 10:30 p.m., and that she had been dead for at least four hours.

Prosecutors alleged that Rodriguez sold drugs to the girls and had a sexual interest in Sandra. Rodriguez denied both accusations but admitted Sandra had told him about her sexual experiences with her boyfriends.

"I was a sounding board," he testified when asked if he thought it was appropriate to talk sex with a young girl. "I never smoked anything with those kids—that would be entirely inappropriate . . . that wouldn't qualify to be a human being."

Rodriguez also said he was standing in the driveway smoking a cigarette at about 10:30 p.m. when Sandra and Beth got out of a dark-coloured car in their driveway. He told police there had been two other people in the car, one a female, and that Sandra told him they'd been at Jack Astor's. She asked if he wanted a hamburger she hadn't eaten. He declined the food and told her to give it to her mom.

Rodriguez also described looking out the window of his townhouse a few minutes later and seeing police leading the girls into different unmarked cruisers. He said Beth looked a little upset and held her head in her hands, and that Sandra stared straight ahead as she sat in the cruiser. The next day, the superintendent told him Linda Andersen had killed herself.

Rodriguez said he drank with Linda about once a month and often heard her arguing with Bobby's father through the thin walls of the townhouse. He had known Sandra and Beth for about ten years and had taken them swimming several times. He knew their mother was often drunk; sometimes she seemed stressed because she didn't have any money or was out of work or was having problems dealing with her daughters.

Under cross-examination Rodriguez didn't remember several significant events, including signing an affidavit or even being at the girls' bail hearing. He also never remembered he had offered to be one of the court-appointed supervisor for the teenagers.

The court was aware that Rodriguez had been convicted for theft, possession of stolen property, dangerous driving, and drug possessions. Rodriguez told police he spoke to Sandra after Linda died. She didn't seem upset when she told him what had happened.

"It seemed like she was telling a story," he said. He thought she was still in shock.

A day before the defence's closing arguments of December 9, 2005, Judge Duncan denied the Crown's request to re-examine ten witnesses who could discredit Ricky Rodriguez's testimony. Their testimony wouldn't provide insight into the sisters' guilt or innocence, the judge said, and it would prolong an already lengthy murder trial.

Defence attorneys said Linda Andersen's death was a tragic accident which happened to occur after the girls talked with their close friends about killing her.

"It was a macabre class project—how to kill their mother....

It was a fable that became the deadly truth as a result of an accidental death," McCulligh told the court.

McCulligh admitted the girls were accomplished liars who told stories to fulfill a need for attention. This time, they took credit for the unfortunate accidental death of their alcoholic mother, whose death was initially ruled by a coroner as an accidental drowning due to excessive alcohol consumption.

"We have an accidental death and a school class project—how to kill Mother—which became a fable when their mother accidentally died. The fact that my client is an accomplished liar doesn't make her a murderer. "The girls were so desperate for attention and to have friends that they created a class project of how to kill mom. Their class project wound up being a joke that became tragically true."

McCulligh painted a bleak picture of how life was for the girls inside their Mississauga townhouse. Their alcoholic mother had abandoned her motherly duties, leaving her daughters to basically fend for themselves, even forcing them to take on the mother role of raising their younger brother. He noted how several friends, who testified as crown witnesses, said the girls' mother was always drunk.

"Their townhouse was party central for their friends—who were free to drink booze and smoke pot and who didn't really care one way or the other for the girls," McCulligh said. "The two girls felt guilty because they left their mother alone and drunk and she died. She was a drunk who finally pushed her luck too far."

McCulligh reminded Judge Duncan about the potentially deadly levels of alcohol that Andersen had in her system the night she took a bath and drowned.

"She was drunk."

None of their friends initially thought the girls were serious when they said they were going to kill their mother, McCulligh said.

"They only told police they took their plan seriously after they were threatened with being charged as co-conspirators," he said. "This case is about a human tragedy. It took place on an urban island in their [townhouse]. Four people lived on this island. The two girls, their little brother, and their mother. They failed to cope on this island. One died, and three lives changed forever."

McCulligh said the girls were used to lying.

"Sandra told her little brother his mom was sleeping when she was drunk and she told her friends her mother was tired when she was drunk. She told herself their lives would get better, but they didn't."

He said the girls lied to most of the Crown witnesses. "Their lies were made amidst their guilt because they left their mother home alone and drunk and she died," said McCulligh.

Of Sandra, McCulligh said:

"She told people she wanted to be a rock star, that she wanted to own a weed farm, that she was pregnant, that she wanted to become an author, that she wanted to go skinny dipping in Europe with a boyfriend—and that she had killed her mother."

McCulligh also attacked David for working as a police agent and getting the girls to confess to killing their mother during the secretly recorded videotapes.

"He raised the question of how their mother died. He was well-coached by Peel Constable Dan Johnstone—Coach Johnstone."

In his closing address, Beth's attorney Robert Jagielski said the teens were compulsive liars. "They had wicked imaginations," he said. "They simply made up stories. It was a way for them to deal with the tragic and unfortunate death of their mother."

Eugene Bhattacharya, who also defended Beth, reminded the court that even a school teacher didn't tell anybody after Beth joked about her mother's possible death as way of getting out of an exam.

"Linda Andersen was an outrageous alcoholic," said Bhattacharya. "She drowned in a highly intoxicated state."

Defence attorneys also urged Judge Duncan not to dismiss Rodriguez. It was entirely possible, they argued, that his conversation with Andersen had occurred. "It wasn't farfetched to suggest the woman, before taking her bath, would want to have a cigarette and some liquor," McCulligh said. "A cigarette, in fact, was found on top of the medicine cabinet and a glass, half-filled with alcohol, was found on the sink."

McCulligh also urged Judge Duncan to listen to the emotions in the frantic 911 call.

Defence attorneys also slammed David's credibility and his motives for going to the police, but Judge Duncan ruled credibility wasn't an issue because the girls spoke on the tape. "He [David] could be Jack the Ripper and those tapes would have the same effect," the judge said. "What he brings here is a real piece of evidence."

CHAPTER 22
IT TAKES TWO
TO TANGO

Linda Andersen's murder was by all accounts a macabre class project in the sense that at least five young teenagers, including the killers, were aware of the plot before and after. Several others also discovered the truth afterwards, yet nobody told anybody, except more friends, and they, too, never went to police. In fact, dozens of high school students, perhaps even hundreds, attending two different Mississauga schools, either heard rumours or had stories confirmed months before David went to police with Sandra's confession.

Yet David was the only "person of conscience," as Judge Duncan would later describe him, who actually said anything.

But it was up to Judge Duncan to decide whether Andersen's death was a result of a "planned and deliberate" killing by her daughters, as Crown prosecutors argued, or "a fable" that became the deadly truth as a result of an accidental death, as defence attorneys insisted.

Prosecutors Mike Cantlon and Brian McGuire believed Beth was just as guilty as Sandra. However, Sandra took most—if not all—of the blame for killing her mother in her now infamous confession, which was ruled inadmissible. She also took full blame when she spoke to David in their videotaped car ride.

But Cantlon and McGuire believed Beth was just as responsible and should also be convicted of first-degree murder.

The selection of Cantlon and McGuire as prosecutors for this landmark Canadian murder trial seemed, to use Ashley's favourite phrase, "so surreal." They appeared to be related. Both had brownish red hair, each wore glasses, and both had beards. Sandra and Beth could have been fraternal twins. Although they didn't look like each other, they shared the same mannerisms and at times it seemed each knew what the other was thinking. They seemed to have a psychic connection. "Here's the headline," Cantlon joked at one point to some reporters covering the case. "Twin Crowns prosecute twin sisters in trial of the decade."

But now their thoughts were deadly serious as they began two days of closing arguments. Once again, the courtroom was packed with curious spectators, including many high school students, Crown colleagues, and interested defence attorneys.

Sandra was described as being the "principal" behind her mother's murder because she held her mother's head under the bathtub water for four minutes until she died while Beth "aided and assisted" her in carrying out their elaborate plan of execution.

McGuire and Cantlon urged Judge Duncan to ignore defence suggestions that the girls were simply "compulsive liars" who told stories as a way of fulfilling their need for attention—and then took credit for an "unfortunate accidental death" of their alcoholic mother.

"They did not lie to get attention—the sort of lies teenagers tell are light years away from the detailed discussions of how they murdered their mother," McGuire said.

The numerous chilling Internet chats and forensic evidence

proved the sisters deliberately killed their mother, prosecutors said. Their friends' testimony not only showed Sandra and Beth "planned" their mother's death, but also carried out their plan with "deadly precision," even to the point of wearing gloves to prevent any bruising on her body.

"To predict in advance the exact manner of her death would be unbelievable," McGuire said.

Cantlon said the sisters talked about their plan—which involved getting their alcoholic mother drunk and nearly unconscious with Tylenol-3 pills—before helping her into her bathtub. It took four minutes, he said.

That was the "exact scenario," Cantlon said, that the teens had talked about with friends "before and after" their mother's death.

"She then dies in the exact manner."

They told friends toxicological information about drugs that would be found in their mother's system—months before police even knew they were there, he said.

Their Internet conversations with friends, which laid out their "plan to murder their mother," were "striking and stark," McGuire said. "Their plan unfolded precisely as predicted and their mother's death wasn't an accident, as defence attorneys suggested, but a designed murder." It was "damaging evidence to the extreme."

To prove his point, McGuire referred to the particularly disturbing online chat between Sandra and Ashley on the afternoon of their mother's death—a conversation he said was held while the accused teens were in the process of getting their mother drunk prior to committing murder. Sandra not only told Ashley they gave their mother four Tylenol-3s but also a bottle of vodka and wine.

"It's the single most chilling piece of evidence of this case. On the day of the murder, the plan is being put in place."

McGuire pointed out how Ashley had wished Sandra "good luck, use gloves," because she already knew the sisters were going to use gloves to ensure they didn't leave any marks on their mother's body.

The videotaped intercepts obtained through the use of police agent also provided details about the crime, McGuire said. The tapes are corroborated by evidence of three teens— Ashley, Jay, and Justin. They were told about the murder and their alibi ahead of time.

"The Internet conversations details the plot that was carried out and reveals forensic evidence days before the murder that wasn't known for more than a year," Cantlon said. "It fits together like pieces of a puzzle. She dies in the exact manner as it was planned."

Prosecutors didn't need to present a motive to gain a conviction. The teens murdered their mother because her alcoholism and pill-popping was ruining their lives and the life of their younger Bobby. But also "a factor," McGuire said, was their mother's $200,000 life insurance policy, which they stood to inherit. Several Internet chats indicated they intended on taking friends on a "European vacation" with the blood money.

Evidence indicated Sandra was the person who drowned their mother but prosecutors said the murder was a "joint venture."

"Beth was very much involved in the planned and deliberate killing of their mother," McGuire said. The only reason both sisters' hands weren't pushing their mother's head under the water was because "the bathroom wasn't big enough" for both of them.

"Beth was just a millimetre away from being a co-perpetrator. She was an integral part of the plan. She was an aider of the highest order."

Beth told a friend how she was "proud of the fact" that drowning their mother in the bathtub was "her idea," he said. She got the pills from a friend.

They intended for their mother's death to be ruled an accident, he said. "They called 911 and said their mother's death was an accident—exactly as they had planned," McGuire said. "They fabricated an alibi to cover-up their plot."

McGuire said it would have been a "cosmic co-incidence" for their mother to have accidentally died in exactly the same way (drowning) they talked to their friends about killing her.

"The evidence shows they murdered their mother. They talked about the murder with friends, they researched the Internet [about drowning] and they enlisted friends for their alibi."

The evidence was overwhelming that they committed first-degree murder, he said.

"Their mother's death happened precisely the way they said it would. They knew there would be codeine in their mother's system months before the drugs were even discovered by toxicological tests.

McGuire also asked Judge Duncan to disregard the evidence of the lone defence witness, Ricky Rodriguez because of his impossible timeline.

"His time anchor is darkness and darkness fell about 5:45 p.m. that night. His timeline was simply wrong."

For the witness to be right, the court would have to overlook all the other evidence, including the teens telling a 911 operator they drew their mother's bath before they went out that night, he said.

After listening to the final arguments, Judge Duncan stunned the courtroom by telling both sides that he would be rendering his verdict within a few hours. (In most trials, judges often take a day or longer to reach their decision.)

Sandra and Beth stared at each other, and then smiled.

As they left the courtroom, still able to wander the halls, ride the elevators, and have lunch in the courtroom cafeteria as free persons, they were still innocent under the law.

But they had to have known they had probably already spent their last night of freedom. They had to suspect they would not be returning to their Aunt Martha's residence where they'd lived under house arrest since their bail was granted twenty months earlier. There would also be no more long bus rides to and from court each day. Most days they got themselves to court because none of their relatives would drive them.

For now, their identities remained protected. But they knew an adult conviction would mean their names would be revealed; their photos splashed across the pages of newspapers and aired on television. Although the general public had no idea who they were or what they really looked like, many people already knew them, especially at their schools, in their neighbourhood and within their ethnic community.

But for the rest of the world they would remain Canada's infamous "Bathtub Girls."

CHAPTER 23

JUDGMENT DAY

Sandra and Beth had displayed little if any emotion sitting in their seats behind their lawyers during their trial. They showed nothing even when a photo of their dead mother, lying naked on the floor outside of the bathroom, was displayed. Often, they whispered to each other. Even found time to share a laugh. Usually they whispered in Danish so nobody nearby could hear what they were saying.

Beth frequently jotted words in a small notebook. On its cover, she'd written the phrases "Don't give up. Don't die. Don't go insane."

But they suddenly seemed tense, and finally a bit worried, when Judge Duncan entered a packed Courtroom 403 just after the noon hour on December 15, 2005. If Sandra and Beth had resigned themselves to a guilty verdict, they didn't let on. Just about everybody else in the standing-room only courtroom was certain of their fate. The publicity generated by their trial was enormous. Amidst the crowd, and now sitting in the front row just behind the girls, were several relatives, including Aunt Martha and their father, Walter. Neither had been allowed in the courtroom during the trial in case they were called as witnesses.

The judge took a few moments to review the case and the key pieces of evidence presented at trial.

"The Crown's position is the Internet chats and other statements made before Linda Andersen's death reveal a plan on the part of the defendants to kill their mother, and her death ensued from the carrying out of the plan. The Crown further alleges statements made to David and others after Linda Andersen's death constitute reliable and truthful admissions of having committed the murder as planned."

The defence, Judge Duncan said, insisted there should be reasonable doubt, and that the Crown had not proven the girls' statements were serious or true. The defence also relied on the evidence of a neighbour, who said Linda Andersen was still alive at 9:00 p.m. He added, "The defence submits with or without the evidence of Rodriguez the Crown has not proven her death was anything other than the accident it was first thought to be."

Judge Duncan explained first-degree murder: the intentional killing of another person that was planned and deliberate.

"The Crown must prove all of these elements beyond a reasonable doubt. The question of whether the Crown had proven its case must be considered separately for each, but there was no issue as to whether this was a case of first-degree murder, if their case was proven. Clearly, the deliberate consummation of a plan to drown another human being fits squarely within the definition of the crime charged. A person commits an offence if he actually commits it, or if he does or omits to do anything for the purpose of aiding another person to commit the offence or encourages a person in committing it. Participation in the formation of a plan to kill, coupled with the presence at the execution of the plan, at a minimum, would constitute abetting the commission of the offence. It is not argued otherwise."

Judge Duncan said a statement made by an accused person is admissible evidence only against its maker. However, where a conspiracy or a common criminal enterprise is alleged, acts and statements of one in furtherance of that common design are admissible against all those proven to be members of a common enterprise. As well, statements about, but not in furtherance of, the common design are not admissible against others.

Judge Duncan quickly dismissed the testimony of Ricky Rodriguez, the neighbour: "I absolutely reject his evidence as having any value at all on the timing issue. I find his evidence to be worthless on the crucial point for which it was tendered."

He turned to the Crown's evidence, which consisted of statements made by the defendants before and after their mother's death. The judge divided the statements into three categories: documented MSN chats, videotaped conversations, and speaking with friends.

Prosecutors called evidence of a number of statements made during MSN chats, which were preserved on the hard drive of a computer seized by the police when they arrested the defendants about a year after their mother's death. The first important issue was whether the Crown had proven they were the statements of the defendants. He was satisfied the record retrieved from the hard drive accurately represents someone's conversations. The main issue was whether it had been proven that "that someone" was one of the defendants. Who made the statements? The statements must be considered with other evidence, including physical evidence, expert opinion, and other statements. What was said in the statement itself and whether the speaker directly or circumstantially identified himself by what is contained in the statement. The judge said, "In my view the evidence establishes [that] the computer, the hard drive, and the chats recorded are solidly connected to the defendants, and they were the chat participants using Exhibit 200 and the authors of the words recovered from it. It may be strictly unnecessary to determine which defendant made which statement since there is ample evidence of common design and ample evidence all of the chat statements before the death were made in furtherance of that design.

"However, there is no need to invoke this rule in that. There is also direct evidence that serves to identify which of the defendants was involved in a particular conversation."

It was clear the computer came from the house in which the defendants were living and was found in a common room between their two bedrooms, he said.

"It is not as if this computer was found on the street or some place not connected to the defendants. The defence makes much of the fact the computer was not hooked up, but in my view that is of no importance. The contents of the hard drive clearly reveal it was the Andersen family computer used during the relevant period."

These chats were with friends of one or both defendants and the email addresses and user names of the participants on one side of each chat have been identified as belonging to the defendants, he said.

"The content of the chats themselves bears a striking correspondence to oral statements known to have been made by both defendants to friends including Jay and Ashley around the same time and to statements known to have been made by both defendants after the event to others, particularly David. The particulars of the plan itself identify the speakers. The speakers planned to meet Justin and Ashley at Jack Astor's; the defendants are known to have done that. In considering who was making statements about drowning their mom in the tub, the court might consider—whose mother drowned in the tub?"

The judge described several passages where specific friends mentioned specific names and specific events that happened in connection with Andersen's death. He pointed out that Justin "did not identify either defendant as his interlocutor [and] he absolutely denied he was a participant in the chat, at least in the form it was presented in evidence. I absolutely reject that evidence, but the Crown still has the burden of proving affirmatively the identify of the person who made the statements. On the basis of all of this evidence, I am satisfied beyond a reasonable doubt the statements made in these chats were made by the defendant to whom they have been attributed. In the case of the chats with Justin, I am satisfied even without direct identification [that) the Crown has satisfied its burden and has circumstantially proven both Justin and Beth were the participants in those chats."

Next the judge considered whether the chats described a real event. "The statements could be true, or they could be lies, jokes, musings, wishful thinking, put-ons, or mistakes. It is not an either-or issue. The Crown must negate any such innocent explanation and satisfy me beyond a reasonable doubt the statements are true." He reviewed the chats and said, "That teenagers would discuss murder in such a casual and open way does not suggest it is a game or a lark, but merely demonstrates the moral vacuity that prevailed. By far the most important feature is this: Linda Andersen, in fact, died in the manner, in the place, on the day, and at the approximate time discussed by the defendants in their chats.

"Unless her death was an astonishing macabre coincidence, the inference is unmistakable that the Internet chat discussions represented a real plan that was carried out in accordance with its terms.

"If there were no other evidence in this case, I would have no hesitation in concluding the possibility of such a coincidence was pure fantasy and the case against each defendant was proven beyond a reasonable doubt. However, there is other evidence and I must consider and weigh it as well before coming to any conclusion."

Judge Duncan reviewed the videotaped evidence and the taped conversations between the girls and David. He said David's personal credibility and reliability were not at issue.

"The videotaped statements are immediately noteworthy in [that] they make no suggestion the death was a bizarre and extraordinary coincidence. To the contrary, at face value, they are highly incriminating. The issue is whether that incrimination is true or a hoax."

He concluded they were the truth: "The description of the convulsions at death corresponds to reality as described by the pathologist—a reality Sandra is unlikely to have otherwise experienced."

When David told Sandra he was bothered by what she'd done, Sandra did not say she had made it all up. "Instead," the judge said, "she said nothing of the sort but rather [described] having murdered her mother. The tone and content of the conversation is serious. Sandra is describing her predicament and her rational but chilling solution to the big problem. She appears to be explaining or rationalizing a real and horrific event, not embellishing a made-up story. She appears to be speaking from the heart about the pain and loss she suffered when her mother was taken from her by alcohol, her concern for Bobby, and her feelings about what she had done.... Her statements do not ring of bravado and cool but rather of pathos. She is seeking his understanding, not his attention."

Then the judge moved on to Beth. "Her response was not outrage or incredulity. In the first segment she might be seen as tacitly accepting. In the second segment she again takes no issue with the truth but immediately refers to background and the need for understanding, much like Sandra did. In the third segment she declines the invitation to agree she wasn't part of it and says she was right there standing behind Sandra. It seems highly unlikely both girls, independently of each other, would decide to pull David's leg about such a delicate, important, and incriminating topic."

Beth's statements during the second recorded conversation with David, show "consistency is the hallmark of truth," he said, because it is more difficult to "remember a false story since there is no grounding in a real memory of a real event."

He said the claiming of a somewhat lesser role in that she was standing behind Sandra may be seen as inconsistent with a false story that is spun "as a put-on" or for "shock value," he said.

"It is one thing to make jokes or false statements that may backfire on yourself; it is another to run the risk of implicating others, particularly those who are close and cared for. Naming her boyfriend as the source of the Tylenol-3s is a detail that did not serve much, if any purpose, and unnecessarily exposed her boyfriend to potential liability. The inference is Beth was talking carelessly but honestly and was not perpetrating a clever controlled joke on David."

Judge Duncan said it was his "firm view" that all of this supports the "clear conclusion" these statements "are true" and they are "not a joke, or a put-on."

"Nothing about these conversations diminishes the strength

of the inference that flows from the concordance of the MSN chat conversations and the circumstances of Linda's death. To the contrary these videotaped conversations emphatically fortify that inference."

Next, Judge Duncan turned to the oral conversations with friends, and said they were mostly superfluous.

The statements before death stand on the same footing as the MSN chats; the statements after death stand on the same footing as David's videotapes. They add more of the same, only in undocumented form.

"As I understand it, from his submissions, Sandra's defence counsel said his client made an exaggerated admission to the effect that [she] told almost every teen in Mississauga she was either going to kill or had killed her mother. At the same time, counsel challenged the credibility of these witnesses and alleged they had been coached by the police or were lying. . . . All these witnesses are friends of the defendants. I see no merit in the suggestion they were coached or they are implicating the defendants to save themselves. The statements these witnesses attribute to the defendants bear a marked consistency with each other and a marked consistency with documented MSN chat statements known to have been made by the defendants and to recorded statements made by the defendants to David after the death."

He added, "With respect to those who said they had foreknowledge, Jay and Ashley . . . they appeared to be genuinely remorseful about their moral shortcomings at the time.[T]he substance of what they related—that the defendants told them they killed their mother by drowning her in the bathtub—is, in my view, unforgettable, unmistakable, and completely reliable. I find the statements as testified to by these witnesses, at least in substance, were made by the defendants."

Judge Duncan turned next to Justin: "He was her boyfriend at the time of her mother's death. He is separately charged…with conspiracy to commit murder and has a preliminary hearing pending. It is alleged he assisted the defendants in the planning and provided the Tylenol-3s. He … provided information that incriminated the defendants. In his evidence at trial, Justin gave no evidence that tended to incriminate the defendants or himself, and…adamantly denied the truth of any incriminating part of his earlier interview.

"In my view…the Crown should decide whether a particular individual is going to be a witness or is going to be an accused, then ride one horse or the other, but not both. I give no weight to Justin's evidence or his statement."

Judge Duncan noted there were some things in the case that couldn't be explained, such as the discrepancy as to how Linda Andersen was found in the tub.

"We will never know. In every case, there are a few dangling threads or circumstances that remain unexplained. That is in the nature of the trial process that tries to recreate past events by imperfect means. While everything need not be accounted for and reconciled, if it did, in this case I would think it is likely (paramedic) Hayes was in error. He had no notes. He may have been mistaken in his evidence, or the deceased may have been moved. Equally the first attending police officer may have moved the deceased slightly, at least enough to bring her head out of the water to check her condition, even though he testified he didn't. It would certainly be odd if he did not do so since the fact of her being dead and beyond help had not yet been confirmed."

To the defence claim that the death of the girls' mother was accidental, Judge Duncan said, "It is a snowflake against an avalanche. When all of the evidence is considered, the possibility of accident has been thoroughly negated." He continued, "The two defendants set out to commit the perfect crime but instead they created the perfect prosecution. The case against them is overwhelming. It is probably the strongest case I have ever seen in over thirty years of prosecuting, defending, and judging criminal cases. I find the defendants guilty as charged of first-degree murder."

Judge Duncan cleared the courtroom before hearing submissions on the sentencing phase of the case.

Outside the courtroom, Eugene Bhattacharya, Beth's attorney, said there would be no appeal of the sentence or conviction for either girl.

"What we dealt with here was the breakdown of a family," he told reporters. "There is no justification for murder. But no matter how you look at it, in the circumstances of this case, I think psychiatric evidence is going to be a factor the court can consider in terms of an appropriate remedy."

Sandra and Beth were visibly upset when the judge resumed about forty-five minutes later; they sat handcuffed beside each other in the prisoner's box.

They were now convicted killers.

CHAPTER 24

DEVOTED,
NOT ALWAYS DRUNK

Sandra, Beth, and their friends portrayed Linda Andersen as any-thing but Mother of the Year. She was a drunk; she masturbated in front of them; she was a despicable mother; she never took care of her daughters or their brother, Bobby; she put booze ahead of family; she was slowly drinking herself into the grave.

But was she really as bad as she was made to appear? Certainly David never believed she was the mother from hell: "I don't know why they killed their mother but their situation wasn't as bad as they made it seem," he said. "She might have had some problems, but they weren't the victims, their mother was."

Several of Linda's hospital co-workers described her as well-liked, a hard-working nurse who always smiled, got along with everybody, and went out of her way to help others. They knew she battled the bottle and sometimes came to work smelling of alcohol, sometimes even drunk. But nearly all of them agreed that Linda was a devoted mother who often worked double shifts and went to night school to get a higher-paying job so she could provide her children with a better lifestyle. She was extremely proud of her daughters and often boasted about their academic accomplishments.

Perhaps Beth's attorney, Robert Jagielski, described Linda best during the sentencing phase. He said there were different images of Linda depending on who was telling the story. One side portrayed her as Mother Teresa, the other as Mary Magdalene. Jagielski reminded the court that her co-workers were unaware of many aspects of Linda's life, for example that she had been fired from jobs for being drunk.

Linda had dark secrets. She was an alcoholic. Her ex-lover had physically abused her. She was deeply in love with Edward Brockman, who found her sexually appealing but had no intention of marrying her. She feared she had lost control of her daughters. She told co-workers she sent Beth to Europe so she wouldn't have to deal with both daughters every day.

Linda was upset and angry with Sandra, who refused to go to Europe. She had stolen money from Linda, money Linda had been saving to buy a new computer and to take upgrading courses. Sandra also cashed in a savings bond Linda had set up for her daughters' educations.

Kim Wiley and Linda Andersen met at the hospital in May 2000. They had a common bond: both had teenagers. They became good friends.

"She called me her 'Canadian friend.' She always made the best of every situation. She was someone whom you could always depend on. She had a great sense of humour. She always smiled. She was always willing to help others. She had a sparkle in her eyes."

Wiley said Linda had become increasingly despondent before her death. She was working several jobs and studying at night to make enough money so her daughters could enjoy a lifestyle like that of their friends. Linda felt she was losing control of her children.

"She loved them very much but didn't know what she was going to do," Wiley said at the girls' sentencing hearing. "Her daughters blamed her for the abuse she suffered at the hands of Doug Landers. It was her fault because she didn't leave."

Linda confided in Wiley about her relationship with Landers. She made a frantic telephone call to Wiley in the winter of 2001. Landers had punched her and held a knife to her throat, then threatened to take Bobby to Holland. He said Linda would never see the boy again. The abuse had been going on for several years. Wiley contacted police.

Linda also told Wiley her daughters made fun of her for dating lawyer Edward Brockman. Dating the lawyer was the biggest joy of Linda's life, Wiley said. But her daughters said he must be old and ugly to want to have anything to do with her.

Linda also told Wiley about the bond Sandra cashed. "She was putting money away but then discovered Sandra had cashed it and wouldn't give it back to her. She believed nothing she ever did for her daughters was good enough for them." Linda was frustrated with Sandra's defiance. Wiley said, "Sandra always wanted to have her own way. And when she didn't get her own way, she would threaten Linda by telling her that she was going to call child welfare on her."

According to court documents, Sandra contacted the Children's Aid Society on February 8, 2001. She was concerned about her mother's volatile relationship with Doug Landers. Police eventually became involved, and Landers was removed from the home a month later. Linda gave permission for a safety assessment of the children. CAS officials said Linda had taken appropriate measures to deal with her domestic abuse issues. They also believed Linda protected her children and was committed to providing them with a safe home environment. Sandra told CAS officials she'd never seen her mother drunk, that Linda was a good parent, and that they had a close relationship. CAS closed the file.

They reopened it on June 14, 2001, when Sandra insisted her mother was abusing alcohol, that their relationship had deteriorated, and that her mother didn't love her anymore. She told them she resented her brother; he was a spoiled brat, and her mother gave him everything. She said she wanted to be removed from her mother's care and placed in a nice rich foster home. CAS officials met with Sandra and her mother twelve days later. By then, Sandra couldn't tell them when her mother had been drinking and said she never saw her mother passed out. CAS officials concluded Sandra's escalating defiant behaviour caused the poor relationship between mother and daughter. There were unresolved parent-teenager issues. Child welfare officials believed Sandra's motives for calling them were questionable.

Linda told CAS officials she was concerned about her daughter's friends, especially one particular boy, and that she was working two jobs and going to night school so she could provide a better lifestyle for her children.

Linda called the CAS in the fall of 2001 and asked for assistance because she couldn't deal with Sandra. An intake worker went to the home two weeks later, and Linda said the situation was under control; she no longer needed their help.

"[Her daughters] were rebellious," said Charlie Boswell, another of Linda's co-workers. "Her daughters were out of control. She didn't seem to feel there was anything she could do to make them happy."

Linda had been concerned about her daughters attending a rave, Boswell said. She wanted to know what drugs might be there. She said her daughters were so upset with a particular

Christmas gift that she had bought them that they threw it at her after they opened it and yelled at her.

"She wanted to do everything to keep her children happy," he said.

Linda got along with everybody at the hospital and never seemed bitter or angry, he said, but he knew she was working three jobs and going to school.

"She said her daughters were giving her a hard time. [They] always wanted to be partying and she didn't want them to." He added, "She never slacked off in front of me. I found her reliable." Other co-workers agreed.

Neither Wiley nor Boswell knew Linda had been fired because of her alcohol problems.

Co-worker Kim Lancaster said Linda told her she was losing control of her children and was struggling financially. She told her that her relationship with the lawyer was an escape from her home life. Kim told police that Linda was living on a fixed budget and was frustrated because her daughter's needs were exceeding her finances. "She returned home one night after working a double shift she found the girls and their friends had eaten everything in their home," Lancaster told police. "Their house was a mess and a Nintendo game that she had bought for Bobby was also broken. She was upset because these incidents were happening more and more. It got to the point where she didn't trust leaving the girls alone. Her daughters didn't seem to care about the sacrifices she was making for them. They didn't care about her financial problems either." Lancaster said Linda bought her daughters designer jeans and expensive clothes instead of fixing her car so she had to take the bus to work.

Not all her co-workers praised Linda. Sarah Rankin told police her drinking was causing problems at work. Meagan Conroy suspected Linda had a drinking problem and told police she smelled alcohol on Linda's breath one day when she arrived at work.

"It reached the point where some of her co-workers didn't want to work with her," she told police.

Irene Dunn told investigators Linda had become unreliable as a worker because of her increasing alcohol consumption. Nursing supervisor Nancy Connors noticed that Linda often called in sick and missed shifts.

Mellissa Conklin noticed a change in Linda's personality midway through the summer of 2002.

"She seemed unhappy. Her mood changed. She regularly missed shifts. She called in sick a lot of the time and it got to the point where nobody wanted to be scheduled to work with her."

Conklin was also aware Linda was having trouble with her daughters.

"She told me one of her daughters offered her a marijuana cigarette and another time one of them jumped on the hood of her car. Linda once baked a cake and put on the windowsill to settle but one of her daughters came along and deliberately pushed it out the window. I thought these girls were mean, especially for a single mother who was working hard for them."

Madison Langdon, another hospital co-worker, told police that Linda often talked about her problems with her daughters.

"They wanted brand new clothes and Nike shoes, in particular. That's why she was working so hard to provide them with these things. She went back to school so she could get a better job so she could make more money. I don't think her children understood she was working so hard to provide things they wanted."

Linda always talked about her children and always called them from work, she said.

When Jen Walton confronted Linda about smelling of alcohol at work, Linda explained that she'd been at a party the night before and didn't get much sleep.

"She said being a working mother of three, and working several different jobs, meant she only got three to fours of sleep each night. She said if she appeared off balance at work it wasn't because she was drinking but because of a lack of sleep."

CHAPTER 25
NOBODY SAID, "NO"

Probation officer Suzie Martin wrote Sandra's pre-sentencing report. To prepare, she gathered information from police, lawyers, defendants, family members—anyone who could give her information that would help Judge Duncan make his sentencing decisions.

Sandra "savoured every moment" of drowning her mother and viewed her death as a "mercy killing," Martin wrote in her report. She was even convinced her mother would "understand" why she had to die and would "forgive her" for killing her.

But Magnus, now a Detective Sergeant, didn't hold back anything when asked for his opinion. He thought that under the right circumstances—"they could kill again."

Magnus told Martin that he believed the girls were "highly influenced by each other." Society would be better off if they were sentenced as adults, he said, so they would remain under restrictions of a life parole, even when released.

"Sandra recalled while committing the murder that she wanted to remember every detail of it," Martin wrote. "She saw her mother's convulsions and her dying heaves." Sandra told Martin she was sober when she murdered her mother, that she was afraid her mother would die from alcohol abuse and that her cousin Derek had sexually assaulted her. She also admitted for the first time that she deliberately killed her mother. She said when she returned home that night, even though she knew her mother was dead in the tub, she still needed to look in the bathroom, and even knocked on the door.

Martin wrote, "She needed to get into a mindset of suddenly discovering her mother dead in the tub." In her interview with Martin, Sandra said she believed getting arrested probably saved her life. "She hated the life she was living," Martin wrote. "Her secret was too big to carry. She was attempting to kill herself with drugs and alcohol." Sandra said the day that she was arrested was her fourteenth consecutive day of being sober.

Magnus didn't believe the murder was all Sandra's idea. He told Martin both girls were "actively involved in planning and researching" their mother's murder.

Magnus said, "They were always concerned about where they were going to get money to purchase drugs and clothing and bragged about their ability to manipulate people."

Both Magnus and Constable Mike Pulley believed Beth had played a much bigger part in the crime than either sister had admitted. Officers were also absolutely certain the crime was partly committed to get their dead mother's cash.

The relationship between the girls and their mother was "very problematic," Magnus told Martin. Linda called police several times. She once even filled out a missing person's report. Magnus said both girls were "disrespectful and verbally abusive" towards their mother, and computer records showed they called their mother "a whore." They were aware of their mother's life insurance polices and were angry when she cancelled one of them, Magnus said.

"The girls bragged about their ability to manipulate people and use their weaknesses against them. They were also angry their mother was no longer dating the lawyer and concerned their lives would return to the way they were before.

"This was no children's crime. It was an adult crime, sophisticated and complex in nature. They are highly influenced by each other and they're dangerous because they know how to manipulate the system."

An adult sentence could place the girls on parole for life, which Magnus and Pulley said would be a "good checking system."

Sandra claimed she would never profit from her mother's murder but Magnus told Martin that Sandra told friends she wanted to sell the movie rights to her story. Canadian law, however, prevents convicted persons from profiting from their crimes.

Family members interviewed by Martin insisted Linda was proud of her daughters and loved them dearly. She was often exhausted because she worked several jobs, and believed her daughters mistakenly interpreted her exhaustion as sign she was intoxicated.

Sandra told Martin she felt betrayed by her mother because her drinking seemed more important than loving her daughters. The more her mother drank, the less she had anything nice to say about her. Even good times faded from her memory. She thought the last happy time she could remember was when they went to Disneyland in 1998.

Even one of her fondest memories of mother was now clouded in hatred. Her mother used to cuddle with her in bed and read bedtime stories. But that ended when she was six. She had wet the bed. Sandra was too embarrassed to let her mother slide in beside her. Soon afterward, her mother stopped cuddling altogether. She felt she preferred the comfort of vodka. Sandra soon became more and more alienated from her mother. Sandra felt alcohol had replaced her.

Sandra once looked forward to her summer trips to Europe. Her mother presented them as "treats" but she eventually realized her mother just sent them away "to make life easier" for her.

"She began to rebel, hang out with negative friends and began to increasingly drink alcohol and smoke pot," Martin wrote. "She was of the opinion it became impossible to have a normal relationship with her. She cried almost every day for years and yearned for a normal life."

Sandra admitted she stole money from her mother.

"She hated who her mother had become and felt betrayed by her," Martin wrote. "She was rebelling to hurt her mother so she would know how it felt."

Sandra didn't like Doug Landers. He abused alcohol and was violent towards their mother and verbally abusive to everybody. She recalled they argued a lot.

"When she was alone with each of them the atmosphere was good but became strained when they were together," Martin wrote.

Her father Walter was extremely hesitant to be interviewed by Martin and declined to answers several questions because he feared his answers would become public.

"He was of the opinion there was no relevance," Martin wrote.

Walter was also very secretive. He had a Masters of Arts degree in sociology, but refused to say what he did for a living, only admitting he held the same job for twenty years. Walter and Linda separated in 1989 and divorced in 1991. Linda granted him access to their children, but she later stopped him from seeing his daughters. She finally gave him supervised visits after he spent three-and-a-half years fighting for his rights to see his daughters. During their initial separation, Beth and Sandra were sent to Holland to live with their maternal grandparents. By the time Sandra was six and Beth was five, he had regular visits with them.

Walter never saw any significant changes in Sandra's behaviour although her grades were falling just before and after his ex-wife's death. He blamed her poor grades on "the wrong company" she was keeping.

"He stated there was no discipline at home," Martin wrote. "His ex-wife didn't show up at school to deal with his academic concerns."

He saw less and less of his daughters as they grew older.

"They were more independent and wanted to spend more time with their friends," Martin wrote. "He spoke to them once or twice a month."

Walter said Linda consumed alcohol back home in Holland but stopped when they started dating and her booze consumption was never an issue during their marriage.

"He was not tolerant of this," Martin wrote.

He gave Linda extra money whenever he could and shared expenses with her involving his daughters' activities. His daughters generally never spoke to him about any major concerns.

"He remembers receiving a call from Sandra when she was in Grade 10 and spoke about their household being disorganized and that their little brother wasn't being raised the way he should," Martin wrote.

Martha Kronwall told Martin that she saw Sandra and Beth every summer when they lived in Holland and when they visited their grandparents, who were both well-respected engineers. Martha immigrated to Canada in 1992 and initially moved into the same townhouse complex as her sister. Sandra and Beth shared a close relationship with their extended family. Martha thought her sister's relationship with Doug Landers had been good in the beginning but she later discovered he neglected the family. She suspected something was wrong in their relationship although Linda never confided in her.

Linda worked long hours and often came home exhausted. Sandra reached out to her about her mother's drinking problems but Linda felt alcohol wasn't a big problem for her and that her drinking was under control. Linda once asked her to go with her to an Alcoholics Anonymous meeting because she felt guilty for drinking after work.

Martha never had any problems with her nieces when they lived with her after their mother died.

"They lived in a basement with two bedrooms, a living room, and a bathroom." The girls shared a good relationship with her and her husband and their two sons, Derek and Hans, Martha told Martin.

Even though Martha saw several liquor bottles under Sandra's bed when police conducted a search warrant, she insisted she'd never seen her nieces drunk or high. She once suspected Sandra might have been drinking based on her behaviour. She confronted Sandra but she laughed it off. Despite Sandra's confessions about her out of control drug use and extensive drinking, even school officials never noticed any substance abuse.

Martha insisted that her sister didn't have a drinking problem. Her nieces saw their mother have a drink after work and then fall asleep and they associated that with alcohol instead of thinking that she was simply exhausted because of working too much.

"Linda was a good mother who always provided for her children," Martha told Martin. "The girls were involved in dance, swimming, Tae Kwon Do, and horseback riding and Linda took her children to Disneyland in 1998.

"Linda wanted to give her children a better lifestyle and in order to do this took nursing upgrades at night school. She worked full-time at the hospital and went to school twice a week in the evenings."

As her nieces grew older, Martha said they took on more responsibility for babysitting Bobby.

"When Linda got home she cooked, cleaned the house, and cared for her children but there were times when she was working shift work that the house was in disarray," Martha told Martin.

Martha last spoke to her sister two days before her death.

"She was in the process of organizing a birthday party for her son," Martin wrote. "She had no concerns for her sister at the time. Everything appeared normal."

Sandra's former guidance counselor, Randy Langois told Martin that Sandra and Beth were the "smartest girls" he'd ever met but their "best skill was their ability to manipulate."

In her interview, Sandra insisted she never "bragged" to anybody about killing her mother but admitted she told people she had committed murder when she was drunk at parties. She admitted telling a family friend details about the murder.

"She regretted telling him," Martin wrote. "She was surprised when she was arrested because she never thought they would get caught."

Sandra now believed getting arrested probably saved her life.

Sandra told Martin she was also embarrassed about sending nude photos of herself, as well as several sexually explicit emails, to the Tucker Max website.

"She thought it was fun at the time," Martin wrote. "Now

looking back she considers this to be one of her worst mistakes." She was also "humiliated" when she learned some info was also on a website called murderingwhores.com.

Martha said Sandra spent most of her time studying while she was under house arrest.

"She wanted to study rather than work," Martin wrote.

Martin also talked to Linda's sister, Martha, who said she had remained supportive of her nieces and had believed they were innocent, but stopped all contact with them after they were convicted of murdering her sister. She was devastated when she learned her nieces admitted killing their mother. "She didn't want to believe what the newspapers wrote and she wasn't allowed to hear witness testimony," Martin wrote. "The girls continually insisted they were innocent."

Sandra told Martin that she never came forward because she was "too scared" and "too cowardly" to face the reaction of her family.

"She was afraid," Martin wrote. "Now, she doesn't want to lie anymore. She wants to make things right so she can heal and people can forgive her."

In the spring of 2002, Sandra said her cousin Derek introduced her to marijuana at her own request and she experimented with it five or six times before she got high. She was an occasional user until that summer when another person provided her with a large amount of marijuana.

"As it was readily available, she consumed it two or three times each week," Martin wrote. "Once her summer stash was gone she returned to being an occasional user.

"She used it on a daily basis after her mother's death. She was trying to get as high as she could to take the pain away. But she never got there."

Sandra told Martin she and Beth consumed amphetamines at a bar in Holland in the summer of 2003. She said she also snuck alcohol from her aunt's liquor cabinet.

Sandra said she didn't attend a lot of parties but when she did she drank heavily until she passed out or vomited.

"She had lots of blackouts and memory loss," Martin wrote. "She thought drinking to excess was normal. She remembers thinking, 'What's the point of drinking if you don't get drunk?'"

"She hated the life she was living," Martin wrote. "Her secret was too big to carry. She was attempting to kill herself with drugs and alcohol."

Walter Andersen told Martin that he had no idea his daughters were drinking alcohol and consuming drugs. Sandra was a sensitive and fragile girl who was afraid to stand up for herself, a follower, especially when it came to his youngest daughter, Beth.

"He loves them and will always be there to support them," Martin wrote.

Martha said her nieces had very different personalities. "Sandra is quiet, shy and sensitive, and intellectually gifted," Martin wrote. "But Beth requires lots of attention. She is assertive, outgoing, and intelligent."

Martha said Sandra rarely asked for anything the entire time she and Beth lived at her house.

"It was always Beth who did the talking for both of them," Martin wrote.

Martha believed Sandra suffered from depression after her mother's death. "She had mood swings and slept often," Martha said. She also said Sandra obtained sleeping pills from her doctor.

"Sandra believed the murder of her mother would rid her of a lack of control and the hopelessness would change," Martin wrote. "Murder was not done out of malice but to end pain."

Sandra also insisted insurance money wasn't the "motivating factor" and she didn't leave her home because of a concern for her brother Bobby. Sandra told Martin that she believed her mother "loved us insanely" and it was "me who fucked up." She never expected to get caught, but admitted she "paid a steep price," and being caught removed the heavy burden of secrecy. Sandra told Martin that she and her sister "spoke different languages." Sandra felt her younger sister always wanted to hurt her. Sandra had been drunk for six months before her mother's death. But she insisted she wanted someone to stop her but nobody did. She wanted somebody to "notice something was wrong."

In her final assessment, Martin wrote that Sandra had accepted full responsibility for murdering her mother and was ready to deal with whatever sentence Judge Duncan imposed. Sandra also understood the consequence of her action.

"She feels freedom through honesty," Martin wrote. "She recognizes her actions have affected more people than she thought possible. She doesn't know how she can possibly repair the damage done to her family."

Sandra also now understands her mother never intended to hurt her.

"She admits her perceptions of her past were narrow and skewed," Martin wrote.

"She's looking forward to receiving therapy and to understanding what went wrong. She understands she needs intervention to deal with the many issues in her life. Her goal is to be able to love and trust herself. It's clear she shares a close relationship with her father. He's attempted to provide structure, stability, and security in her life. But he seems more concerned with her education and spiritual needs than dealing with the issues that brought her to court.

"She wants to obtain a master's degree in psychology and to become a psychologist and help others like her. She wants to become a writer. She would like to write fiction, children's books, and scripts.

"The violent crime against Linda Andersen was premeditated and well-researched. She wanted to remember every detail of the offence. She admitted she never expected to get caught. She appears to have manipulated her family, her community, and the police into thinking the death was an accident. The police involved indicate she is dangerous and knows how to manipulate the system."

Martin recommended that Sandra receive a lengthy sentence of incarceration where she could receive the necessary rehabilitation and treatment for her eventual re-integration into society, thereby giving long-term protection for the community.

CHAPTER 26
"I DID IT TO SAVE BOBBY"

Probation officer Stephen Lane wrote Beth's pre-sentencing report. Like Martin, Lane gathered information and talked to many people before putting his report together. He knew Magnus believed Beth was the most evil of the two sisters, and that she was driven by greed. But Beth told Lane a different story.

Beth believed she and Sandra were being "merciful" by ending their mother's miserable life in a "painless" way rather than risk her suffering in a car crash while driving drunk and possibly killing them, their brother, or another innocent person or family.

But Beth provided another far more important reason. With her mother dead, she could raise Bobby.

"If she and Sandra got away with killing their mother then they could raise Bobby and do what was best for him. They carefully planned the murder to be able to look after each other and Bobby. They could not look after him if they were in jail."

Beth's life was a mess. She couldn't run away because she didn't want to leave Bobby behind with her mother. She was afraid her mother would harm Bobby when she was drinking. She recalled the day her mother drove the wrong way down a street while impaired.

"She said it was inevitable her mother would injure herself," Lane wrote.

Like Sandra, Beth also thought about killing herself.

"She was ready to die but her brother held her back because it would be difficult to fathom leaving him alone," Lane wrote.

Beth was also sad because she hadn't been allowed to see Bobby since her arrest. "It hurt her not to see Bobby," Lane wrote. "She felt as if her first-born had been taken away from her. It was painful for her not to have any contact with him. She knew he was suffering. She was powerless to help him. It was a huge punishment for him not to see his sisters. His sisters were his whole world."

She and Bobby had a special bond.

"She implemented a survival strategy," Lane wrote. "Neither her mother nor her stepfather would raise Bobby. Their mother even neglected Bobby when she was sober. Sandra told her that Bobby would unfortunately have to the "sacrificial lamb" in their mother's murder.

Beth, like Sandra, vehemently denied there mother's life insurance money played any role in their decision.

"It was not about money," Beth told Lane. "The money was never a motive." Beth understood all the insurance money was paid to her Aunt Martha.

"Beth's friends not only supported their decision to kill their mother but also encouraged them to go through with it," Lane wrote.

"None of her friends said to her this was a bad idea. Her friends supported the killing. She felt she was being swept along by the crowd. There was no vengeful aspect of the murder. She discussed it with others and instead of trying to stop the process they made suggestions such as 'wear gloves.'"

Beth said Sandra was "adamant" the murder was going to happen "regardless" if she participated, Lane wrote.

"It was like trying to stop a tidal wave in terms of preventing the killing."

Beth insisted the decision to murder their mother was Sandra's idea. She initially tried to talk her out of it, but she decided not to "interfere negatively" with the killing. Beth cried when she told Lane that she had made drinks for her mother the day she died. Her mother was happy when drunk.

"There was no suffering."

To make sense of the killing, Beth told Lane "drastic actions are called for in drastic situations."

In his view, Lane believed her mother's alcoholism as being the "degeneration of her mother as a human being."

But she insisted the "murder wasn't done out of malice," and it was "done to end the pain" of their mother's alcoholism.

"She wasn't particularly angry with her mother. She felt hopeless dealing with the family situation," Lane wrote. "Drinking left her mother incapacitated and out of control."

Her mother was drinking herself to death. She and Sandra wanted to "speed up the process" in a way they could control. It would be "quick and painless" and "merciful" to kill her mother.

Beth recalled how her mother's drinking got worse when she was in her early teens. Although she insisted there was no anger involved in the killing, Beth believed she "had a right to hate her mother," Lane wrote.

"She felt her mother should be a mother, the authoritative figure in the family, not an alcoholic. She wanted out of the shitty situation at home. She felt helpless with her family situation."

Beth claimed she and Sandra often went to school hungry. They wore shabby clothes as children because their mother used her money to buy alcohol instead paying the rent, buying food, and making sure the utilities were paid. Her mother mismanaged their household by spending her money on alcohol.

Despite this, Beth also told Lane her mother taught Beth and Sandra compassion. "But she was not able to provide her children with a normal and stable household," Lane wrote. "'We cannot afford it,' was their mother's standing response when the girls asked for anything. A lack of money to buy things was a prevailing theme in the family."

Beth told Lane that Sandra ran the household, and that the fridge was empty most of the time.

Beth saw things differently after their mother was dead. "I never thought I would regret it so much," Beth said. "I never thought it would be so permanent." She had been insensitive to her mother's alcoholic problems and lack of control: "All I saw was a drunk." But she now realized her mother was trying to help them; she learned a lot about her mother after her death.

"If she could have looked past her mother's alcoholism, she would have seen more of her mother's positive qualities," Lane wrote.

She believed she and Sandra had been wronged because the CAS and family members never helped them deal with their mother's alcoholism.

By the time of the murder, Beth was a regular marijuana user and had tried magic mushrooms several times "to be a cool teenager" because her friends encouraged her. She drank at parties. She smoked pot daily with her friends. She went through several phases—from being a nerd at thirteen, to a skater at fourteen and a Goth girl at sixteen. "She was Tom Boy, slightly androgynous and focused on sports," Lane wrote. "She wore tight clothes to emphasize her feminine attributes."

Beth insisted she and Sandra never had many discussions about the murder until January 2003 when Sandra outlined her plan. She didn't know Tylenol-3 was going to be used until a few days before the murder took place when Sandra told her it was to be used. Beth conceded she wasn't present during the final moments of her mother's life. "She was pacing outside of the bathroom," Lane wrote. "There was no noise, no struggle."

Beth told Lane she didn't recall what was said at Jack Astor's except she felt "horrible" and started to "deny to herself" that her mother was gone.

"Her mother meant well and in some twisted way, they meant well, too."

Neither she nor Sandra was thinking clearly about the permanence of death or about their mother's alcoholic problems. "She wished somebody told them to think twice about committing murder," Lane wrote. "She said her mother was suicidal. She said controlling their mother's death seemed more merciful, although now she considers it to have been selfish."

Lane believed Andersen's death emanated out of narcissism —a sense of entitlement that they deserved better and more.

"Beth said her mother rebelled against her own parents' wealth by drinking and getting pregnant," Lane wrote.

In the weeks leading to the murder, Beth's mood was very low and she had suicidal thoughts. Like Sandra, she believed she had few options—kill herself or kill her mother—as the means to fix their lives. Beth described herself as a perfectionist, but said she lacked guidance in her life. She often criticized Sandra, and told Lane she felt her sister always wanted results without putting in the effort needed to achieve her goals.

"She felt Sandra was often self-serving and when she was angry she wanted to hurt others," Lane wrote.

She and Sandra learned to communicate better when they found themselves under house arrest, Beth told Lane.

"She would like her nightmares to stop," Lane wrote. In them, she was "running from something," was being "attacked by others," and having to "fight back," and "arguing with her intoxicated mother."

When asked what she would wish for if she were magically granted three wishes, Beth said she'd wish that her mother could return and that she wasn't a drunk. She couldn't think of anything else. But she didn't think Sandra wanted her mother back. She also admitted she told lies to cover her faults and failures.

"She said she wasn't manipulative like Sandra," Lane wrote. "She often felt abandoned by her sister. She considered herself to be responsible and not impulsive."

Beth told Lane she had wanted to plead "guilty" but her family insisted she plead "not guilty" and she was very unhappy about that.

In the interview, Beth told Lane she was groped when she arrived at the Syl Apps Youth Detention Centre, that she was threatened with sexual assault, and that her cousin had sexually assaulted her.

Beth liked to read the classics such as Hugo, Dickens, Twain and Steinbeck, and admitted she once was a "chocolate merchant" for "Students Against Drugs." She used her money to buy friends gifts and pot for herself during the two to three months she worked for the company. She also worked part-time at a pet store but found the job "slow and boring." She worked at a bakery while under house arrest and often helped her aunt at her architectural office.

"She felt overwhelmed at life," Lane wrote. "And bored at her jobs."

Lane also reviewed several statements of various friends, including one who said Beth bragged about her own alcohol use after their mother's death and how she was going to get $50,000 when she turned eighteen. Even though Beth seemed depressed after her mother died, several friends said she told them her mother was "so stupid they wanted to kill her."

Beth said Justin and Billy were her close friends. She thought Ashley was a snob.

"She was bright but lazy," Lane wrote. "She was cool and fit in." Ashley was also "manipulative" and "domineering." She described Jay as being "pleasant" but suffered too much from an "unhappy family life." Donny was "quiet" and "passive" but loved her sister.

Beth told Lane that she "dearly loved" Justin, her first sexual partner. They met in one of their gifted classes. Justin was outgoing and intelligent. She felt safe with him and there was never any violence or infidelity between them in the "eight months and eleven days" they went out. Beth felt so strongly about Justin that even after she was convicted she was still bothered about how their relationship ended. She wished there had been a better closure because she missed him and his family.

Others interviewed said Beth had "a controlling boyfriend" and that she abused alcohol. They described both sisters as being drug users. Richie Drake, a boy whom Beth met through their cousin Derek, described her as being "bubbly, energetic, and logical" while Sandra was more "reflective, intelligent, and quiet." Both sisters were "nerdy" and both "hated their mother." He said Beth seemed "depressed" after her mother's death.

Beth didn't really enjoy drugs and only took them to fit in with her friends, Lane wrote. Although she insisted she had a low tolerance for drugs, she admitted she sometimes liked to get high, and experimented with magic mushrooms.

"She vomited and didn't like the effect," Lane wrote. "Her peers encouraged her to try different amounts and different types of drugs."

Drugs made her "lose control" and she always liked to be in control, Lane said.

"They took her out of the natural swing of things," Lane wrote.

She smoked pot daily although she insisted she wasn't high or drunk when their mother was murdered. She started drinking at fifteen and smoking pot at fourteen and her cousin Derek introduced her to pot.

"She smoked pot for fun and to fit in with her peers, not to relieve stress," Lane wrote. For Beth, smoking pot enabled her to "feel lazy" and "waste ten hours" out of the day. "She used it to be a cool teenager. She did it for show," Lane wrote. "Drugs don't appeal to her now."

As far as alcohol, Beth usually passed out after three shots.

"She didn't like it but liked an occasional shot," Lane wrote. "She drank tequila, vodka, beer, wine, and champagne. She drank for show to fit in at parties. She claimed alcohol and drugs clouded her judgment."

In kindergarten, Beth liked to "play by herself" and described herself as being "confident, independent, and logical." But her grades initially deteriorated in 1998 and 1999 and really fell apart in 2002 and 2003.

Beth thought Doug Landers had the "mentality of a child" and was "short-tempered, verbally aggressive, intimidating, bullying, demeaning," and she was "afraid of him." She and Sandra were both verbally abused by him and she hated living at home when he was there.

"It was torture to live with him."

He had weak hearing and blasted the television at midnight or in the morning and woke her up when she was trying to sleep. She felt smarter than him and would contradict what he wanted her to do. He would yell at her and her sister.

Landers was "cruel and very simple," and "if you disagreed with him, he would beat you and make you agree with him," Beth told Lane.

Beth thought Landers moved out when she was about twelve, after their mother got a restraining order against him.

"He hit her with belt buckles," she told Lane.

In Grade 2 or 3, Beth said Landers gave her money to buy a specific book at a book fair but she bought a different one.

"She got beat for that," Lane wrote. "She disobeyed him just to infuriate him. She recalled being punished for the least little infraction."

Beth remembered when she was seven she was sick at home and her mother brought her some cereal but accidentally dropped the bowel.

"Her mother confronted her and she was afraid her stepfather would yell at her and beat her," Lane wrote. "Her stepfather would find reasons to destroy her possessions."

Her parents divorced when she was just two or three. Her mother couldn't tolerate her ex-husband's "tyranny." Her father was "very rigid" in that he always expected things to be done a certain way. She saw her father once or twice a month when she was growing, but they began to have more contact with him when she was about ten after Sandra asked to have more contact with him.

Because her family moved so much she ended up going to about ten different schools.

"She said her family's financial situation was very difficult,"

Lane wrote. "She described wearing shabby attire and was hungry at school. They had no money to buy food."

Despite her hard life, Beth's education didn't suffer. By Grade 3 she was in a gifted class and taught other students. She eventually shifted into an advanced class and was in French immersion from kindergarten to Grade 4.

"But she was frustrated moving to different school and used the word 'estrangement' to described her feelings about it," Lane wrote. As far as her schooling was concerned, Beth felt she was "meticulous" in her schoolwork and because of that often withdrew from others.

All Beth wanted to do before her mother's death was to "please her peer group" instead of "thinking for herself," Lane wrote. She wanted to drop out of high school and felt "not worthy" and "had no ambition."

But she now saw her future more clearly, Lane wrote.

"She wants to get her high school credit, and attend university and get a master's in psychology in order to understand people and their behaviour," Lane wrote. "She wants to get a law degree, She also intends to seek therapy."

Beth believed her mother's drinking began in her own teenage years in Holland and got worse after she gave birth to Sandra and her. She thought her mother made "poor choices" when it came to the men in her life.

"She blamed her mother for choosing a tyrannical boyfriend, who physically assaulted her," Lane wrote. "Her boyfriend exasperated her mother's drinking and forced her to drink.

"She wanted her mother to stop drinking. She tried to get help from her aunt Martha. But she denied her mother had a drinking problem and her uncle agreed with her."

Beth saw herself one day living on her own or with her new boyfriend, whom she didn't identify but said was twenty. She didn't think she could ever live with her father or her aunt and uncle again.

"She may live as a roommate with him (her boyfriend) and Sandra and her could share the costs," Lane wrote. "She also intends to seek therapy."

"She described herself in a play of words as 'loving to learn and 'learning to love.' "She's headstrong and battles issues that affect her. It was hard for her to accept kindness from people. She didn't think she deserved their kindness. She felt hideous when somebody did something nice for her. She had attachment issues. All of her life her trust has been betrayed. Beth has experienced a great deal of fear, despair, hopelessness, and anger in her young life. Now she strives in isolation."

The stress at home caused her to have sleeping problems as a child but that stressed vanished whenever she went to live with her maternal grandparents, Lane wrote.

"She had a feeling of being overwhelmed in life," Lane wrote. "She thought she was somewhat bipolar. In the past she had gotten emotionally high and then depressed. She felt there was way too much sacrificing in her family."

Beth admitted that she "wanted help" to deal with her issues. "She said it was a new thing for her to be able to step back and see her feelings and actions from a third person.

Beth also described herself as being previously passive, but now thought of herself as being far more assertive, although she believed she would fail in life if she weren't efficient in everything she did.

"At times she felt disgusted with herself for what she had done," Lane said.

She described herself as being headstrong and had trouble recognizing positives and dwelled on negatives. Lane continued, "Beth believed she's been a good role model for other offenders. She's organized reading groups, taught yoga, and tutored math to other offenders. She expressed surprise and was unaware that others thought of her as being somewhat demanding and unreasonable although she knew that she liked to have things done on her own terms. . . ."

Under house arrest, Beth told Lane she had two bunnies and two cats for pets.

"She said pets didn't get angry at you and they loved the warmth you gave them," Lane wrote.

Lane said Walter believed his daughters were "cooler" towards him as they got older.

"He said his daughters wanted to be more independent and he told them they could call him when they needed him," Lane wrote. "He described himself as being old-fashioned. He saw drinking and smoking as stupid."

Walter believed Beth was extremely focused on her health and exercise.

"She had been eating junk food a lot and that had a negative impact on her health," Lane wrote. "She learned a new way of nutrition from her father." The diet involved eating and preparing food that consisted primarily of 70 per cent fat, 20 per cent protein and a combination of carbohydrates.

"He told his daughters to get their education, find happiness, work to maintain food health and try to get a good job and arrange their life according to their own wishes," Lane wrote. "He stressed the mental, spiritual, and physical" aspect of their lives.

"He believed the murder was motivated by mental stress in their family not insurance money."

Martha said her nieces cooked most of their own meals when they lived with her because they stuck with their father's strict diet, instead of eating what they ate.

"Beth would like to get help and participate in treatment programs but she is adamant about what type of treatment she's to take and where she's to take it," Lane wrote. She also prefers to remain at Syl Apps. Beth was sorry for her involvement in the murder of her mother. She knows this will not bring her mother back. She cannot change what happened. The only thing she can do is to try to help as many people as she can. She didn't actually commit the physical act of murder. But she feels like a failure because she could not help her mother."

CHAPTER 27
THE BAD SEEDS

Forensic psychiatrist Phil Klassen testified for the defence at the sentencing hearing. The only question left unanswered was what really turned the two brilliant young students into mommy killers. Were Sandra and Beth monsters? Or sick, misguided youth? Did they believe their mother's alcoholism left them with only one course of action? Or were they greedy teenagers, who saw killing their mother as a means to get rich with her life insurance so they could run their lives? Were they psychopaths? Or manipulative, narcissistic teens—bad seeds—because of their environment?

Klassen was the deputy clinical director and associate head of education for the law and mental health program at the Centre for Addiction and Mental Health in Toronto. He reviewed statements, court documents, pre-sentence reports, and an assessment written by forensic psychologist Percy Wright. He spoke with Sandra for seven hours, and with Beth for five.

When he wrote his report, Klassen didn't mince words. He said Linda's murder met Sandra's need for status, attention, and power. "She was motivated by excitement or novelty in committing the crime. She was excited by the process of planning to kill her mother.... The fact so many needs might be met by a single action may have been one of the most intoxicating qualities of planning and affecting the murder. The planning and carrying out of crime was intoxicating for her to improve her life."

It met Sandra's need for "status, attention, and power," he said. It gave her "a sense of control over her environment." Her life experience "was deteriorating" because she wasn't able to get her mother to change or receive any help from family members or child welfare authorities.

Beth's role stemmed from a combination of influences of Sandra, and a "sense of loss of control, growing resentment, and uncoupling from more pro-social or corrective adult or peer influences," he said. He thought Sandra was the "principal driver [and] the engine of the murder," and that Beth, after some initial resistance, became a full partner in the enterprise. He said Beth's personality traits included a sense of loss of control, over-controlled hostility, and resentment.

Neither girl suffered from any major mental illness. They had very little in common except that they murdered their mother.

Klassen used a psychiatric test to rate the psycopathy of both girls. Sandra scored 22.4 out of 40, which put her in the 66th percentile among all incarcerated females in North America. Beth scored 13.7, a little higher than the average person, but a low to moderate score, and consistent with her history.

In his view, Sandra had a mild conduct disorder with adolescent onset, common to many teenage offenders. Even if she never received treatment, he didn't think she posed any significant risk to society.

"One of the most striking aspects of the murder was that all of their academically gifted and close friends not only did nothing to stop them but also encouraged them," he said.

"I've not seen one iota of resistance from anybody about the murder of their mother," Dr. Klassen said when he testified at their sentencing hearing. He was "stunned" how their friends, none with any previous criminal records, would be so "seemingly blasé" about the murder.

"They spoke and told them how to improve the plan."

One friend, Ashley, who knew about the murder in advance, described it like "watching a movie," he said.

"For them it was all about the drama, the excitement, the collaboration." He said many variables led to the murder: Sandra and Beth were both developing adolescents; they lived with an alcoholic mother; they believed nobody would help them; and all the adults in their world were dysfunctional in one way or another.

Their friends' cavalier attitude and approval "deepened their commitment" to murder their mother.

Unlike Magnus, Dr. Klassen didn't believe they would kill again. In his view, keeping them in a youth facility was also "a better fit."

"Sandra admitted a steep price was paid but she doesn't regret she was caught. The process saved her from a more problematic life and also removed the burden of secrecy weighing on her for more than a year."

In his view, Sandra's need to kill had more to do with her deep psychology than receiving a life insurance windfall. The murder was a "highly egocentric" and "distorted response" to what was happening in her life. Her "grandiose self-gratifying fantasies were fuelled by poorly channelled anger and resentment." Sandra has "moral vacuity" and shows narcissistic, histrionic and anti-social traits.

Even though both girls experienced a role reversal, in that they increasingly took on a role of the parent, it was still not an excuse for their "grievous behaviour," he said.

Sandra sought to make changes in her circumstances by contacting child welfare. They told their aunt about their concerns.

"This is no way justifies the murder of their mother but they did make every effort to bring changes to their circumstances."

Dr. Klassen said a "host of variables" had to be present for the murder to occur. These variables included the personal traits and inter-relationships of them and their friends. Sandra and Beth were both developing adolescents. They lived in a household with an alcoholic mother. They believed nobody would help them. Most important, all the adults in their world were dysfunctional in one way or another and contributed to their overall situation.

"There would not have been a dead mother if only one of these variables had been different. A lot had to go wrong for things to go terribly wrong."

Their mother was "falling off the radar screen" in terms of her responsibility and significant neglect, he said. The girls felt they were "emotionally abused" by their mother.

"It appears to be a tsunami of evidence that she was seriously alcoholic."

In many ways, his interview with Sandra was far more revealing, far more open and forthcoming, than Beth's.

Sandra wanted to marry one day and have a family and admitted she was "such a girl underneath the murder." She "loves to be loved." She wanted to be "reborn" again with her current knowledge "preferably into a rich family" and wanted to be "enlightened so wishes wouldn't matter."

She has dreams of being a pathologist, and a feature film director. She wants to write and direct and become "financially comfortable" making successful films under the "Andersen Films" name. She "feels like a millionaire already" and "all she needs is money."

Her films will "make people think." She wants to own a ranch and attend university and enjoy various recreational pastimes. She finds film director Alfred Hitchcock to be "funny" but admires Beatle John Lennon for his "love for humanity," and his "refusal to give up on people." Her role models are Thomas Edison, Albert Einstein, and Abraham Lincoln.

She believed her mother drank when she was pregnant. She didn't suffer from any childhood illnesses. Her parents told her she "cried for hours on end" as an infant. She was a quiet and shy girl growing up in a Roman Catholic family. Her parents divorced when she was four, and she had no memories of them living together. She didn't blame her father for any of the problems she had with her mother.

She said she was her own worst enemy; that she procrastinated and lied to herself. She made bad decisions and lacked discipline. She thought her best quality was her comedic genius.

Sandra now realizes her mother was sick and "could have been helped." She was surprised to learn her mother wasn't dying from cirrhosis of the liver.

She has a substance problem and always needs "instant gratification" from things in life. She often lied to her mother about completing homework, school attendance, and stealing money but wasn't "manipulative." She's impulsive, irresponsible, and lacking in self-discipline. At home, she was left to her own devices when it came to discipline.

Sandra admitted to having six different sexual partners but two of were more than one-night stands. Her first real sexual encounter happened inside a movie theatre with a friend as part of a dare.

"I tend not to back down from dares."

They spent all day in the movie theatre on one ticket. The

sex involved oral and genital stimulation. She wanted to lose her virginity and asked him to do it.

She was serious when she told Tucker Max she wanted to have a sexual relationship with him. She "talked her sister" into having a threesome sexual encounter.

"I guess I like to push her envelope."

Another sexual partner fell asleep during sex because they'd been drinking. She also had sex in her Aunt Martha's house while under house arrest.

At school, Sandra was "socially retarded" and always uncertain how to react to people. She described Ashley as her best friend, and said Ashley convinced her to become more socially acceptable by criticizing her posture, her weight, the way she talked, and the way she walked. Ashley manipulated her life and exploited her. At times she felt "attacked" by her. Ashley invited large groups of people to their home for parties. Ashley seemed giggly and told her "you have this homicidal look in your eyes."

Sandra enjoyed the attention she received from classmates, teachers, and friends when she returned to school after the murder. "I milked that so horribly."

She missed a lot of school afterwards but skipped classes even before her mother's death. She did drugs and drank before her mother died with "like-minded people" and people who "made it easier to get drugs."

She ran away from home three or four times and stayed out all night, usually ending up at her aunt's home. She has no previous criminal history and denies having any history of vandalism or fire setting. She stole candy from a store three times when she was younger. As a teenager, she shoplifted bras several times after her mother died even though she had money. She wanted to use the money for pot and alcohol.

Besides smoking pot, Sandra also did magic mushrooms at least six times as well as cocaine and amphetamines.

"She enjoyed mushrooms, feeling out of control, and hallucinating," Dr. Klassen wrote. "She wanted to sell drugs, but she always consumed them." She drank semi-regularly before her mother's death but then drank almost every day afterward, and every time she could get her hands on alcohol.

"She stole her Aunt Martha's liquor until she caught her. Afterwards, she asked friends to purchase it for her," Dr. Klassen wrote. "She felt unhappy without drugs. She said lying "drains and burdens your soul." Sandra said the "endless lies were killing" her but now she's "tasting freedom through honesty." She once carved the word "stop" into the back of her hand when drunk.

"She drank to overcome depression and anxiety but she rarely felt anger," Dr. Klassen wrote.

By the summer of 2002, Sandra believed her mother was a hopeless alcoholic, and the more critical she became of her mother's drinking, the more her mother drank. Instead of arguing with her, she "exploited her mother's drunkenness" by getting her to order food and give her money. She stole cash from her. She used drugs about six months in the year before her mother's death to "feel good" and "to laugh" and her behaviour deteriorated. She wanted someone to notice that everything was wrong, and to stop her. When they didn't, she continued to "push the envelope" by stealing money from her mother. Using pot, her future seemed "fuzzier and fuzzier." She stopped telling her mother about her life, neglected chores, skipped classes, and purposely failed classes.

"I was a mess."

"She felt certain her life would improve if her mother was dead," Dr. Klassen wrote. "She wanted her mother's alcoholism to stop and blamed it for everything. Her mother was bringing all of their lives down and was responsible for all of her pain in life."

Sandra convinced Beth to go along with her plan. She was surprised that people were upset when Linda died.

"She felt no one would be upset and everybody would see her mother's death as she did," Dr. Klassen wrote. "She was struck by seeing people crying over her mother's death."

Sandra cried at her mother's funeral and also helped her Aunt Martha dress their mother for the casket, an experience she described as being "unforgettable." Sandra, however, insisted she apologized to her mother during a private moment at her open casket.

Sandra became more isolated and consumed more drugs and alcohol. After the murder she skipped classes. She stopped believing that she would see her mother later and saw the murder as "a cold permanent outcome." She might have killed herself if she didn't go through with the murder but never intended on "harming" anybody else.

She and Beth became closer under house arrest. Beth was very depressed and upset. Beth would cry to her "I want my mommy!"

Sandra initially told Dr. Klassen that she got the Tylenol-3 pills from her mother's purse, but then requested another interview with him. This time she said Justin provided the pills. She initially lied because she didn't want to involve anybody else.

"All I ever do is hurt people."

Her family convinced her not to plead guilty.

She had no major mental illness such as schizophrenia or bipolar disorder; she suffered from a personality disorder and one or more substance abuse disorders. She had a number of personality features that could be considered criminogenic. She expressed a sense of entitlement to wealth. She wanted a life of leisure. She felt like God when she was murdering her mother.

Her father wasn't an "effective buffer" in regards to her problems with her mother. Her mother was raised in a privileged family in Holland, but rebelled by using alcohol and she experienced a downward drift in terms of her relationships with men.

"It appears Linda Andersen suffered severely from alcohol abuse disorder to the extent it interfered with her capacity for parenting, healthy attachments, and employment," Dr. Klassen wrote. "There was little structure in her home. She was easily manipulated. Her relationship with Edward Brockman was self-defeating."

In his view, Sandra possessed a number of personality features that could be considered criminogenic. She expressed a sense of "entitlement to wealth." She wanted to live with a "rich foster family." She seeks a life of leisure. She felt like "God" when she was murdering her mother.

He wrote:

She has been described as being drawn to power. I suspect she was envious of others in her immediate environment and experienced a feeling of shame and consequent rage at her socio-economic circumstances and at her mother's behaviour. She dislikes manifestations of weakness in herself or in her environment.

Shame, envy, and ultimately muted rage likely coalesced into feelings of contempt for her mother, contempt that led to her experiencing her mother in unidimensional terms, and which led to rationalization of justification; the benefits of the murder of her mother.

She was excited by the process of planning to kill her mother, and her subsequent self-disclosure may have been predicated on similar grounds.

In non-criminal ways, she seeks to have the upper hand in her relationships with others. She rejected her father's discipline. Her sense of not being able to reason with her aunt might be understood in her inability to manipulate her. Her behaviour towards her sister and teachers has been described as being manipulative. [Her] drive for power and willingness to manipulate in the service of that power are not typically part of the adolescent developmental course. When Sandra planned and carried out the murder, it was also about the same time she went from pubescent conformity to adolescent rebellion. It was also the same time Linda Andersen suffered from alcoholism and a loss of her ability to function. Sandra stepped into the power vacuum left by her mother's increasing dysfunction. Sandra might have tried to model her behaviour on her mother. Andersen appeared to be more emotionally needy than Sandra but both had difficulties with self-discipline, substance abuse, manipulation and facultative sexual behaviour.

As the parent-child boundaries dissolved in a milieu of alcohol abuse and loneliness it may at some level be that Sandra not only responded to what she saw but modeled on it. Her increasing parentification may also have contributed to feelings of omnipotence and entitlement.

Sandra had a history of conning others, of theft, of physical cruelty. All were signs of a relatively mild conduct disorder. Klassen wrote:
Sandra might best be diagnosed as seemingly suffering from a personality disorder with narcissistic, histrionic,

and anti-social traits. She presents anti-social traits insofar as there is a history of deceitfulness, a failure to plan ahead, reckless disregard for the safety or self or others, and a lack of remorse for her misdeeds. She presents some histrionics as she is attention seeking, her interaction with others is at times provocative, and her emotional expressions appear to be shallow. She presents some narcissistic traits as there is some evidence of grandiosity, fantasies of unlimited success, a sense of entitlement, a history of interpersonal exploitation, and difficulties with empathy. . . . Sandra does suffer from significant personality difficulties. There certainly is a sense of some degree of moral vacuity. Her relationships appear to be superficial. Her lines of thinking leading up to the murder show remarkable entitlement and rationalization. She appears to have suffered from one or more substance abuse disorders, currently in remission in a controlled environment.

Klassen turned to Beth.

He saw her as a perfectionist, detail-oriented, and said she was inclined towards stability, predictability, and a sense of control over her environment, but enjoyed little of this during her formative years.

"She is clearly intellectually endowed but socially awkward. She found solace in her mastery of her academic work. [Her] efforts to return the family home to a position of greater stability and security by means of attempting to enlist the assistance of relatives or child welfare agencies seemingly went unrewarded and perhaps contributed to her sense of a loss of control."

Beth's poor academic achievement had much to do with her feelings of hopelessness and meaninglessness and the inevitability of her mother's murder. In her, he saw tension, pessimism, hostility, and defiance.

"She became an active participant in the murder of her mother reportedly after a period of token resistance a perceived dearth of available alternatives, combined with a high degrees of resentment and bitterness, led her to participate."

Although she denied anger, in his view, Beth has significant levels and bitterness. She's been let down by others. She has feelings being repeatedly abandoned; he said Beth struggled with anger, tension, and emotional stress but did not have a conduct disorder.

Klassen wrote:

She meets many of the criteria for having a narcissistic personality disorder. She has some traits of grandiosity, entitlement, arrogance, and lack of empathy. Individuals with obsessive-compulsive traits often present with perfectionism, orderliness, and a need for mental and inter-personal control at the expense of others. They are prone to becoming upset or angry in situations in which they aren't able to maintain control. Individuals with passive-aggressive tendencies may be sullen [and] complain of being misunderstood or unappreciated by others. Self-confidence is often poor despite superficial bravado.

According to Klassen, Beth demonstrated some post-traumatic stress symptoms.

He continues:

It is not clear she does suffer from post-traumatic stress

but she reports nightmares and distressing recollections of various aspects of her childhood and of the [murder].

Her post-traumatic stress symptoms are more related to her persisted family difficulties than the murder. Beth's vulnerabilities would likely continue into adulthood.

There is a history of substance abuse and vulnerability.

Her thinking leading up to and including the murder was egocentric and lacked perspective and she was in a dependent position with respect to [Linda]. She [feels] down at times but perks up when she reads or does homework and spends her time writing in her journal and creating children's stories. She feels nothing worse can happen to her and denies she has any suicidal tendencies.

Beth told Klassen she had a major depressive disorder, an avoidant personality, a generalized anxiety disorder, and post-traumatic stress disorder. She also had a tic disorder. She thought she had narcissistic personality disorder and lacked empathy, although she didn't think she was arrogant. Klassen thought she was perfectionistic, controlled, and emotionally detached. She presented a resentful, hostile personality with intellectual insights, and her goals were more pro-social than anti-social. She wasn't particularly happy.

Asked about her mood following her mother's death, she said, "You can't work through a murder with a smile on your face."

She rated her mood a two out of ten in the days leading to the murder. She had suicidal thoughts but never attempted to kill herself and never had any plans to commit suicide despite feeling intensely depressed and upset after her mother's murder.

She didn't get out of bed for the first few months of her house arrest. She said nobody seemed to care. She admitted feeling anxious because she couldn't control her own fate. She used to have panic attacks that lasted from a few minutes to a few hours. Smells triggered certain memories. She never had delusions.

She said that when she was angry, she often insulted people, or became cynical or sarcastic towards them. She thought she might be passive-aggressive. She said she was never physically aggressive.

Klassen said many factors drove Beth to participate in the murder, among them peer influence, situational factors, and a lack of perspective.

In his view, Dr. Klassen said he didn't believe the sisters would kill again; he thought a youth facility was a good fit for both sisters. Recidivism among females, never mind adolescent females who commit violent crimes, is generally very low.

"There is little violent or criminal behaviour in their background particularly in comparison with the grievous nature of the predicate offence, does support the notion that developmental and situational factors were salient in the commission of the offence."

But both Beth and Sandra could be at risk of substance abuse, mental health problems, and aggression with a partner or children, he wrote. "When adolescent females convicted of serious violent offending do engage in criminal and criminally violent behaviour in their adult years this is often directed towards persons in their environment with whom they have a close relationship, for example children or intimate partners."

CHAPTER 28
THE SENTENCE

Prosecutors wanted an adult sentence.

The sisters knew the difference between right and wrong, Brian McGuire argued. "It was a planned and deliberate murder of the highest level." Only an adult sentence would hold the girls accountable.

Judge Duncan wasn't swayed.

On June 30, 2006, he ruled that Beth and Sandra would be sentenced as youths, placed in secured custody for no more than six years, then in open custody for four more years. (Canadian law allows a maximum ten-year penalty for youths convicted of the most serious criminal offence.) Their identities would be protected forever.

Had they been sentenced as adults, their names and photos could have been published. An adult sentence would also have been a life sentence in name only. In fact, Sandra would have simply been banned from seeking parole for ten years while Beth would have needed to wait between five and seven years before the National Parole Board could consider releasing her.

Judge Duncan left no doubt how he felt about them.

Until they were arrested, he said, their feelings about what they had done were at best ambiguous. Remorse, assuming it is truly present today, was a slow train coming. They carried out the plan with chilling detachment. Sandra held her mother's head under the water in the tub for four minutes while Beth stood or paced nearby. As they had hoped, the death was treated as an accident by authorities for almost a year, until Sandra revealed her secret to someone of conscience and character.

The offence was premeditated to an extreme degree. It was a plan months in the making. It was researched, discussed, and fine-tuned. There were plenty of opportunities to retreat or abandon the plan. Yet that never seemed to have even been considered. The debate seemed to be merely one of methods and logistics. Sandra and Beth also involved friends in the scheme, he said.

The plan was carried out without hesitation or falter and without abhorrence or revulsion or a flicker of moral compunction. Sandra, by her own admission, savoured every moment, and the defendants followed through with their pre-planned false alibi and cover-up, including an Oscar performance in the 911 call and during the subsequent police investigation.

In their favour, Judge Duncan noted they sought a "humane way to kill" and the act was carried out "without cruelty or unnecessary infliction of pain."

He praised them for their openness with the people who interviewed them for pre-sentencing and psychiatric reports, and for not trying to take the stand to lie their way out of their predicament. Then he said, "These girls at one time loved their mother. The circumstances that turned love to hate were not [of] their making. The adults in their life created their environment and left them to cope and find a solution."

He agreed with Dr. Klassen that none of their friends did anything to stop them, and he agreed with defence lawyer Jack

McCulligh that these friends shared some of the blame for what eventually happened.

He noted how McCulligh told the court "Had any of them made one phone call (to police), three lives could have been saved," McCulligh said in his sentencing arguments. He also noted the sisters' clean records, then described their home life: "They appeared to experience the same sorts of anxieties as many teenage girls and were socially awkward. Linda Andersen did have a serious drinking problem and her children deeply felt the effects materially and emotionally. Her children suffered a level of poverty not in keeping with her relatively good income. They were left with age inappropriate responsibilities for maintaining the house, and in particular in raising and caring for Bobby." There was a "lack of parental guidance, authority and companionship." He described their home atmosphere as being "depressing" and "degrading."

"They saw she (mother) was not there for them. Not that she was working double shifts to provide for them. They saw her as a passed out drunk. Not an exhausted mother trying to cope and taking comfort in alcohol."

By the end of summer of 2002 there was little positive to be seen, he said. The impact of Linda's drinking on her family reached a "critical level." Their feelings were aggravated by what must have been lingering resentment towards her for having brought Doug Landers and his abuse into their lives. It was further compounded by their frustration in being left to find "a solution" to what they perceived to be an "intractable problem" neither their mother nor any other adult would acknowledge.

"I find the combination of these factors caused the defendants to develop a mindset that was a complex of hatred and pity towards their mother, concern for their own future, and for Bobby's, a longing for things to be better both emotionally and financially, and a hopelessness that things would ever change on their own or any adult would intervene. From this mindset, their teenage minds came up with a grim and extreme solution."

Unlike Magnus and Pulley, and to some extent the prosecutors, Judge Duncan didn't find their mother's life insurance money played a "dominant role" in their vision of a better future with mother being dead. He thought Sandra was deeply troubled by what she had done, and that she felt compelled to talk to others about it. "Up until her arrest, I do not think it could be said she was remorseful. In fact, I think she was still inclined to think she did the right thing in the circumstances as she felt them to be at the time." Since their arrest, both girls had gone through considerable introspection and were genuinely remorseful, he added.

He saw neither sister as any danger to the public; he thought the public could be properly protected, and the sisters rehabilitated by a youth sentence.

Parliament could have enacted any punishment for murder under the Youth Criminal Justice Act [YCJA]—ten years, twenty years, or life. But ten years was chosen as a maximum. In providing for the punishment, Parliament has determined such punishment is both consistent with the principles of the YCJA, consistent with sentencing principles generally, and capable of being sufficient to hold the offender accountable in the cases to which it applies, namely first- or second-degree murder. Whatever the Court or . . . the public thinks of the sufficiency of that sentence, Parliament has determined it is capable of being sufficient to hold the offender to account.

Their offence was premeditated to an extreme degree. The defendants are not intellectually challenged. Far from it. Neither was suffering from any psychiatric or psychological disorder or impairment. Their plan was the product of fully functioning, unusually bright minds. Clearly the degree of participation and responsibility is very high for both defendants. There is some distinction between the two. Sandra, the elder, conceived the idea and brought Beth into it. Sandra was the one who actually committed the act of murder.

They were probably more mature than most [youthful offenders] due to their intelligence, life experience, and the responsibilities that were thrust upon them. On the other hand, they had little guidance or positive parental influence and were largely left to develop their own value system. Despite these factors, they did not otherwise get involved in criminal or serious anti-social activity or develop criminal ideation.... Their conduct in custody has been exemplary.

Judge Duncan said that all of these features—their ages, lack of a record, the situational nature of the crime, co-operation, compliance, and progress in custody—demonstrate [that] the prospects for their rehabilitation and re-integration into society are excellent and their risk of re-offending is low.

Would a youth sentence hold them sufficiently accountable? Judge Duncan said:

It cannot be said the maximum youth sentence ... is not a meaningful consequence. It represents, in total, more than half their lives so far. To the contrary, it permits some allowances for the mitigating circumstances while the adult sentence does not. It cannot be said it is not proportionate to the offence. It is the most serious punishment provided by law for the most serious offence committed by one who is to be treated as a youth.

The decision for Beth was easy. The sentence was of "sufficient length" to hold her accountable. But Sandra was more difficult because she bore a greater degree of responsibility. The law asks the Court to treat similar cases in a similar way and nothing would be more similar in this case than Beth's case.

While Sandra's case differs from Beth's, it's not . . . different [enough] to justify the huge disparity [that] would result from subjecting her to an adult sentence.

They had already spent nine months in pre-sentence custody and had been under house arrest for about 21 months. They appeared to have abided by all of the conditions of their bail release. As a result, he gave them credit, at least on paper, for eighteen months for time in custody and on bail.

In the end, Judge Duncan decided to only use the time served credit of 18 months in pre-trial custody in his decision to choose a youth sentence over an adult.

"In my view it would be wrong to deduct it from the eventual sentence imposed. The law requires time spent in custody be taken into account, no that it should be counted twice. Accordingly, the sentence will be the maximum with no further credit for the pre-sentence detention."

Defence attorneys had asked that Sandra be sentenced under intensive rehabilitative custody supervision, but Judge Duncan said she didn't meet the necessary requirements—a mental illness or disorder, a psychological disorder, or an emotional illness that required treatment.

Because she was twenty, Sandra had to serve her youth sentence in an adult facility. Beth, nineteen, remained in a youth facility. Both were ordered to submit DNA samples for the national DNA databank. The judge also ordered the forfeiture of the life insurance money as proceeds of crime.

Outside the courtroom, Jack McCulligh, Sandra's attorney, said, "They have a chance to do something with their lives. They're talented young women who have learned from the experience."

In years, there wasn't much of a difference between an adult and youth sentence.

Had they been sentenced as adults, those sentences would have carried a life component. But even McGuire conceded they would have been paroled after ten years. McGuire also condeded their "minimal risks" didn't require them to be monitored for life.

Sandra started her youth sentence in an adult provincial facility, but was transferred a few months later to Grand Valley Institution, a federal women's penitentiary in Kitchener, Ontario. Grand Valley more or less is a campus-style prison and includeds a secured unit that holds 15 maximum-security inmates, which is where Sandra was placed. Beth, meanwhile, returned to the Syl Apps Youth Centre in Oakville, Ontario.

When Sandra was transferred to Grand Valley in September 2006, she became eligible for government-paid university courses. She could also have family visits of seventy-two hours.

At her transfer hearing, her new attorney, Stephen Gehl, said she wanted to become a social worker or a psychiatrist: "She is desirous to get on with her life. She hopes one day to become a functioning and useful and productive member of society."

According to court documents, Sandra had been under protective custody at Vanier. When she was transferred to Grand Valley she requested to be moved into the general population.

She could also get counselling.

CHAPTER 29
LOOSE ENDS

Had the murder occurred in the United States, no doubt the Bathtub Girls would have been discussed nightly by crime commentators Nancy Grace, Larry King, and Greta Van Susteren, Court TV anchors, and an assortment of crime and court analysts on CNN, Fox News, and MSNBC. Someone would have dubbed them the Menendez Daughters—a reference to the high-profile California brothers Lyle and Erik, who after years of emotional, physical, and sexual abuse murdered their parents.

The Bathtub Girls were never mentioned by a major American media outlet.

Then Sandra contacted the Tucker Max website, and thousands of people read about the sisters on www.tuckermax.com. According to site operator Luke Heidelberg, the site receives thirty million hits annually.

Sandra used the website's message board to post information about her trial and to describe the allegations against her. In one of her thirty posts she said a young relative had been sexually assaulting her for years. She also posted three nude and several sexually explicit photos of herself. One was sent at 4:22 a.m. on December 15, 2005—about nine hours before she and

Beth were convicted. She logged into the website again at 8:16 a.m., one of the last things she did as a free woman.

Prosecutors and defence attorneys had no idea the site existed, never mind that Sandra had been posting blogs and sending emails to Tucker Max. Peel Police never knew about it either. Even their friends never knew about Sandra's online antics until a Toronto reporter covering the case revealed the existence of the site to Magnus just before Christmas 2005.

Some of Sandra's blogs provided information that hadn't been presented at the trial. Soon after she began posting information, a companion site—www.murderingwhores.com—was launched. The new site described the case as "Canada's Murdering Whores—Two Canadian whores—One alcoholic mother—A wacky feel-good murder case that's fun for the whole family." The site posted all the latest news about the trial and asked visitors to vote for Canada's hottest murdering whore. Sandra clearly out-shone her nearest rival, Karla Homolka—the ex-wife of Canada's notorious sex predator and killer, Paul Bernardo. Homolka spent twelve years in prison for manslaughter in return for testifying against Bernardo, who was sentenced to life in prison and later declared a dangerous offender. He committed fouteen rapes during a reign of terror in Toronto. He murdered two young teenagers girls, and with Homolka's help, drugged and raped her fourteen-year-old sister, who died after choking on vomit.

Visitors to the site offered comments about Sandra:

"I bet she drowns the competition."

"Better leave it up for a while I'd hate for someone to pull the plug too soon."

"I'd hate to see this idea go down the drain."

Sandra sent her first email to Tucker Max in early September 2005, several weeks before her trial began. Using the name "Sunshine," she sent a series of blogs to the message board.

Who is Tucker Max? In the biographical section of his website he says: "My mother told me I could grow up to be anything I wanted. So I became an asshole." His favourite celebrity is Sirhan Sirhan. The former Duke law student was born in Atlanta in 1975 and grew up in Kentucky. He's the author of several books, including the *New York Times* bestseller *I Hope They Serve Beer in Hell*. He describes himself this way: "My name is Tucker Max and I'm an asshole. I get excessively drunk at inappropriate times, disregard social norms, indulge every whim, ignore the consequences of my actions, sleep with more women than is safe, or reasonable, and just generally act like a raging dickhead. But I do contribute to humanity in one important way. I share my adventures with the world. They are known as the Tucker Max Stories."

Heidelberger, director of information technology for Max's company, Rudius Media, said his friend and employer "defies convention" and "rebels against the notion that you have to do things a certain way."

Information from the murderingwhores site was discovered too late for prosecutors to use at the sisters' trial, but was included in the documentation given to Judge Duncan for the sentencing phase, to probation officers preparing pre-sentence reports, and to forensic psychiatrist Phil Klassen.

In her first email to Tucker Max, two months before the trial, on September 7, 2005, Sandra said she was nineteen and from Canada. She wrote: "I love you. Damn smart motherfucker. We'll fuck one day when my legal issues clear up and I can leave the country. You seem like one of the few sane people alive. I'll send you some pictures later."

Max didn't immediately reply. He explained: "I get emails from girls wanting to hook me up all day."

Beth sent Max an email at 11:28 p.m. that night. The subject line said, "Do you do threesomes (sisters)? NEED RESPONSE." The text of the message said, "What would you like to see two girls do to each other and to you? We're eighteen and nineteen." The email was signed "Beth and Sandra."

Max replied one minute later:

"Baby I used to date a bisexual girl. Of course, I like threesomes. Where do you live?"

Beth replied: "You didn't answer our question. Toronto."

Max answered: "Fuck, of course. What else would we do? Read to each other?"

By this time Max was intrigued. He'd never had sex with two sisters at the same time.

A few days later, Sandra posted several provocative photos. In the first, she was a topless, wearing only a man's necktie and a hat. In the second, she wore a one-piece bathing suit. Her back was against a life-size picture of Doors lead singer Jimmy Morrison. Sandra also sent two photos of Beth. In one she wore a Roaring Twenties-style dress. In the other, she leaned against a tree wearing a large Cat in the Hat outfit and holding a Canadian flag.

At 9:57 a.m. on October 5—about a month before the trial—Sandra and Max exchanged sexual emails again, this time under the subject "Tucker Made My Day."

"I dreamt about you fucking me four times last night. It was awesome," Sandra wrote.

Two minutes later, Max replied. "Toronto is not far from Chicago. Come down and I will."

Sandra: "We will. Just not now. Do you go to bars with girls that are under twenty-one?"

Max: "If you have ID, yeah of course."

On October 6, Sandra signed up as an official contributor to the message board. In the biography section of the sign-up, she wrote, "When life gets hard, fuck it." She said her interests included reading, writing, and masturbating. Under occupation she wrote, "Ha ha—I'm an artiste."

That night Max asked Sandra about her Hallowe'en costume. She replied: "A while ago, I was arrested naked. I walked out of jail in their full getup so now I have a costume."

On October 7, at 11:37 a.m., Sandra revealed more: "Once upon a time, I found myself in the surprising situation of incarceration, with many lovely ladies to spend my days with. Most of them were seventeen to nineteen-year-old crack whores. At first, I silently passed my days reading and as an observer. But before I knew it, girls were spilling their guts to me, and then taking me for a friend (other than the fact that no one had any friends in that hell). The whore babbles were never ending, so one day I suggested a game of chess. Long story short, I ended up teaching half a dozen crack-addicted prostitutes how to position chess pieces on the board. A few of them managed to master the knight's movement."

At 10:30 p.m., Sandra posted another blog: "Once upon a time . . . I'm about to start trial (end of October) and it'll be in the papers, so I can't give any good details until it clears up. I'm looking at a life sentence over stories that were told by me and believed by kids. One guy had a camera hidden in his car, so he caught my bullshit. Now I'm under house arrest. If I'm not convicted, I'll fill in the specifics. I can't explain more because my lawyers will crucify me. In response to someone, I'm not a pedophile, just a nineteen-year-old girl. I meant 'teens' when I said 'kids' because they're kids to me. Someone died in an accident and I'm getting blamed. I am in awe of my stupidity. Regardless of the verdict, my story will be posted somewhere. The trial will take a few months though. Only MMMEEEEEEEEEEEE!!!"

On October 10, at 11:28 p.m., in response to a request for favourite daydreams, Sandra wrote: "I daydream about being a famous movie director/writer. Once I'm rich enough, I'll own some land in foreign countries where I won't overpay for a horse ranch or the help. I'd own a manor with my personal wing (off limits to my damn family). The servants' wing would be facing east, so that they can rise with the sun. Mine would be facing North-north-west. I'd like a few orchards so that I can pass out in them with no fear of ever being disturbed. And with my millions of dollars, I'd afford nannies and tutors for my many children, so that my kids can learn languages and an instrument of their choice. I'd spend my time travelling and doing tons of crazy shit. I'd learn to surf. I'd scuba with whales. I can go on and on. If I end up being ridiculously lucky, I'll also find a husband who'll like sticking around and fucking me everywhere. Otherwise, I'll be nice to my young, manly help. I give myself ten years before I'll be publicly rich."

On October 13, at 4:34 p.m., in response to a request for info about the most incredible fight you'd been in, Sandra wrote: "My sister and I have been to hell and back together. We've also learned how to provoke insane fits of rage in one another. Many girl-on-girl amateur wrestling sessions have resulted. A few years back, we were home alone and watching TV together. We were sitting in opposite ends of the room. We started arguing, probably about what to watch. Before I knew it, my sister whipped the TV remote at my head, effectively breaking both. I screamed and jumped up so she ran into the kitchen. She grabbed a GOD-DAMN BUTCHER KNIFE!! This freaked me out a bit so I made it to my room and grabbed a tennis racket. That's as interesting as that got. We faced each other and yelled for a while before putting our 'weapons' down. Pretty soon we were laughing about our sisterly love. I ended up telling our Mom that I stepped on the remote, seeing how I was the one who broke it. The welt on my head was hidden by my hair. Angry people are funny."

On October 15, at 3:38 a.m., Sandra replied to the question "What makes you happy?:" "My understanding of happiness is the right balance in fulfilling the needs of the body, mind, and soul. I'm still working on figuring out my balance. Things that make me sinfully happy are beer, sex, certain stories, and some of my dreams. I also like to push the envelope. My Dad taught me pain is inevitable, suffering is optional."

On October 18, at 5:10 p.m., Sandra replied to a request for info about overcoming addictions or experiences involving interdictions. Under the heading "Mother You Had Me But I Never Had You," Sandra wrote:

"I've learned more than I ever thought possible. Maybe that's because I keep fucking up. If anything, I'm learning how to deal with any possible shit that can be flung at me. I'm bipolar and an alcoholic. But I've got a lot of potential. Fuck. Anyways, I'm up to my ears in shit.

"I feel as though I'm walking on the edge of a knife. This is corny but my understanding of love and the soul keeps me sane. I love my sister and my soul is worth whatever I'm accomplishing. Only my death will hinder the realization of my goals. Luckily, I'm still young."

On October 19, at 8:56 p.m., Sandra wrote about the day of their arrest:

One night, I was up until 4 a.m. There was to be no school that morning because the term had ended and students were writing exams. I had no exams so I was planning on watching movies and drinking beer with a friend. I drifted off to sleep without setting my alarm clock.

"Sandra!"

"What the fuck is going on?"

"Sandra!"

Holy shit there's a lady in a suit blinding me with a flashlight.

"Get up!"

"No, I'm naked." (I sleep naked.)

I sit up. I grope for my pjs, which are under my pillow.

"Don't move! Show me your hands!"

Now there's a uniformed male officer in my room too. The house is alive with heavy footsteps. I am utterly confused. I absent-mindedly keep searching for my pjs when the woman grabs my arms and yells, "Show me your hands!"

They're empty and two male officers are getting a free show because now I'm fully exposed to them.

The lady shows me a badge and arrests me. She undoes the cuffs so that I can pull my pyjama top on. I put the bottoms on with the cuffs double locked. She hands me mismatched socks and after telling me not to say anything to anyone, leads me upstairs. She undoes my cuffs so that I can put my winter jacket on and locks them before I put my boots on. I end up leaving in my sneakers.

From the time that the cops appeared at my door to the moment where they drove away with me, nine minutes had passed. Then I spent eleven hours in an interview room. Also, I now know what a paddy wagon is.

All of these events seem entirely surreal. How the fuck did everything get so insanely out of control?

On October 25, at 10:23 p.m., in reply to a question about who inspires you, Sandra wrote: "I'm inspired beyond words by Leonardo da Vinci. I can't think of anyone who would be greater to talk with. I'm also deeply impressed with Abraham Lincoln. The accomplishments that these personalities represent blow my mind."

On November 1, at 2:00 a.m., seven days before the trial began, Sandra posted a naked shot of herself kneeling on a table and a second shot in which she was topless, standing in her bedroom, holding a feather between her breasts and wearing sunglasses. She told Max the first picture was a few months old and the second had just been snapped.

On November 3, at 11:27 p.m., in reply to a question about how you'd react if you were a celebrity, Sandra wrote: "I would travel and surf, and write children's books for a living. Maybe some books about travelling and surfing as well. I'd make some movies too. I'd ride horses and surf in my movies. I'd have a casting couch. I'd also buy a small plane and learn to fly it. I'd love to tip everywhere with fives and twenties.

"If I could afford it, I'd be myself all the time. Instead of being quiet and polite, I wouldn't spend my time around people that I didn't like. I'd probably get some goats on my ranch and spend time with them. And I'd make goat cheese."

On November 24, at 7:27 p.m., Sandra replied to a question asking what people were thankful for. "Never approach a goat from the front, a horse from behind, or a fool from any side. I'd be thankful if I wasn't surrounded by fools."

Twenty minutes later she wrote: "I am thankful that I am Sandra. I'm content that I can breathe and laugh. I'm surprised and overwhelmed at the unsurpassable quality of love that a few people have shown me. I do not deserve any of it. This developed at a time where many more people than I know want me to hang or rot somewhere. Fuck I'm thankful for life in its entirety, even the red dots that pepper my validation."

On November 25, at 9:32 p.m., Sandra answered a request for info about inner secrets. "My cousin sexually abused me for years. He still lives in the same house as I do. I can't get away for a few more weeks because I'm under house arrest. I want to take a shotgun to his balls. I have too many secrets."

On November 26, at 1:54 p.m., she posted a message titled, "I Can't Get Away."

"By 'get away' I mean that I can't move away for now. The last time that he cornered me, I stopped him from putting me through hell by freaking out loudly. It worked well enough. Occasionally, he'll still grab me and do light and quick things, but these are easy enough to walk off. What's the one thing that's true everywhere? This too shall pass. I get raped and I walk it off. I feel fucking crazy.

"Ah well. It's such a nice day today. Here's another secret: I'm a retarded optimist.

"And one more: The fisting thread inspired me to give it a try, so I got out my lube and went to work. Eventually, I was slipping my fingers in to the third knuckle. At this point I got impatient and came all over my bathrobe anyways. Looks like I have some more work to do tonight. And some laundry."

The next day, at 9:28 p.m., Sandra wrote in reply to a request for secrets:

I don't believe in sin or salvation. As a child, I teased my girl cousin about being skinny. She was fat when I saw her a few months later. I teased her about being fat and now she's an anorexic. I thought she had a thicker skin.

I convinced two vegetarians to start eating meat again.

I once stole $1200.

I managed to talk someone into writing about twelve essays within a week for me. The story isn't interesting. I was simply amazed that it worked. It was for a course that was due that month and I had put off doing it all year long.

I somehow convinced a parent to call my school and tell them that I was on vacation for a week. All I did was waste my time wandering around.

I've consciously lied every time I was in a confessional. I didn't want to be there.

In Europe, just like my mom, I stole countless bottles of booze from my retired engineer grandparents. They had so many wines, cognacs, vodkas, everything that they never noticed...until I started coming home drunk. I never want to black out again. Apparently I'm an animal.

I want to film Hamlet *in its entirety. I already have an Ophelia and maybe a Hamlet. My interpretation is that they fuck. I don't think that I can start this within this year. If need be, I'll devote years to this.*

I don't channel my energies well. I like sunshine and I love the lack of it.

The murderingwhores website got about 35,000 hits daily when it went on line in December 2005. By the end of January 2006, it had had more than 400,000 visitors. The idea for the site came to Heidelberger on Christmas Eve 2005. He was drinking a few beers and working on a project when he thought it would be cool to create a site devoted entirely to the "wacky" Canadian sisters. He contacted Max, and the site was running within a few days. Heidelberger was a network engineer and Linux systems

administrator when he discovered the Tucker Max website in
early 2003. Max and Heidelberger soon became friends, and
Heidelberger started handling the website's technical side part-
time. After he created murderingwhores.com he became mod-
erator for the Tucker Max message board. By March 2006, he
was a full-time employee for Rudius Media. Heidelberger said:

> Most of the people who visit the Tucker Max website
> keep their crazy at least somewhat disguised. However,
> about ten per cent are clearly a little wacko. So when
> people make extraordinary claims, [we] generally tend
> to be a little leery. A good number of the people who
> say they want to sleep with Tucker aren't really that bal-
> anced to begin with. But these two Canadian girls took
> the cake. From the emails we got and information from
> people who knew them, it really sounded like the sisters
> were textbook sociopaths. It seemed like their mother
> certainly wasn't the mother of the year, but this case
> seemed twisted in so many ways.

Max never posted any information until he read about
their conviction in the newspaper:

> I realized they were telling the truth and I thought it
> was pretty funny. She [Sandra] started posting on my
> message board and started making these vague allu-
> sions to certain things. She mentioned house arrest and
> whatever. But I didn't pay too much attention to it. I
> didn't really care. But then she started writing more
> and more. I didn't think she and her sister were going
> to come and hook up with me. I wasn't going to go to
> Toronto. I had no idea if what she was telling me was
> true [and] I really didn't care.... This place, the Tucker

Max Message Board, has had a long, weird three-year history. We have seen underage girls pretend to be old. We've seen old women pretend to be young. We've seen faux-superheroes get owned, military posers get their shit called, pedophiles called out. Trashing, throwing, Guido gets fired, an engagement that began here, prostitution deals struck here, and just about everything in between. And this doesn't count the shit that I've done. But we've never had a convicted murderer on the board. . . . You don't get many criminals posting messages every day on a message board. They sent information. She [Sandra] killed her mom. You don't expect normalcy from this girl. Clearly she wasn't a professional killer. She was just a really fucked up girl.

Heidelberger said, "It appeared from her postings that she and her sister really expected to walk out of the courtroom after being acquitted. I'm not sure if it was a denial, hubris, or bravado, but in my opinion, Sandra didn't appear to think this would be the last post she would make for several years. She even spent the last few moments of freedom surfing the message board."

On January 13, 2006, at 11:23 p.m., murderingwhores.com received an email from "Ominous Anonymous."

Be forewarned . . . that your site is offensive enough that you have most certainly already upset more people than me and I cannot stress enough that I myself found it hard not to want to attack back. Others may not have that reserve. I wouldn't worry too much, however, as chances are no one would ever attempt retribution.

Think about we who deserve no more pain. I am not a bad person. I am not in any negative lights. I'm a decaying soul who has witnessed more world-ending misery in the past few years than anyone should ever see. Think about a person in my position, who has been brought to their knees, who has defended their friends at the sake of their own credibility against the world. I will not say for sure whether the verdict is fair or not, as it is no longer a question as far as legality is concerned. It is now a moot point, and along with it is gossip and insults that now continue to decay what I have strived to hold onto through all that has happened. They have a family. They have friends. And none of us deserve to be put through any more than we already have. I implore you from the depths of my soul just to end it.

We are suffering no longer at the hands of onlookers, media, and the police. Now we are suffering from [what] you have created.

The laughs and random enjoyment that site browsers are deriving means nothing to them. It doesn't tear away at the remaining parts of their souls. They can happily laugh it off and walk away. Such is not the case for us. I wish I could show you the pain we have felt.... For those involved, this has been horrific, and endless. We need no more pain. We need no more crying. We need a chance to try and scrape up our pieces before they are blown apart once again. It is a struggle to maintain sanity. And people's needless hate is tearing us apart.

You may all think this case is clear and that they are terrible people, but why on earth would I be begging in such a degrading way if I felt such things were true?

When you have good friends, it's hard not to defend them but efforts to defend are quickly stomped out when phrases such as "the friend of murderers" destroy what shred of credibility we have left. You have caused a pain that no one in this country could have caused. You have put faces and names together with stories and allowed anyone with a computer access to this right, which should not be one they hold.

You may feel that since the girls' lives are already destroyed, it hurts no one to continue positing methods for others to learn hate but it destroys lives of those of us who did nothing to deserve this. You have told the world something that Canadian law would have easily suppressed had it not been for the girls' foolish postings.

Just after midnight on March 13, 2006, a person using a female name sent a message to murderingwhores.com with the title "U THINK U ARE SMART, EH!"

I am appalled to see that u posted their names. No offence but it is against the law to publish their names under the youth criminal act. They are protected. If their names are not removed I will be informing their aunt of this website. I don't agree with what they did but I think you should respect their right to privacy. Remember you don't know what was really going on in their heads that had a lot happen to them and these so-called friends should know about it. And as for my friends that killed their mom you didn't really know them if all you can do is talk shit about them for real. They may have killed their mom but they were good to me. And I will always stay at their side no matter what cause THAT IS WHAT FRIENDS ARE FOR. You got one week to take their names off this site or else u will face the heat just like they are you asshole.

Several concerned readers warned Max he might be breaking some laws by posting nude photos, particularly if the pictures were taken before Sandra turned eighteen. Some people
thought Max was playing with fire by publishing their real
names, because such information was prohibited in Canada.

Max never worried.

"Look, I didn't find them, they found me. Everything she
[Sandra] posted on the site was posted by her, not me. It's not
like I went and found her and coerced her into putting things
on my message board. It's their business if they want to use
their real names. They posted them. Not me. It's not my fault. I
didn't kill their mom."

Justin

Justin was an enigma in the story of the Bathtub Girls. Even
after a jury found him guilty in December 2006 of conspiracy
to commit murder, he maintained his innocence. He thought
the sisters' murder plans were a joke, and he never thought they
would drown their mother.

On February 5, 2007, Madame Justice Francine Van Melle
sentenced Justin to a year in jail and an additional six-month conditional sentence. He immediately appealed his conviction and
was freed within a day. His fate is in the hands of a higher court.

Justin played a role in the story of the murderous daughters. But what role did he play, morally, ethically, and legally?

Jurors legally couldn't reveal why they convicted Justin but
it seemed clear they must have been convinced he offered real
advice on how to murder Linda Andersen when he chatted
online with Beth just five days before the murder. To convict
him, jurors must have believed Cantlon; Justin was either a full

member of a three-way party to murder Linda, or he helped, assisted, and encouraged the sisters to plan and carry out the murder, including helping them with their alibi.

The morning of December 4, 2006, Sandra testified against Justin as a Crown witness. It was the first and only time she spoke in public about her mother's murder, and she took centre stage. Craving attention was in her nature.

According to Sandra, Justin gave Beth the Tylenol-3s. Then Beth gave the pills to Sandra in a sandwich bag. Sandra thought she gave her mother at least four pills; she threw the rest away. Her mother had bought alcohol the day of her death or the day before. About a week before the murder, Beth said Justin was meeting them at Jack Astor's. "My sister told me Justin was coming and he was assisting with the alibi," Sandra said in court. Beth had a relationship with Justin, but Sandra didn't know him very well.

Defence attorney Alison Mackay asked Sandra why she initially told police she got the Tylenol-3s from her mother, and not from Justin.

"I didn't want to involve anybody else," Sandra answered. "In my mind, it didn't really matter what Justin did or didn't do because I would have still gone ahead. I told the police my sister was only five per cent involved but I wanted to say zero. I was the only one that did almost everything. Today, that's still my belief."

Justin never took the stand. MacKay never called a single witness.

In his closing argument, Cantlon said that when Justin provided Beth with Tylenol-3s, he was "putting bullets into a gun used as a murder weapon." The disturbing online chat between Justin and Beth five days before Linda's murder was like "a wiretap of a mob hitman about to kill someone." There was more than enough evidence to show Justin "assisted and encouraged" the sisters to murder their mother—either as a "full partner in a three-way murder plot" or a "party" to the crime committed by the sisters. Justin, then just fifteen, had offered advice and knew specific details about their plan, Cantlon reminded the jury. Justin told them what to do if Linda suddenly woke up while being killed. He gave them an alibi. He provided the Tylenol-3s they used to render their mother nearly unconscious before drowning her, Cantlon called the online chats "a recipe for murder."

When Justin was arrested on August 13, 2004, and presented with his incriminating chat, again, Justin told Detective Mark Armstrong the conversation was nothing but "hot air" and he was merely "talking shit with his friend" and that they always talked "stupid stuff because it's funny."

Cantlon told jurors that Justin was one of five people who knew the murder was going to take place. He was the person who suggested they go to Jack Astor's afterwards for a nice celebration dinner. The chats showed that Justin wanted to help, and that he also wanted to be there when the murder took place.

Justin's extremely incriminating interview of January 21, 2004, the day of the girls' arrest, was never presented in full to the jury hearing his trial. But jurors did hear how he had access to codeine pills because his mother had been prescribed one hundred pills in late 2001 for a chronic jaw problem.

Mackay said Linda's death was a tragedy, but urged jurors not to create another tragedy by convicting her client. She said the murder chat might not have been a joke for Beth, but it was certainly a joke for Justin. She described the chat as "ridiculous banter" that involved drugs, music, skipping school, and sex. She reminded jurors how Beth and Justin "laughed" throughout their chat and she insisted Justin's role was merely "bravado to impress a wild girl" and nothing more.

"Do you really believe a fifteen-year-old boy would seriously talk about murdering a woman whom he didn't know with a girl, whom might have had a crush on him, but he barely knew?" Mackay asked jurors. "It was late at night. He was tired. He was studying for a drama exam. He was role-playing, not having a serious conversation about a murder. It's a scary thought to think a fifteen-year-old boy talking nonsense to a girl, who might not be talking nonsense, could be convicted."

Mackay reminded jurors there was no evidence that Sandra spoke to Justin about the murder. She also suggested Sandra might have been lying when she testified that Beth told her Justin gave her the Tylenol-3s. Then she asked the jurors to consider Sandra might have been telling the truth when she initially told police she got the pills from her mother's purse.

In the end, the jurors needed less than four hours to convict.

Cantlon asked the court to sentence Justin to three years in custody, the maximum allowed under Canada's Youth Criminal Justice Act for a conspiracy-to-murder charge. Mackay suggesting he was already rehabilitated and urged the court to keep him out of jail.

Madame Justice Van Melle noted from his pre-sentence report that Justin was a model child at home and in school. The present charges came as a shock to the parents. They believe he did not do it. They could not match up the image of a model boy in the offence.

But she was also concerned by some of things in the pre-sentenced report.

He stated his email chat with the girls, who killed the mother, was a joke. He admitted it was in bad taste, but that was all. When the probation officer asked him why he had not been suspicious after their mother was killed, he said the thought had crossed his mind. But he refused to consider it. He said it was too absurd to think it would have happened.

Justice Van Melle also noted that Justin had no previous criminal record, and before his involvement in this case there was no evidence to suggest he presented any behavioural problems at school, at home, or in the community.

The judge knew she must render a sentence that held Justin accountable for his actions but allowed for his rehabilitation. The Youth Criminal Justice Act said custody was to be used only if a young person committed a violent offence, or an offence for which an adult would spend more than two years in prison.

"Although I formed the opinion, from Sandra's testimony at this trial, that she was the primary moving force behind the murder, Justin's role in the murder must not be minimized," Judge Van Melle said. "Despite having had a lesser role in the murder, he did encourage Beth to commit the offence, discussing with her on MSN the pros and cons of different methods [that] would result in the death of Linda Andersen. There was no evidence to suggest at any time he made any efforts to discourage Beth from committing murder.

"Justin shows little insight into the harm to which he contributed and the fact his actions assisted in a murder. Justin is by all accounts a very intelligent young man and as such should have been aware of the harm his actions could bring about."

Nothing in his background explained his involvement in the crime, she said. Mitigating factors included the fact he had no previous criminal record and was only fifteen when the offence occurred; that he was not a leader in the offence and he had complied with very strict conditions after his arrest. However, she noted an adult might receive a life prison sentence for the same conviction.

She said, "Although Justin was not a leader in the offence, he contributed to the offence. He must be held accountable for his participation in the conspiracy, which led to Linda Andersen's death. My review of case law of similar situations leads me to conclude there are no available sanctions other than custody in this situation. No other disposition would be reasonable."

She sentenced him to eighteen months—a year in secured custody followed by six months conditional supervision in the community. She also ordered a DNA sample be taken for Canada's national DNA databank.

While he was out on bail pending his appeal, Justin twice broke his conditions of release. Once he failed to report in as required. And he was arrested and charged with having a small quantity of marijuana.

Letters from a classmate

On January 12, 2006, a young man who knew Beth well suggested in an email sent to the murderingwhores website that she had pulled the wool over the eyes of investigators: "These girls committed murder. There is no justification for that act. They should not be receiving any pity and understanding."

The author, who remains anonymous, hated Beth and admitted his observations might be biased. He said he'd known her since elementary school and even then suspected she was a frightening psychopath:

Beth was in my class... and in fact the two [sisters] even came to one of my birthday parties when I was young and decided to invite the whole class. Knowing what I know now, the thought disgusts me no end. Beth was really a star pupil. She easily achieved some of the best marks in class. When adults were present, Beth was a polite, shy, and respectful young girl. She not only fit the stereotype of the perfect student, she created the stereotype. Lacking any form of accountability for their actions, the teachers marked us all based entirely on the effort we put into our work. And on our personalities and behaviour. Funny how checks and balances did not seem to be present in their vocabulary. Beth's grades reflected this pitiful excuse for an educational system.

When adults were not present, however, she was a much different person, if the word person can be applied to a matricidal lunatic. She lacked anything that could be considered a moral centre. She was manipulative and ... the complete opposite of the way she acted around authority figures. When I told adults or even my parents about this, it was disregarded or ridiculed. It was suggested I was jealous of her success or perhaps had a crush on her. I've heard of boys pulling on the hair of girls they like, but how many claim they are frightening psychopaths to any that will listen?

I hated Beth with all the passion a fourth grader can hate someone and later on, with all the passion a twelfth grader can hate someone. Does that make these observations irrelevant or biased? Perhaps. Like I said. Take from this what you will.

Beth I told you once in all seriousness I would get my revenge even if it took fifty years. If you're reading this, consider that debt paid. There's nothing I can take from you now that you haven't thrown away yourself. Keep that in mind as you rot in prison.

The author sent another email later that night:

Beth started off with almost a split personality. She had the perfect little girl setting they used around anyone with authority. And the raging psychopath setting they used the rest of the time. In fact, back in the early grades, they pretended to be perfect even when authority figures weren't around. It was very rare to see the crazy setting, unless you ignited her very short fuse. That's when the whole glass house would shatter.

As the years passed it would start to blur together. She still dressed like Daddy's little girl stereotype despite the fact their father never had custody of them in all the time I knew them. But she was acting more and more, well, I'm not sure exactly. It just kept intensifying until one day, very suddenly, her appearance changed from being Daddy's little girl to Dracula's little Gothic corpse. I didn't know it at the time. But it coincided exactly with the date of her mother's murder. They fit in reasonably well with both of these groups—the Do-Gooders and then, later, the Goths.

There is one thing you must absolutely realize, and this is critical. Beth is the brains of this macabre little operation. Sandra is not the sharpest knife in the drawer. ... When Beth says jump, Sandra says how high, then fails to achieve the required height by a wide margin.... Sandra left virtually all the clues the police had to follow. If she hadn't been around, I'm sure Beth would have gotten away with it.

I would bet all my worldly possessions Beth orchestrated this entire thing and that Sandra simply followed along like a puppy, a puppy with admittedly great tits.

I have a little story to tell you that at the time seemed inconsequential and yet now it is rather disturbing. When I was in Grade 7 the class had a trip to a skating rink but I was sick and couldn't go. Since we lived right by the school and the ice rink, the teacher asked if my mom could swing by and help them out very briefly just to get the kids organized and into the rink. My mom agreed, and later when she was leaving, Beth stopped her and asked where I was. My mom told her I was sick and she replied, "Oh well, let him know I hope he dies."

Money

Sandra and Beth maintained their mother's life insurance money never played any role in the murder. Under the terms of the insurance policy, underwritten by Manulife, Sandra and Beth were to split evenly about $133,000 of $200,044. Bobby would get the rest. Prosecutors Brian McGuire and Mike Cantlon decided to seek the remaining funds as "proceeds of crime." They believed the insurance money was part of the sisters' motive for murder, and wanted Judge Duncan to consider the money in his sentencing decision.

In total, $133,674 of the $200,044 was paid to Martha Kronwall, the sisters' legal guardian, to be held in trust for the girls. Doug Landers received $66,823.95, to be held in trust for Bobby. McGuire learned that by the time the sisters were sentenced only $48,487.04 of their $133,600 remained. Bobby had already received $66,823.95 as his share of the policy and was to receive what was left once the funds were seized. McGuire said their investigation determined the rest had been used to pay down debt on credit cards and to pay income tax bills.

Judge Duncan would not hear the Crown's application to

seek the funds as proceeds of crime. He said the remaining funds had nothing to do with the sisters' sentencing.

"The defendants were not in control of the money and not responsible if it was misused," he said, and it would be inappropriate for him to hold them responsible. If family members wanted to seek the remaining $48,000, they might try the civil courts.

McGuire and Cantlon wanted Judge Duncan to consider the insurance money in his sentencing decision because it was their theory that part of their motive for killing their mother was to obtain the insurance money. But Jagielski insisted there was no sense trying to locate the rest of the money. "It had already been consumed and wasn't hidden in a house or a boat."

Neither Sandra nor Beth was ordered to repay any of the money; Aunt Martha never had to account for the missing cash, either. Defence lawyers Robert Jagielski, Terry MacKay, and Jack McCulligh agreed to turning over what was left of the insurance money to Bobby; they all agreed he was the rightful beneficiary of his mother's insurance funds.

CHAPTER 30

IT COULD HAVE
BEEN WORSE

Had Sandra and Beth been eighteen when they committed murder they would have received a life prison sentence with no possibility of parole for a minimum twenty-five years. Down the road, they could apply under Canada's Faint Hope Clause, for early release after fifteen years. Their names and faces would have been splashed across newspapers and displayed on television newscasts.

But an entirely different set of rules came into play because they were just sixteen and fifteen at the time.

It didn't matter they were adults when sentenced. They remained under law of Canada's Youth Criminal Justice Act (YCJA), which replaced the Young Offenders Act on April 1, 2003.

The YCJA dramatically changed how Canadian courts dealt with youthful offenders, particularly killers, would-be killers, violent repeat offenders, and rapists. It required judges to steer youthful offenders away from jail and prison for almost every crime except for the most serious and violent offences, mainly murder, attempted murder, and aggravated sexual assault, along with those found guilty of a pattern of violent offences such as three assaults. The new Act required judges to dish out sentences proportionate to the seriousness of the offence and the degree of the offender's responsibility. Sentences had to be crafted so offenders had the best chance for rehabilitation. Custody was to be reserved for only the most serious of offences where a judge saw no other alternative, and if their crime would send an adult to prison for more than two years.

Sandra, being sixteen, fell into a different class of kiddy killers than Beth, at fifteen.

As murders go, Andersen's drowning was nowhere near as horrific as some other youth-committed homicides, including the heinous slaying that took place eleven months later in Toronto when a sixteen-year-old boy brutally murdered his own young brother on November 25, 2003. Johnathon Robert Madden, twelve, was found with seventy-one cuts to his head and neck in a basement crawl space of his home, his throat slashed, his carotid artery severed.

This vicious crime is mentioned because it shows how things could have been a lot worse for Sandra and Beth.

Madden's older brother Kevin, who like Sandra, was sixteen when he killed, was sentenced at the age of nineteen on September 29, 2006 as an adult, not as a youth, for the first-degree murder of his brother and the attempted murder of his stepfather. He received a life sentence with no possibility of parole for ten years, a lifetime criminal record and probation. He also received seven years concurrent for the attempted murder of his stepfather because consecutive sentences don't exist in Canada. Unlike Sandra and Beth, Madden's identity was revealed along with the identity of his dead brother, who until then had only been known as "Johnathan" in media reports.

A friend, Timothy Ferriman, then fifteen, like Beth, was convicted of manslaughter. He was eighteen when he received an adult sentence under the youth Act of two years in jail and three years probation. His identity was also revealed. Ferriman tried to impress girls by boasting he was a vampire. He also gave Madden the kitchen knife used in the murder, which he watched.

Before the murder, Madden, Ferriman, and another teen, who was acquitted, played hooky from school. They drank booze and smoked cigarettes at Madden's home while his parents were at work and Johnathon was at school. The plan called for both parents and their little brother to be murdered. The teens vandalized the master bedroom and trashed the basement with baseball bats. Ferriman also bragged to a girlfriend about the plot, but he was secretly taped and police were contacted afterwards, resulting in their arrests. Madden and Ferriman were convicted November 14, 2005, almost a month to the day of Sandra and Beth's conviction.

Andersen's murder actually occurred when the YOA was still in force. But under Section 160 of the YCJA, presumptive adult sentencing for murder committed before April 1, 2003 applied only to offenders who were sixteen and over. That meant Beth never faced an automatic adult sentence although she still faced the possibility of being sentenced as an adult once convicted. Unlike Sandra, prosecutors initially needed to prove Beth should be sentenced as an adult, while Sandra's attorney Jack McCulligh needed to prove that she shouldn't.

But the entire sentencing issue was turned upside down when a successful Charter argument changed the playing field before Judge Duncan sentenced them.

When the trial began, Cantlon and McGuire made no secret they wanted an adult sentence. In the trial, defence attorneys operated under the assumption that they, and not the prosecution, needed to prove Sandra shouldn't be sentenced as an adult.

But the roles were suddenly reversed on March 24, 2006, when Canada's Court of Appeal ruled the presumptive adult sentencing under the YCJA was unconstitutional and the onus to prove a young person should be sentenced as an adult now rested with the Crown, and not the defence. When Justice Duncan put his mind to how he was going to sentence Sandra, he had to start from the premise the ball was now in the Crown's court to show why he should increase her sentencing to adult status instead of the defence proving he shouldn't. Beth, however, started out with a youth sentence, so nothing changed. Prosecutors still needed to prove she warranted an adult sentence.

Judge Duncan also needed to decide which Act applied, the former YOA, or the new YCJA. Charter law mandated Sandra and Beth received the lesser of the sentences if two different findings resulted from the Acts. The YCJA was clear in what Judge Duncan could impose.

Although Sandra and Beth were fortunate they were sentenced as youths and not adults, they could have conceivably faired better had they received a youth sentence and committed the crime several years earlier when the YOA still ruled the criminal landscape for offenders aged twelve to seventeen. Under the old Act, a youth could only be sentenced to a maximum five years if sentenced as a youth but still faced the traditional adult sentence of life with no parole for at least twenty-five years as an adult, provided they were at least sixteen. Beth would never have been considered for an adult sentence under the old Act. But Sandra would have likely been transferred to adult court and sentenced as an adult if convicted, and her name and photo might have been revealed even before her trial.

Ironically, Beth being sentenced as a youth under the new YCJA resulted in her getting more time—a potential six years in custody—than she might have if she'd been sentenced as an adult, which carried a minimum parole ineligibility of between five to seven years. However, the difference was far greater in Sandra's case—six years as opposed to ten. The big difference between a youth and adult sentence was their parole ineligibility. A youth sentence carried a ten-year maximum sentence; an adult sentence and its ten years of parole ineligibility was just a component of the life sentence.

Regardless, even sentenced as youths, Sandra and Beth still face the possibility of spending their entire ten-year sentence in secured custody if they're ever deemed too dangerous to be released back into society.

Under the YCJA, the most severe penalties are to be reserved for the most severe crimes. As well, special sentences can now be imposed for youthful offenders suffering from mental or emotional disorders, which mandatory treatment being part of their in-custody sentence. Also, children under twelve remain outside of the criminal justice system.

Arguably, Sandra and Beth's crime certainly fit with the parameters for in-custody sentencing of the YCJA, and not with the general idea of keeping non-violent offenders out of jail wherever possible. Again, Judge Duncan really had no choice when it came to deciding whether they deserved to be incarcerated.

Under the old YOA, children fourteen and fifteen weren't transferred to adult court for adult sentencing. The new YCJA lowered the age to include youths as young as fourteen for possible adult sentencing once convicted. Once Sandra and Beth were past the age of fourteen they always faced the possibility of an adult sentence. In fact, Sandra would have faced the same consequences for the past century even when the Juvenile Delinquents Act was in place. Youths committing crimes in

Canada fell under the Juvenile Delinquents Act from 1908 to 1984 when the YOA came into being to make twelve- to seventeen-year-olds more accountable for their crimes. In 1992, amendments to the YOA increased the maximum length of a sentence in youth court from three years to five years for murder. By 1995, further amendments increased the maximum sentence for first-degree murder for youths to ten years, and seven years for second-degree murder and allowed for youths committing murder and other serious crimes at age sixteen and seventeen to be automatically transferred to adult court. Under the old YOA, it was presumed a sixteen- and seventeen-year-old charged with murder, attempted murder, manslaughter, or aggravated sexual assault, would be transferred to an adult court, and if convicted, usually received an adult sentence unless their attorney demonstrated why a youth sentence was more appropriate. The federal government undertook a complete review of youth justice in 1996. In March 1999, the first version of the YCJA was introduced into Parliament with Bill C-3 being submitted in October 1999. A federal election delayed the bill's third reading before Bill C-7 was introduced in February 2001. On February 4, 2002, Parliament passed Bill C-7, a.k.a the Youth Criminal Justice Act, which became law on April 1, 2003.

Canada's lawmakers and critics pushed for new youth laws because they felt the old system didn't prevent troubled youths from becoming career criminals, and there was also a need for courts and judges to better deal and be fairer with violent youths as compared to youths who committed non-violent crimes such as shoplifting and break and enter. Critics believed the criminal justice system was sending too many youths to jail when alternative measures could be chosen instead of incarceration. Those pressing for change also felt society needed to provide better rehabilitation for youths returning to society once they served their sentences. As a result, the YCJA included major changes to sentencing principles, sentencing options, the elimination of transfers to adult court, and custody and integration policies.

According to Stats Canada and Justice Canada information for the year 2000, the year before the new Act came into law, more than 40 per cent of cases in youth court under the old YOA Act involved less serious offences such as theft under $5,000, possession of stolen property, failure to appear, and breach of probation. Minor assaults made up of the majority of violent offences. Under the YOA, judges had no mandatory power to order convicted youths to serve any period of community supervision once they were released from custody. That meant youthful offenders could be released back into society with no direction or support to assist them in their transition back into society or help them stay away from a life of crime.

The new YCJA changed that, which is why Sandra and Beth will be under community supervision for all of the years of their sentence once they're released from secured custody. Every person placed in custody following their conviction under the new YCJA is required to be under community supervision as part of their overall sentence, even if they're convicted and sentenced for murder. But if Sandra and Beth breach any condition after their release from custody, they run the risk of being sent back to prison to serve the remainder of their sentence.

Unlike the old YOA, the transfer process for youths to adult court was also eliminated altogether by the YCJA. Instead, youths such as Beth and Sandra needed to be convicted first before any decision was made as to how they would be sentenced. Judge Duncan, like all judges, was also required under the YCJA to decide before sentencing whether a youth sentence would be of "sufficient length" to hold a young person "accountable" for their crime. As a result, under the Act, Judge Duncan had no choice but to impose a youth sentence if he found such a sentence would be "sufficient" to hold Beth and Sandra "accountable" for murdering their mother rather than imposing a life prison sentence as an adult.

Beyond everything, one of the biggest benefits Sandra and Beth gained with their youth sentences was keeping their identities secret forever. Even their dead mother's real name remains protected by law. Lawmakers decided to make the non-publication of identities a cornerstone of the YCJA. Revealing the names of youths might hinder their re-integration back into society. Under the old YOA, an offender's name could be published as soon as they were transferred to an adult court, even before their trial, even before they were convicted or acquitted. The YCJA corrected that. Identities of youthful offenders are protected until they're convicted as adults. Even then, Judge Duncan could have still ordered their names not be published if he felt it was in their best interests. No doubt media lawyers would have fought such a ruling.

Although Andersen's real name remains forever protected, the new YCJA generally provides for victims' names to be revealed once their killers are sentenced as adults, provided parents give permission, if the victim is under eighteen. The decision to reveal or not reveal their son's name came into play during the trial of the very first person to be charged with first-degree murder under the new YCJA. On the first day the Act was enacted on April 1, 2003, Justin Morton, a psychotic fourteen-year-old, strangled classmate Eric Levack, fourteen, with his own belt. The brutal and prolonged killing took place in a wooded area behind their Heart Lake Secondary School in Brampton, Ontario. Like Sandra and Beth, Morton came from an unhappy home life, and a life, which he felt, had too many rules and restrictions on his freedom. Like the girls, he also thought about suicide. He even thought life in jail might be better than life at home.

Morton eventually pleaded guilty to first-degree murder and was sentenced as an adult at the age of fifteen on April 22, 2004. Although Eric's parents, George and Debbie wrestled with revealing their son's name after Morton was convicted, they resisted until his killer was sentenced as adult, after which they allowed the media to publish their son's name, putting a face and an identity to him. They had been caught between the law and their desire to put a name and a face to their beloved son, whose identity had been kept from the general public because they mistakenly feared if their son's identity was revealed that somehow his killer would get off with a lighter sentence than the law allowed. Because Morton was just fourteen at the time he committed murder, his parole ineligibility was set at seven years for his life prison sentence, the same sentence Beth faced had she been sentenced as an adult.

Ironically, at the time this book was being written, both Morton and Ferriman were believed to be among the inmates tutored by Beth inside Syl Apps Youth Centre, where by all accounts she was considered a role model for other inmates.

CHAPTER 31
FINAL WORD

On any given day, according to Stats Canada, about 13,000 youths are either in secured or open custody or under supervised probation in Canada. Only about 700 are actually locked up. Very few are serving time for murder.

Sandra and Beth are the only sisters in custody for killing their mother.

Legal experts, however, are of the same opinion. The Bathtub Girls crime stands alone when it comes to Canadian murders despite some elements of this chilling case being similar to other youth slayings.

"Certainly this case is an atypical youth offence," said Queen's University Law Professor Nicholas Bala, one of Canada's foremost experts on youth crime and youth justice and author of *Youth Criminal Law Justice.* "In fact, it's not even a typical youth homicide. It's probably not even a typical homicide committed by a woman."

Although a landmark murder for Canada, youth-committed murders aren't rare in Canada. According to Stats Canada, 59 of 549 murders in 2003 were committed by youths twelve to seventeen. It's unknown if these stats included Beth and Sandra.

The murder took place in 2003, but they weren't caught until 2004 when 44 of the 624 murders were committed by teens.

Canadian Youth homicide had taken a dramatic increase by time of their 2005 trial. Then, 65 of the 658 murders were committed by youths, the highest number in more than a decade. More than a third (37 per cent) had previous criminal records. About half (54 per cent) had previous convictions for a violent offence besides homicide. Males were more likely to have a criminal past. Police and youth experts said gang violence, although not totally responsible for the increase, played a significant role.

Regardless which year they fell into or the state of youth crime in the years immediately following their convictions, one thing is certain about teen killers. Most are adolescent males, and when they kill, experts say, their killing usually is spontaneous; from a fight, a robbery, or a drug deal gone terribly bad. In 2005, nine out of ten persons accused of homicide in Canada were males. Most were between eighteen and twenty-four. As well, almost 73 per cent or 480 of the victims were male compared to 178 female victims.

But young females can be extremely violent. Consider the high-profiled murder of Reena Virk, fourteen, who was swarmed by a group of seven young females, aged fourteen to sixteen, and one teenage male. She was beaten to death under a bridge in Victoria, B.C. on November 14, 1997. Kelly Ellard, sixteen, and Warren Glowatski, seventeen, were convicted of second-degree murder.

Young female murderers generally are a rare breed in Canadian society. In 2005, only nine teenage girls were accused of homicide. If included in 2003 stats, Sandra and Beth were just two of ten females charged with homicide. Included in

2004, then they were only two of five females charged with committing homicide.

Young sisters killing their parent had been unheard of in Canadian society until Beth and Sandra. But it isn't particularly uncommon for family members to murder other family members. Based on the latest crime statistics, data compiled by Stats Canada consistently show people are far more likely to be killed by someone they know rather than a stranger. Of the 658 homicides in 2005, 478 were solved, about half (49 per cent) were committed by somebody known to the victim, and a third (33 per cent) were done by a family member. In 2005, twenty-seven sons or daughters killed another family member. Strangers accounted for 18 per cent of the killings.

Ironically, while there were thirty-four more homicides in 2005 than in 2004, fewer parents killed their children in 2005 than any year since 1964, according to Stats Canada.

What made the Bathtub Girls case extremely unique in Canadian criminology as far as Professor Bala is concerned was the amount of planning and forethought that went into the execution.

"Certainly the planned and deliberate murder of a parent is rare," Bala said. "One of the common things about adolescent crimes is most youths aren't particularly good criminals in the sense their crimes are easy to prove from a forensic perspective. They're tragic but police very quickly find lots of evidence. Often a ton of evidence.

"These girls almost got away with it. It was a very deliberate and planned murder. They took unusual care. The vast majority of youth crime is unplanned. In fact, when you ask them afterwards, they often don't know why they did it. They genuinely have trouble explaining their motivation. Most murders committed by youths are also typically poorly executed. But not this one."

Their reasons for this murder also takes it out of the norm, Bala said.

"Usually when a youth kills a parent or an immediate relative there's lot of anger behind it," Bala said. "And again, the killing is usually spontaneous. Of course some spousal homicides are carefully planned for insurance money but that is a tiny fraction of familial homicides. These girls planned the murder of their mother for months. They also didn't seem to be driven by anger. That makes this murder even highly unusual among adult murderers."

For Bala, one of this crime's most striking aspects was also typical to many youth crimes. The sisters couldn't keep quiet.

"The perfect crime is one that is not detected," Bala said. "This was essentially a perfect crime. But they opened their mouths. They did themselves in."

The fact adults are often able to remain silent once they kill is a big reason why police don't solve some cases, he said.

"But these girls told their friends. Youths who commit crime absolutely tell their friends. That's how most serious crimes involving youths are solved. Once police know who committed the crime then they're able to start collecting the necessary forensic evidence."

Bala, however, isn't surprised they told their friends.

"There are some cases where teens have taken their friends to see the body. The fact these girls told some of their close friends is both very common and very naïve on their part. But it shows the role peers and friendships played in their lives."

Most youths who commit crime also feel extremely safe even when they tell their friends, Bala said.

"Believing nobody will ever tell on them is very common among youthful offenders. There is often a sense of invincibility among adolescents. They won't get caught. None of their friends will ever turn on them. Trust in peers is very common.

"Adolescents place a tremendous amount of importance on friendships and peer relationships. That's part of the adolescent culture not to rat out your friends."

Youths who kill often also believe they're justified, Bala said.

"There is also, at least initially, a lack of remorse. One of the ironies is that over time, as these girls mature into adults, they will become more remorseful. Often, among youths, there is no real appreciation of what they did in their early teens. But afterwards, in their twenties, they develop a much deeper appreciation."

Most homicides in Canada are committed by one person against one victim. In 2005, 95 per cent or 594 of the 623 different incidents involving 658 victims were one-person homicides. When more than one person is killed, it's usually a family-committed homicide and 94 per cent occur in a private residence.

In his view, it appears it was extremely important for Sandra and Beth to carry out their plan together. Sandra insisted she would have still murdered her mother if Beth never agreed to help, but Bala doubts whether she would have gone through with the murder had her sister not been on side.

"They gave each other courage. On their own, neither likely would have had the capacity or inclination to kill but together they did something neither one probably would have been able to do on their own."

Most youth-committed homicides are committed by more than one teen. Of the fifty-one incidents that resulted in sixty-five youths accused of homicides in 2005, more than half were committed by two or more people. Historically, teens are more likely to kill other teens or young adults. Of the solved homicides committed by youths in 2005, more than half or 56 per cent of the victims were between the ages of twelve and twenty-four.

Since their incarceration, correctional officials have repeatedly described Sandra and Beth as being role models for their fellow inmates, including other youthful offenders. Generally, youthful male offenders rarely if ever are described in these terms. It's far more common for adolescent males who commit homicide to get into fights with other inmates.

Despite the callous and disturbing nature of their crime, Bala disagrees with those who say parents shouldn't view the case as a cautionary tale.

"The vast majority of kids who say they want to kill their parents, never do. There is no indication these girls ever threatened to kill their mother or harm her before they planned her death and murdered her. They never told her they were going to kill her if she didn't stop drinking.

"I wouldn't want parents to look at this very unique homicide and start fearing they have to be careful around their teenagers because they might turn on them and kill them. There are good reasons to be concerned about your children and adolescents. Kids have senses of invincibility. They sometimes make bad decisions and show poor judgment and then ruin and profoundly affect their lives. But I think fearing your kids will kill you should be way down on every parent's list of worries.

"This case shouldn't be viewed as the tip of the iceberg. It would be wrong for parents to worry their child will stab them because they've had a fight with him or her. Parents should worry about their relationships. But nobody has a perfect relationship with their teenagers. There isn't a kid out there who doesn't think their parents are too strict at one time or another. Every single adolescent has had tension with their parents. If you look at teens who kill their parents, some were profoundly abused, sexually and/or physically. But many were not. In this case, these girls were once good students. Sure, their parents were divorced and there was a lot of tension in the family. But many kids grow up in divorced homes, and some end up living with an alcoholic parent, but few ever end up committing homicide. There are a lot of teenagers with problems. Most grow up to be healthy productive adults. In this case, their mother obviously wasn't a model parent. But I don't think you can conclude that if she had paid more attention to them, that her daughters wouldn't have killed her."

Even though Bala believes there is a good chance the sisters will likely be released before their mandatory in-custody portion of their ten-year sentence has been completed, he doubts whether there would have been a different outcome, even if they knew they might spend their entire lives behind bars if caught. It's naïve for the general public to think stiffer sentences for youthful offenders would make much of a difference.

"These kids were not thinking about getting caught. And if they were, they certainly weren't thinking they would only get ten years. We've had a pretty consistent homicide rate for youths in Canada over the past thirty to forty years. No doubt there has been a deterioration of social issues and an increase in gang violence. We've always had problems of youths and poverty and kids growing up in single parent families and having access to weapons.

"We live in different times. The Internet is affecting how youths perceive their world. Video and culture influences tolerate aggression and encourages violence. Young people certainly have a different attitude towards authority figures. We live in a society where youths respect adults less and less. But adolescents have always been rebellious and alienated from adults."

Bala also thinks keeping their identities protected forever will help them and society in the long run.

"They eventually will get out and be able to start their lives again but if their names and photos had been in the newspapers, they'd never be able to put this behind them and that wouldn't do them or society any good."

As for the method of their crime, there are so few drowning homicides in Canada that it isn't even listed among causes by Stats Canada. Just over a third (34 per cent) or 222 of the homicides in 2005 involved a shooting with 58 per cent of the firearm deaths coming from handguns. Stabbings accounted for 30 per cent or 198 of the deaths. Another 22 per cent or 145 were beaten to death and 7 per cent or 45 were either strangled or suffocated. Even twelve babies were killed by shaken baby syndrome.

Another aspect of the Bathtub Girls case that is out of the norm is that most homicides are solved within a week. Very few, about 5 per cent, take more than a year to solve such as was the case with this murder. Interestingly, statistics compiled between 1991 and 2005 show that 81 per cent of the 1,998 homicides committed by family members other than a parent were usually solved within a week whereas homicides committed by one criminal against another took an average of six and a half months to solve. Stranger homicides took an average of four months to solve.

Of the 429 victims aged seventeen and under killed by a family member between 1995 and 2004, 90 per cent were murdered by their own parent, which means Beth and Sandra were more likely to be killed by their mother than their mother being killed by them. And based on general trends, had they been killed, Linda Andersen might have then committed suicide.

Home-grown killers

As one of Canada's top experts on youth homicide, Dr. Mark Totten has seen it all. Despite never interviewing them, he still has some strong, perhaps even controversial thoughts about what drove them to become Canada's first and only sister act of a matricide murder.

"When you work with these types of kids for years as I have and do therapy with them you truly come to understand why they did what they did," said Dr. Totten, who in 2002 co-authored the ground-breaking book *When Children Kill* with Katharine Kelly, an associate professor of sociology at Carleton University in Ottawa. "I've never been surprised. If I interviewed these sisters, I'm positive I wouldn't have been surprised they killed their mother."

Although their crime was unique in the annals of Canadian criminology, the life story behind them is in many ways is similar to the backgrounds of other young killers whom Dr. Totten has encountered as director of research at the Youth Services Bureau in Ottawa as well as through his extensive work for his co-authored book, Canada's first qualitative study of youth killers.

"There are so very few kids in Canada who murder that there are no real trends. If you look back over the past fifty years, it's always been around thirty-five to thirty-six each year and generally the ratio for males to females in about ten to one.

"But the reasons why they kill, who they kill and how they kill are very different from males to females. Young woman usually kill somebody they know very well, particularly a family member.

That's very different from young males, who might kill an acquaintance, who isn't even a friend. They usually kill strangers."

Certainly, this murder fits the general pattern of young females committing homicide, he said.

"As well, the means they use to commit homicide are also very gender specific. Young women tend to find quieter means whereas young males don't. I'm not aware of any young woman in Canada who has ever used a gun to kill anybody."

For him, this murder appears to be a textbook killing for young females. Judge Duncan remarked during sentencing how Sandra and Beth had at least chosen "a humane way" to kill their mother in a sense the drowning wasn't particularly violent.

In looking at why youths kill, one has to closely examine the social context, especially the social situation and relationship of the young female killers to explain or analyze their homicidal actions, Dr. Totten said. For young males, it's quite different.

"I worked with a couple of guys who were convicted of a brutal beating of a cocaine dealer. They beat him to death simply because he owed them money. There was nothing more to it. That doesn't happen with young females."

For their book, Dr. Totten and Professor Kelly studied nineteen different young people convicted of murder and manslaughter, male and females, who weren't born bad but became killers because of their social and family environment. They found that based on their social-psychological development from their childhood to their teens, there were three clear and distinct pathways that each offender followed en route to taking someone's life.

One of the pathways to homicide is a willingness to take aggressive risks. Sandra and Beth don't seem to fit this group of killers.

"This group would involve kids who aren't necessarily doing any criminal activity but their lives are such that they take extreme risks and seek thrills in ways that could end up with either their death or killing somebody else," Dr. Totten said.

In this group, Dr. Totten recalled a case of a young man who was convicted of multiple counts of manslaughter when he played chicken with his car and another group of kids in another vehicle.

"They slammed into a gasoline tanker but he had never been involved in any criminal activity before. This is a kid who said he would have strapped himself into a rocket if he could."

Another common pathway to homicide is for youths involved in "ordinary violence." This group includes gangs and other anti-social groups, who commit violent behaviour such as home invasions day in and day out. Again, Sandra and Beth don't fit here.

"Those in this group are likely either going to kill somebody or they're going to be killed themselves as a consequence of their actions."

In his view, Dr. Totten is certain Sandra and Beth's descent into homicide clearly falls within a third pathway. They found themselves frustrated by their life circumstances. They clearly appear to have been victims of very serious and prolonged maltreatment.

"If we assume their mother's drinking problem started when these girls were very young, then you could assume their psychological mistreatment was very severe. What we know about kids who endure severe psychological mistreatment is that some go on to kill. They typically commit murder by themselves or with a very close family member."

Although there is absolutely no evidence Andersen ever

beat her children, Dr. Totten said emotional maltreatment is often just as damaging. When a kid grows up in a household like these girls did, their sense of self-worth would have been pretty much at rock bottom, he said.

"These emotional wounds leave scarring. I work with a lot of survivors of maltreatment who wish they'd been beaten because the physical scars heal. But the deep emotional wounding never goes away. Living with an alcoholic parent and the impact of that emotional scaring would have been equivalent to somebody being beaten up for many years."

As children in this pathway grow up, Dr. Totten said they develop "coping mechanisms" to deal with their maltreatment, including "splitting" from reality.

In looking at why children kill, Dr. Totten said there are often several factors that come into play, including an influence of a boyfriend.

"You need to peel away the layers of the onion to understand why kids do these things."

Often, there is a sexually abusive or emotionally controlling boyfriend involved when young women kill. Often, there is also a large age gap such as the disturbing case in Medicine Hat, Alberta, where a young twelve-year-old girl was convicted in the spring of 2007 of murdering her parents and her eight-year-old brother because her parents wouldn't allow her to continue her relationship with her twenty-three-year-old boyfriend.

Although there was no evidence either Sandra or Beth were abused either sexually or physically by their boyfriends, prosecutors Cantlon and McGuire clearly showed during the trial that Beth's boyfriend, perhaps, had some influence over her, although it's debatable whether he convinced her to kill her mother.

"But one must ask if this young woman would have done

what she did in the absence of her boyfriend. It's not an excuse to let her off the hook but you have to look at what she did in context of her social situation."

Although Sandra and Beth always denied their mother's life insurance money played any significant role in their decision to end her life, homicide investigators, prosecutors, and even some of their friends clearly believed money, and a lack of money, played an important part of their mindset. Dialogue with their close friends, both in person and over the Internet, indicated they planned to use the life insurance to take some friends on a vacation.

Such ideas aren't uncommon for young killers, according to Dr. Totten.

"Sure it's crazy, these Romeo and Juliet ideals of driving off with each other into the sunset. But quite often, they also have suicide pacts, if their ideas don't work."

While it might seem odd that Sandra and Beth would both become heavy drinkers and drug abusers before and after they killed their mother, when they hated their mother's own alcohol abuse, Dr. Totten said there was nothing unremarkable about this seemingly contradiction. In fact, he would have been surprised, given their circumstances in their household, if they didn't abuse alcohol themselves.

"It's not bizarre for offspring of parents who have substance abuse problems to mirror the same behaviour even though they hated that behaviour. We know children who grow up in homes where parents abuse substances are likely to abuse substances themselves despite the fact they despise their parents for doing so."

Dr. Totten is convinced Sandra and Beth developed what he describes as a "breached attachment" to their alcoholic mother from a very young age.

"What we know about parents who tend to be substance abusers is that they're not often available as caregivers. They're also distant. Their punishment practices also usually tend to be random. Kids don't know when they'll get punished. And punishment doesn't have to be physical.

"Like moths being attracted to a flame, kids are attracted to the same self-destructive patterns that they learned in their families. They feel safe. It feels consistent. It feels comfortable even though they're highly destructive. It's easy to say these girls had it good. They had parties. But I doubt they would have been drinking booze and using pot at such a young age had they not grown up with a parent who was abusing alcohol. They saw it day in and day out. When that happens, you're likely to mimic it even though it's very destructive."

It would have also been surprising, he said, if Sandra and Beth never told their friends, or confided in their friends about their murder plan.

"Despite the fact these girls were exceptionally brilliant, most kids who commit extreme acts of violence are really dumb. They tell people and that gives them a sense of status. Quite often kids see themselves as being above the law, They don't think the law applies to them. They've constructed this alternate reality where the rules don't apply to them. Where they are masters of their universe. They believe they'll never get caught. These kinds of acts aren't surprising at all."

The fact none of their friends ever told anybody about the murder is also extremely common among youth killers, according to Dr. Totten.

"It's fits with the pattern of many high-profile murders in North America. Look at the high school shootings. Sure these are males doing the extreme harm. But it's rare for these killers not to leave very concise clues specific to their plans. It would have been a real surprise had these girls not told their friends even before they went through with it. And peers just don't act on this kind of knowledge. They want to protect their friends. Not wanting to be a rat is so prevalent in today's youth culture. Kids will do just about anything to not tell on their friends."

Dr. Totten was also not surprised these girls murdered their mother even though they were brilliant students with high IQs. Although many young killers suffer from some form of brain damage or from fetal alcohol problems, others fall into the complete opposite of the intelligent spectrum.

"It's not unusual for smart people to kill. I worked with a young man who at two was severely beaten with a hanger by his stepfather and wound up in hospital for several years. But when he got out, the beatings never seemed to affect his ability to learn. He could read a book in twenty minutes. His parents often abandoned him for months growing up and he took care of his little sister. He made sure she did her homework and he stole from the local supermarket. He went on to murder a friend but he was brilliant."

Although most parents don't have to fear being killed by their kids, Dr. Totten said he believes parents who abuse alcohol and drugs should view the story of Sandra and Beth closely.

"The lack of emotional care and maltreatment arises when adults do drugs and alcohol around their kids. People shouldn't see these girls as being monsters. They did a monstrous thing but what they did was highly predictable. It was really the worst outcome for a parent who abused alcohol. This could have been totally preventable if these kids got care.

"Like many kids who kill, these sisters likely felt totally helpless and hopeless about their situation. The cruel irony is at the same time these kids are homicidal, they're also suicidal. What we see a lot with these kids is their emotional wounds are so profound that their soul is barely alive. They do the most extreme things to develop a coat of armour emotionally around them. They learn they can't trust adults and that adults are only going to hurt them. They don't want to take the chance they will be harmed again."

By the summer of 2007, both were no longer incarcerated in youth facilities, something Dr. Totten considered to be a mistake.

"One of the things not well understood by the general public, even the judiciary, is that when young people get transferred up into the adult system or are sentenced as adults, the chance for them to be rehabilitated goes down the toilet. Kids are far better no matter how heinous their crime is, to remain in the youth system, they're exposed to a whole lot of risks from people who are older than them. I call this the close proximity thesis. The minute you stick a young person in with adults, who are there for murder and other serious crimes, there is a chance the young person will pick up more deviant behaviour. Of course, the women's federal system is far different than the men's system and a lot safer. But you can't escape the fact by putting a young person close to an adult offender, the potential for harm is quite high."

Dr. Totten also remains convinced that Sandra and Beth likely experienced some sexual trauma during their life. Indeed, both claimed their cousin sexually abused them.

"There is a very distinct and clear pattern in Canada that girls who have been sexually traumatized are highly likely to go on to commit extreme acts of violence. You can almost say that prolonged sexual trauma can predict violence. So I would be surprised if there wasn't a pattern of sexual trauma in their lives. The fact they never revealed this is also normal."

Based on what Sandra and Beth told their friends, their defence-hired psychiatrists, and their probation officers, it's clear their mother freely talked about her own sexual escapes with men. It's also clear Sandra, at least, was involved in sexually daring antics. But it's also clear there was no evidence whatsoever these girls had ever been sexually abused by their mother, their father, or any of their mother's boyfriends, only that they alleged their cousin had been sexually molesting them since their early teens.

"Their case has sexual abuse written all over it. Nine out of ten times there is sexual trauma involved in these types of crime," Dr. Totten said. "I would be very surprised if there wasn't sexual abuse somewhere."

EPILOGUE
HOW COULD THEY?

Sandra and Beth were pros when it came to lying and manipulating people. They thought they were better and far more intelligent than their friends and adults in their world. But just how far would they go? Would they lie to get even? Would they spread rumours to send another relative to prison?

Beth told probation officer Stephen Lane that sometimes "drastic actions are called for in drastic situations."

Did Beth and Sandra think by portraying themselves as victims of sexual assault, that in some way, they would gain sympathy from the court, and from Judge Duncan in particular, when it came to their sentencing?

In June of 2006, and just days before they were sentenced, Peel Police arrested their cousin Derek, twenty-one, and charged him with sexually assaulting both girls.

Aunt Martha was devastated. She never wanted to believe her loving nieces murdered her sister, and their own mother. Now they claimed they had been groped and fondled by her youngest son. Their allegations suggested some of the sexual assaults took place while they lived at her home under house arrest.

Derek was released under his own recognizance. But a

cloud of suspicion remained for more than six months until all charges were suddenly withdrawn in early 2007. Prosecutor Vickie Reid told a Brampton court there was no "reasonable prospect" of gaining a conviction based on the "totality" of the evidence. Reid was filling in that day for prosecutor Mike Morris, who was in charge of the case but involved in preparing for another murder trial.

Outside the courtroom, Derek said he was relieved. He could now get on with his life. He would have more to say in the future. He believed his cousins had "falsely accused" him simply to gain public sympathy.

"I guess they wanted people on their side and they wanted sympathy," Derek said, just moments after Judge Vibert Rosemay withdrew the charges.

"I was the only convenient one. Nobody else had much contact with them when they were under house arrest. I was their age, and their friend. I'm happy it's over. But I wished it didn't have to take so long."

Sandra and Beth had basically grown up with Derek and his older brother Hans. They were more like brothers than cousins.

Defence attorney Robert Ash accused Peel Police of "rushing to judgment" when Derek was initially charged. He was still angry, but praised Morris for "making the right to decision" to withdraw the charges.

"They should never have been laid in the first place," Ash said outside the courtroom. "He was totally innocent. These girls had zero credibility. None whatsoever. They murdered their mother. Draw your own conclusions."

Derek had been under tremendous stress. He had been charged with two counts of sexual assault in connection with alleged multiple incidents of non-consensual fondling of the girls between 1997 and 2005. The girls were between ten and nineteen when the alleged assaults occurred. None of the alleged sexual offences involved any allegation that Derek had sexual intercourse with either girl. Based on the date of the allegations, some would have occurred while the girls were under house arrest.

Both girls had told their probation officers and psychiatrist that Derek had been sexually assaulted them.

Also, Sandra previously revealed the sexual attacks but never named her attacker, during a series of sexually explicit blogs that she posted on the Tucker Max website.

Sandra also told probation officer Suzie Martin that her cousin fondled and masturbated her. In Grade 9, she said she told a priest about the repeated sexual assaults during a high school retreat. She never told her father, or her Aunt Martha. She told Martin the alleged sexual assaults involved kissing, touching, and masturbating. They had been happening since she was a young child although she wasn't certain if sexual intercourse had ever taken place.

Beth told probation officer Stephen Lane that Derek fondled her under and over her clothes every week from the age of about thirteen. He also climbed into bed with her a few weeks before she and Sandra were convicted of murdering their mother.

"She freaked out," Lane wrote in his pre-sentence report. "She said nobody would believe them. She pleaded with him to stop. She felt unsafe. He offered her drugs for sex."

Beth also alleged the sexual assaults took place in their Aunt Martha's residence and her own townhouse. Beth told Lane that she never told anybody because nobody would believe her. Beth also claimed Derek had a collection of child porn.

Sandra told Dr. Klassen that Derek had sexually abused her, including fingering her more than a dozen times. He slept in her bed and called himself "her husband." She told herself that she wasn't abused because she never wanted to perceive herself as being an abused person. These sexual acts involved genital contact. When she threatened to tell his mother, he dared her to, but she never did. He fingered aggressively when she was in Grade 5 to the extent that she felt he had taken her virginity away. She insisted her aunt didn't believe her disclosure.

Despite insisting he wanted to tell his side of the story, Derek changed his mind and decided against granting any interviews for this book. Neither Sandra nor Beth ever gave evidence against Derek in court. Neither girl remembered if these alleged sexual assaults ever progressed to full-blown sexual intercourse.

What they told investigators remains a secret as does why charges were suddenly dropped. However, it was clear it would have been difficult for prosecutors to convince a jury, even a judge, to believe the word of convicted killers. Even in cases where evidence seems overwhelming against an accused, judges usually caution jurors about how they view the truthfulness of claims made by convicted felons, and unsavoury witnesses. It's not that judges want jurors to think the person on the stand isn't telling the truth. Jurors just need to understand "who" is telling their version of the truth, and whether they might have any ulterior motive for shades of gray.

Magnus and Pulley remained convinced money played a major part in the decision to end Linda Andersen's life. They remained just as certain Beth played as important a role, and might have even been the driving force behind the murder.

"In my opinion, Beth along with Justin, were all parties to the offence with Sandra," Magnus said. "Sandra and Beth contrived an idea they would have a better life and Justin got involved and gave them advice on how to make it happen.

"Even though Sandra insisted it was her idea, Beth was the more evil of the two. They both decided to kill their mother. Beth had as much to do with the planning as Sandra did. Sandra may have come up with several ideas. At the end of the day, it's Beth who is talking online with Justin about drowning and researching stuff.

"Beth never told a soul about it. Sandra at least had a minor conscience when she was drunk. Either she wanted people to feel sorry for her to impress them. Beth wasn't happy, Sandra told people. I have no doubt that she took her big sister aside and told her if they ever got caught, that she had to take the blame because she was the one who couldn't keep her mouth shut."

Regardless of who came up with the idea, Magnus said once they realized they could "get rid of the mom" and then "do what they liked" and had "all this money to spend" and have a "better life," there was no turning back.

Magnus never believed Linda was as bad of a mother as the girls made everybody believe.

"Most of their friend's opinions were based on what they told them. They lived in a strict house environment but their mother had a lot of expectations for them. That was their main problem with her. She wouldn't let her daughters do what they wanted to do. They felt they had a right to do what they wanted to do when they wanted to do it.

"Linda tried to take an active role in their lives and they didn't want her to. They didn't like the fact she told them who they could hang around and who they couldn't see. They didn't like the fact she insisted they study hard and go to school. They didn't like her checking up on them from work.

"It was very difficult for her as a single mother having to support three children. She was holding down several jobs to accomplish things and give her girls a better life. But they didn't see it. They felt they could have a better life once their mother was gone because they would get to live with their aunt and live happily ever after."

Magnus believed money was one of the key factors in their decision to get rid of their mother.

"Their lifestyle had changed. They had once been good students but now they were with a new group of friends who liked to party hardy. They believed once they got their mother's insurance money that their life would change for the better."

Pulley agreed: "All of a sudden they were hanging around other teens from pretty good homes. They were being exposed to a different aspect of life and a different income levels. They wanted to achieve more."

Eventually, they realized their mother wasn't as bad as they thought, Magnus said.

"One of the big problems they had with their mother was that she wanted to send them to Holland each summer so they could spend some time with their grandparents, Pulley said. "But they had reached the age where they had new friends and wanted to hang around with them, not their aging grandparents in Europe. They were starting to grow up.

"That's why Sandra called the Children's Aid Society the year before the murder. Mom wanted to send them to stay with their grandparents like they had done almost every summer. But Sandra called the CAS and made excuses about her mom just so she didn't have to go. She had a boyfriend and she wanted to stay at home, not in Europe.

"One summer she ended up having to purchase new plane

tickets to get them back because they made such a stink over in Holland. They were supposed to stay for two months and wound up staying only about two weeks. Their mother always wanted them to visit their family, to keep in touch with their grandparents and their roots. But they just wanted to party with their friends."

They were also upset when Edward Brockman ended his relationship with their mother, Magnus said.

"As long as their mom was dating him their financial situation would possibly be better. Once he breaks up, they see their lives returning to what it was before. As long as mom was working and dating him, the more she was away from the house and the more their friends could party. But if mom doesn't work, then she's at home more and if she's there, then they can't do what they want to do.

"So they're miserable again. It's like the teacher's back in the class. Their mom breaks up. She's not working. She's back at home and keeping tabs on them. So life turns miserable again."

In the end, the story of the Bathtub Girls would have been told entirely differently in the media, and in this book had it not been for a decision by Peel Police homicide inspector Mike MacMullen to keep Linda Andersen's real name under a publication ban right from the beginning. Had police released her name as the victim in this sordid crime, nobody would have been able to report that her own daughters were charged with murdering her because that would have identified them. The decision not to release Andersen's real name turned this crime into a far more sensational story.

"We recognized public and media interest would be extremely high," said MacMullen, who by the end of 2007 was now the Inspector of Peel's street crime unit. "Given the uniqueness and unusual background of the case coupled with the ages of the culprits, there was a clear obligation to provide a brief history. To do so meant disclosing the family relationship. It was obvious we had to provide the community and the media information on the unusual nature of the case of children killing their parent. I believe we struck a fair balance in terms of public interest while protecting identities."

By the end of 2007, Beth and Sandra had already served about two years and one month of their ten-year maximum sentence. But just how long they would have to remain in custody remained to be seen. As with other aspects of their case, the girls presented new challenges for the legal system, now as convicted offenders. Even learned legal experts weren't exactly sure just how long they would remain locked up because this ground-breaking case entered entirely new territory for teens convicted of first-degree murder, as youths, and not adults.

By the time the clock struck midnight on New Year's Eve 2007, Sandra had been incarcerated in a federal women's prison for long-term offenders for about a year and in custody for twenty-five months in total. Though some aspects of her case continue to be dealt with under the YCJA, including the protection of her identity, in other aspects she was being treated as an adult offender. While there remained some uncertainty among legal experts about exactly when and how her case should be dealt with, it seemed clear she would be considered eligible for parole or early release well before serving half of her sentence. If she does not get an early date for a release hearing, you can bet her lawyer would be seeking one through the courts.

However, whether or not Sandra ever gets released before spending no more than six years in custody, depends on her progress inside the penitentiary. Further, if she's considered a serious danger to the public after six years, the National Parole Board could order her to serve her full sentence in custody. Given her situation, it seemed unlikely she would serve more than six years, and, in fact, could get out of prison before then, although she would remain under community supervision for the full ten-year sentence.

As for Beth, she received her first youth court review in June of 2007. Once she turned twenty, she was transferred to Vanier Institute for Women at the Maplehurst Detention Centre in Milton, Ontario. In mid-October 2007, Beth was transferred to a maximum-security wing at Grand Valley. Following several months of assessment, she would have been moved into a less restricted area of the women's federal prison. Once there, she and Sandra would again be able to see and speak to each other for the first time since their sentencing on June 30, 2006. Like Sandra, it also seemed unlikely that Beth would ever serve more than the required six years in secured custody.

Regardless, whenever they finish their sentences, after ten years, their youthful criminal records won't automatically be expunged as they would have been under the old Young Offenders Act. If they re-offend, their youth records might be used against them, but if they don't, the general public may never learn their true identities.